CARP... NOW AND THEN

by

ROD HUTCHINSON

Beekay Publishers

This book is dedicated to the late Richard Walker and to Fred J. Taylor, whose written words enlightened, entertained and inspired me; and to Ann, who picked me up when I was down, and made this book possible.

Thanks go to Brian Naylor for his excellent drawings and diagrams, Tim Paisley for his contribution and to Dave Watson for helping me put the book together.

The first edition of Rod Hutchinson's Carp Book was published in 1981. This book contains that material plus the development of carp fishing since that date.

CARP... NOW AND THEN

by

ROD HUTCHINSON

First published 1988
Reprinted 1990

Published and distributed by
Beekay Publishers, Withy Pool, Henlow Camp, Beds. SG16 6EA

Designed and Produced by Print Solutions
London W6 (01-748 9898)

CONTENTS

Foreword

'Rod Hutchinson's Carp Book' was written in 1980 and published in 1981 by a small firm in Nottingham, Hudson-Chadwick. Only 2000 copies were printed, as it was the intention of the owners of the copyright to make the book a collectors' item. At the time 2000 probably represented about one third of the active carp anglers in Britain.

In the intervening seven years, carp fishing has blossomed to become the fastest growing branch of angling, not only in Great Britain but in Holland, Belgium, Germany, Austria and France. At the annual conference of the British Carp Study Group held at Wembley Conference Centre in 1987, carp anglers from eight different countries attended, giving a measure of the huge popularity this fish now holds.

Carp including good sized specimens are now available to every angler in Europe and the knowledge on how to catch them is passed on each month through the various magazines of those countries. Yet they still represent a challenge as carp have a unique ability above all other freshwater fishes to learn. To learn what is dangerous, be it a food, a method of presenting a bait or an area which is no longer safe to feed in. This learning is what keeps the carp angler on his toes, it is what maintains the challenge. He has good days, good catches and wants more of them but the method used for those catches and the area he fished no longer produce as they did and so the angler has to learn, to try and catch up with changing habits, to try to be one step ahead. The original 'Rod Hutchinson's Carp Book' is to be found within this publication in its entirety. Each chapter being followed by Rod's comments at this moment. It represents the changes he has gone through in those seven years, seven very successful years; how he and his friends have kept up with the carp. Since 1961, carp fishing has been Rod's life; today he still has the same enthusiasm as when he started, the same ability to tune in with his quarry and yet while he admits to being obsessed by it, he still carries a humour and is able to laugh at himself for his obsession. To Rod carp fishing is just a way of life.

Author's comment

This book has been produced because I'm skint, sorry, because there was such a limited print of my first book, that many of today's carp anglers have expressed a desire to read it, but have been unable to obtain a copy. My apologies to those who do own an original for the repetition involved in producing "Carp, Now and Then" in this format, I hope that does not detract from your enjoyment of this volume.

Rod Hutchinson
March 1988

Introduction '80

"What is a carp angler?" asked the speaker.
"An idiot" shouts a man from the back row.
"Shut up Arnold, you're showing me up", says his wife.
"No let's be serious" says the speaker, trying to calm down his audience. "I was serious" cries the same man in the back row, laughing loudly. His wife, the cold look of an assassin in her eyes, knees him in the groin. He falls to the floor, his eyes going round like the tumblers of a fruit machine.

Is a carp angler an idiot? No, surely not, crazy, certainly, but not an idiot. What is this obsession that drives a man from the arms of a good woman on warm, perfumed nights in June, and pulls him from the warmth of a blazing fire in the depths of winter? The pursuit of a fish? The man's got to be an idiot!

Carp fishing has been likened to drug taking, but drugs can only end in despair. Carp fishing is more like love, with time it gets richer and more rewarding. There comes a time when you can't let go, to do so would render part of you null and void. At the start it's a challenge, but really the only challenge is in your head. Man against fish, superior thought, the power to reason – there can only be one winner in the end. So at times we deliberately make things difficult for ourselves, just to keep up the challenge.

Then it happens, nothing will go right; how can a fish make a fool of a man? We trot out the old excuses – too much natural food, it's too cold, or the fish haven't finished spawning. But surely with our superior intelligence we should be able to overcome these minor difficulties? Man can fly to the moon, so catching a stupid fish should be easy meat! Yet it isn't always the case.

On top of man's great knowledge, we develop animal cunning. We start to think like an animal, and move like a fox. Keeping out of sight, yet darting in when the opportunity is there. We move in with the sunset, blending with the trees, or we ghost in upon the water at dawn, as light of foot as the morning mist. Instincts come out in us which have lain dormant since the time man was a hunter. Maybe we are all still hunters, but society and convention condemns such thoughts and so they are forgotten. Is it the kill, the capture, we still crave for?

It all sounds so earnest, yet for something taken so seriously, how come we enjoy it so much? I wish I knew the answer, but I don't. What I do know is there isn't a night at home I don't wish I was at the waterside. On the other hand there have been a few nights when things have gone wrong and I wished that I was at home. Having some success, but not quite enough is, I think, the key to it all.

It's not my intention to lay down a statement of absolute facts, or "This is how it has to be done", because quite honestly sometimes things just happen, and I'm at a loss as to why I've caught a fish. But I do believe in certain things which will, I hope, point you in directions that may end in successful fishing. Hopefully you'll keep an open mind at all times, read my book, digest and analyse it, and take the directions you believe are right for you.

Introduction '88

When the book first came out, I thought that the introduction was the best part of it. Yet even as I was writing things were changing around me. "Keeping out of sight, moving in with the sunset, blending with the trees. Ghosting in upon the water at dawn, as light of foot as the morning mist." This was carp fishing in its purest form. Carp fishing from a bygone age. A time when few carp were caught, but when captures only played a small part of being a carp fisherman. There always were lakes which held big fish, yet in the fifties, sixties and early seventies many were not fished because the lakes were not beautiful. The carp man just could not conjure up in his head that carp fishing atmosphere when sitting beside them. He wanted to be alone with his thoughts, to become part of the landscape. He wanted to sit in beautiful surroundings and dream of catching beautiful fish. Fish which had never graced a net before. Scales which had never reflected the first rays of the sun. A fish whose form had never leapt from the pages of the angling *weeklies*. It was a very personal thing. Man the master of his environment, pitting his wits against the queen of the water.

I had been part of that scene and while I still craved at times the loneliness of it all, there was a new excitement, a realization that big carp were there for the taking. Much of this realization came about not because of new baits or new rigs, it was much more simple than that. Anglers simply had more spare time. The late seventies had seen the growth of unemployment, others working were doing fewer hours. Established waters became crowded. Anglers who could not handle the crowds tried larger pits often hitherto unfished. Pits where carp had been left alone to grow large, but carp which had never had to learn from their downfalls and so were very naive when it came to anglers' baits.

A carp anglers' grapevine had been established. Each night lines buzzed as carp men compared notes. The veil of secrecy which had for so long shrouded carp fishing was being lifted. The membership of the carp societies exploded as each week it seemed the papers would let out another secret. There became an urgency to go and fish waters, lakes which for years you left alone before the "lifers" moved in. Even in established lakes, fish which had sought refuge in areas far beyond the range of the carpman's hooks, were now well within the scope of the angler, as new materials made rods which could cast fantastic distances. Where before it had been "if only I could get a bait there", it was now "I want to get a bait there first", because it was becoming apparent that first in with a method, or new type of bait had the true bonanzas.

Yes carp fishing was changing. By 1981 it was a million miles away from the carp fishing I had grown up with. Maybe I should have written in that original introduction, "moving in at dawn, stamping my feet, to blend in with noise of mallets driving in bivvy pegs." The days when a buzzer sounded at night and I leapt for my rods were long over. Now when one sounded I wondered "Whose is that?". The times of sitting alone with one's thoughts were forgotten. Alone! At times I had more binoculars on me than the Derby winner!

But life changes and you change with it. In truth the actual fishing was far better than in years gone by. From dreaming about catching big fish, there were now times when you could expect to catch big fish. There were still disappointments, you need those to appreciate the good times, but the disappointments were fewer than before. As more lakes were fished, as more carp were caught, as the information was passed around, one thing became apparent. A carp is a carp, should it live in Lincolnshire, the south of France, Germany or a concrete basin in the local park. None at the outset is more intelligent than the others. A good bait will be a good bait anywhere. If one lake is more difficult than another, it is not down to the carp at the outset. True carp in waters of high natural food stocks that come under a great deal of pressure will get harder to catch but that is due to pressure and the fact that those fish don't actually need the anglers baits to live and grow large, while carp in over-stocked waters will remain easier to catch simply from the fact that there is not enough natural food to sustain them but their basic intelligence is the same. Most problems encountered during carp fishing however have nothing to do with carp themselves, they are what I term technical problems, i.e. the distances at which the carp may feed from the angler, heavy weed growth, thick silt upon the bottom, line chafing gravel bars, diving ducks and coots and seagulls which appear as if magic every time a catapult elastic is pulled back. All are problems which can at times have you pulling your hair out but there are ways and means of overcoming them. Probably the most frustrating time is when you know the carp are feeding in a certain area but you can't get anywhere near them because of other anglers, but I think you just have to grin and bear it, knowing that your time will come and when it does make the most of it.

Every dog has its day, just try and make sure you get more than one. Don't dwell on past memories too much, work to create making new ones. I think that one of the main reasons I've retained my enthusiasm for carp fishing is by moving around trying new waters. I don't like to know too much about a new venue, in that way it's like starting all over again and when eventually I strike into a fish, size is irrelevant; whatever it is, it will be new to me. As much as I enjoy catching the fish, I could never become obsessed by sheer size. To become so would limit me to very few waters and I would miss out on the beauty of other lakes and the sheer joy of playing hard fighting, though often quite small carp. I love carp for their sporting qualities and have to admit a sense of disappointment when my two largest fish to date both came in like wet sacks. But that is life, that is carp fishing. You can't expect a grand old lady to fight like one bristling with the vigours of youth. For me the joy is when the rod hoops over and you've no idea what's on the other end. As long as it's a carp, to me they're all beautiful.

In the original introduction, I said it was not my intention to lay down absolute facts and stated that there were times when I had caught fish when I didn't understand why. Those times still happen occasionally but more often now you are likely to ask yourself "why didn't I catch?". The fact is that I and my friends knew a great deal at the time but because we were open minded and things were changing fast I was always loathe to make conclusive statements such as this or that will work. However seven years is a long time and many ideas we had have been proved correct and there are now many things about which I can say "this is the best way" and many baits about which I can say "this will work on your water, providing it has not already caught those carp".

The objective of updating this book, is to show fellow carp anglers what phases I and friends have gone through on our own lakes. How we overcame problems at a given time. Hopefully the reader will be able to use this knowledge we have gained and apply it to the circumstances on his own water at a given time.

Chapter 1

Location of Carp '80

THIS is the real nitty gritty of carp fishing, what it's really all about. Without knowing where a carp feeds or is going to feed at some time, consistent success cannot be achieved. There is not a top carp angler in the country who is not good at the location of fish. Some are not aware of it, seemingly being pulled by a subconscious force in the direction of carp. But regardless of whether they know it or not, they can locate carp, and without locating carp, you can't catch them.

Feeding areas

To identify the feeding areas, we should first look closely at the carp. As a wild creature it is governed by two basic instincts, the need to breed, and the need to feed to survive. Being a master of its environment it soon becomes aware of the places where it can find its food. The nature of that food changes as the carp grows, the infant carp feeding on far smaller items than a full grown carp would, in ordinary circumstances. The angler has to identify the food items natural to a particular water, and where the carp are most likely to find them. A feeding carp is one that can be caught. A carp not feeding is difficult to catch, to say the least.

Having decided where the feeding areas should be, the angler should then try to observe any movement in those areas, in order to confirm his beliefs, by watching the area from the best vantage point possible. I've climbed up trees, telegraph poles, stood on top of my car, and even once climbed the jib of a lakeside crane to gain a good vantage point. Unfortunately many waters are not clear and observation of fish becomes difficult. Here the angler, whilst still trying to identify feeding areas in his own mind, must be acutely observant of all movements of carp. It can take a long time before definite feeding areas are located. To do this, the precise location of all swirling and leaping of fish must be noted, and preferably at what times this takes place. The same applies to any bubbling and colouring up of the water, again when and where. Work out which areas receive the most attention and you're well on the way to finding a feeding area.

The fact that carp may be seen regularly in a certain spot does not necessarily mean that that area is a feeding spot. During the day, when not feeding, carp appear to choose some place where they can lie up, safe from anglers and their baits. The angler has to differentiate between feeding areas, and the safe, holding areas. In a small lake, under five acres, the observant angler should quickly be able to track down the feeding areas. If that lake is very coloured, then careful plumbing to find its contours will help identify areas where food accumulates.

Big Pits

It is on the large open gravel pits where the angler has most problems. Some seem to forget the basic rules, just fishing swims where they know that in the past fish have been taken, but although through sheer size these waters are more difficult, the same rules apply. The carp will feed in those areas where they are accustomed to finding food. I find it beneficial to break the lake up in my mind's eye into a series of smaller lakes, and then attack each area independently. Once this has been done, they are then all pieced together again. Where large waters are concerned, one of the greatest aids to the angler is the echo-sounder. Using this, the angler can make a detailed map, and the areas most likely to hold high stocks of food can be estimated with a fair amount of accuracy. Not all clubs, however, will allow the use of boats on their waters, which is essential if the echo-sounder is to be used. So in many cases all the angler can do is observe and plumb to find food stocks.

Given that the angler has done his work, by whatever methods are at his disposal, he will still be left with a variety of alternative areas. How does he decide which of these areas will attract fish in different weather conditions? It is the opinion of myself and my close friends that the greatest factor governing the movement of carp in large waters is wind direction. The stronger the wind, the greater the impact upon the fish. There are several reasons as to why this is so, each probably having some bearing on the matter. A strong wind creates waves which in turn oxygenate the water. Where the waves hit a particular bank or an obstacle, so a greater concentration of oxygen is created. This in turn appears to attract carp, an example of this being that on hot days at Billing Aquadrome, carp will follow boats. It seems that they are taking advantage of the extra oxygen created in the boat's wake. This extra oxygen may arouse a feeding urge within the carp – or it could be coincidental to other factors.

The pounding of the waves upon a bank or underwater obstacle also disturbs the bottom or weed growth in those areas, so much so that food is released. Much of the food ends up in suspension along with fine silt. The removal of the top layer of silt from the bottom also lays bare other food items too heavy to be taken into suspension. These items include molluscs, crustacea, advanced forms of the fly cycle, and leeches. As I pointed out at the

PREVAILING WINDS & SUB-SURFACE CURRENTS '80

prevailing wind

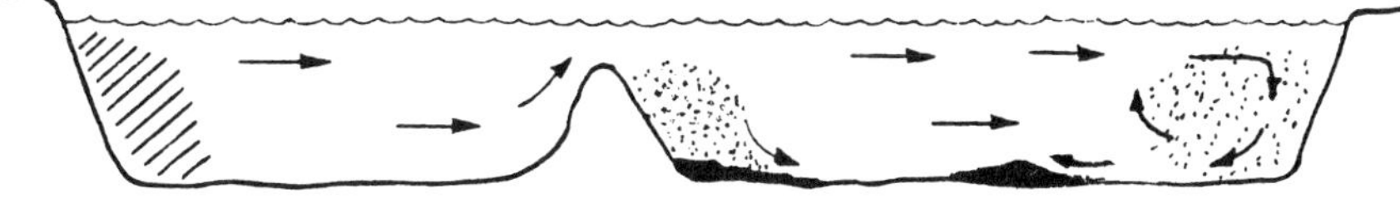

calm area protected by bank

gravel bar - note silt area

silt area formed away from bank

BIRD'S EYE VIEW OF GROUNDBAIT PATTERNS

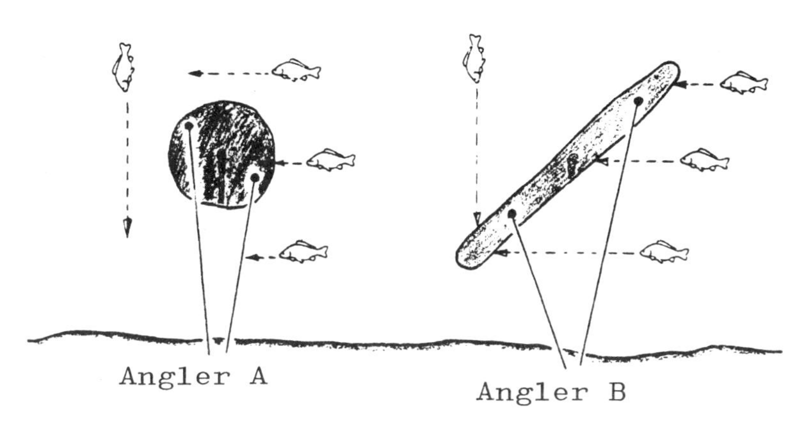

Angler B's diagonal groundbait pattern intercepts more patrolling fish than angler A's patch.

beginning of the chapter, the carp is a master of its environment and is well aware of this reaction of wind on certain areas and will expect to find food in such conditions. Also I believe that the colouring-up of the water by the suspended food is in itself an attractor of carp and, I might add, other species like roach and tench. The reason is most likely because the fish associate the colouring-up with suspended food; but the colouration alone is enough to attract. I've seen so many examples of this reaction that I could fill a chapter just recounting them. I will, however, illustrate by giving just three instances.

When I was in the Redmire Pool syndicate, the nature of the overgrown banks often meant that I had to wade out from the bank in order to net a hooked fish. The bottom of the pool consisted of a very fine reddish clay, from which the pool got its name. On wading in, the movement of the feet in this clay created reddish clouds in the water. It was common to see carp come in to investigate these clouds, and in one instance a carp in fact bumped into my legs, quite oblivious to my presence.

On one complex of gravel pits I fish regularly, some of the lakes are joined up by narrow channels. Should the wind be such that it blows into or across the mouth of one of the channels, then silt is disturbed forming a cloud where the channel comes out in the adjoining lake. Within minutes of the cloud forming, carp appear on the scene. These channels are also favourite haunts of swans; their grubbing about in these areas again creates clouds which the carp soon investigate.

Coloured water

I first became aware of this fascination of carp for coloured water back in the mid sixties. I was at the time fishing the then very popular group of lakes at Horton Kirby in Kent. On one particular day a strong wind sprang up out of nowhere, taking my brolly with it. The brolly drifted down the lake until it sank at a point approximately two-thirds down the lake. The area where the brolly sank appeared for some reason to be pretty barren of carp; at least it was very unproductive. An angler who had seen my brolly float off soon appeared on the scene, offering the use of his inflatable dinghy. Exhaustive dragging of the bottom eventually produced the brolly, and also created a large patch of coloured water. Within minutes, the area was full of bubbling, leaping carp feeding in gay abandon. Myself and several other anglers soon picked up on this, between us taking something like half a dozen fish in the next hour.

This leads us to two significant points, the first of which is the need to look for areas capable of creating clouds, that is, areas of fine silt. Happily the silt and food go very much hand in hand. Silt is far more easy for insects to penetrate, and so create the fly cycle, than is gravel. So we should be looking for areas where silt carried in suspension by wind action on the lake is likely to be deposited. This would also explain the popularity of gravel bars for carp (and carp anglers). Any such obstacle, be it gravel bars, islands, peninsulas, large snags, or weedbeds, will create a barrier to water flow and so collect deposits of silt. These will eventually mount up, providing a home for much of the carp's natural diet. It should also be remembered that the most effective barriers are the banks which confine the lake, and as such one would expect to find the largest deposits of food in the margins of the lake.

Undertows

Another point to look for on waters of fairly uniform depth, is the occurrence of undertows. While the action of wind upon a bank creates an upwards circular flow which holds the silt and food in suspension, it often creates an undertow beneath that flow. The undertow goes back in the opposite direction, and carries with it a certain amount of suspended food and silt. As the undertow moves further away from the bank it becomes weaker, and so the silt gets deposited. On some waters, these deposits reach almost gravel bar proportions, adjacent to the bank receiving the prevailing winds. It is not on every water however where this occurs, so it is wise to check for this condition. This can easily be done by dropping light float tackle just out from the margin with the lowest shot set just off the bottom. Open the pickup, and if an undertow is in operation then the float will steadily move against the wind. On those waters where it does occur, the deposits appear to collect mostly between 20 to 25 yards from the bank.

The second point concerning the silt cloud/carp combination is this. If the combination is of such importance, would it be worth dragging a swim for carp, in much the manner tench anglers have been doing over the years? I believe in certain circumstances it would. However I see no point in dragging a swim when you are achieving good results by conventional methods. There are some lakes in which I would not consider it, because of the atmosphere. The ends don't always justify the means. There are times however when I could see it being beneficial. For example, in periods of high summer when the carp bask frequently and seem to have no inclination towards feeding. The creation of an area of coloured water may well lead them to investigate, and bring on a tendency to feed. Another time when I could see advantages in its use is when using a tiny non-visual mass bait, the success of which is dependent on carp feeding in a certain area. Though ideally you should have chosen the correct area in the first place, it might be that the area you wish to fish is well covered by other anglers. In this case, a cloud could help draw fish into your swim and onto your bait.

One final point on the gravel bar/island situation and the accumulation of silt, is that not all areas of a bar or island will receive the same amount of deposits. This will depend on the prevailing wind direction over the course of the year, one side of an island or large bar often being quite barren of food. How many times does the angler find it necessary to cast to one spot precisely, in order to get a bite? The fact that this is a regular occurrence illustrates, I think, the point I am making.

Weedbeds

It goes without saying that weedbeds are natural havens of food. (A chicken and egg principle going on here.) Accumulations of silt promote certain weed growth, which in turn collects suspended silt, promoting more weed growth. Besides its "larder" qualities, weed also provides cover, lending a feeling of safety to the fish, which again can promote feeding. In many waters, carp at some time of the year begin feeding upon weed. Whether it is for the food content of the weed itself, or for food carried upon the weed is irrelevant.

FOOD AREAS IN A TYPICAL GRAVEL PIT '80

Remember that silt = natural food = carp, so try to assess where the silt deposits occur on your water.

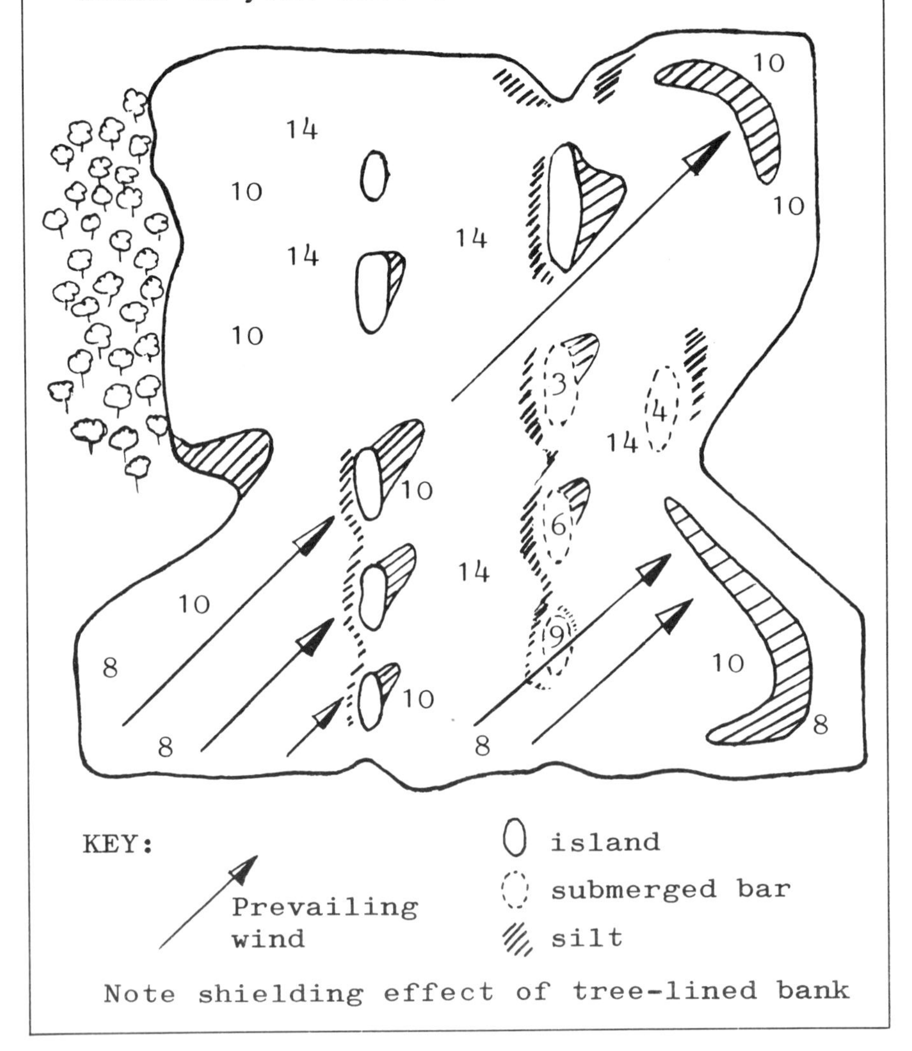

Although it is very difficult to tempt fish to take a bait at such times, you must have your bait amongst the carp to stand a chance of catching one.

On waters of irregular depth containing extensive areas of both deep and shallow water, I would expect the shallower areas to have the largest concentrations of food, for the reasons already stated. However, if a good force wind was blowing into a bank surrounded by deepish water (but not much over a depth of twenty feet), then that is where I would expect to find the fish. I would expect a combination of well oxygenated water, coloured conditions, and food, to outscore an area containing just an easy food source. Given conditions of stable humid weather, with very little wind, then I would expect the easier feeding in shallow water areas to be more to the carp's liking. That is in the period between June and mid-November – after that carp seem to react differently, as I point out in the chapter on winter fishing.

I personally believe that in summer temperatures have little bearing upon where a carp will feed. Carp will feed well right through the scale from around 50 degrees Fahrenheit up to approaching 80 degrees. While thermoclines (a phenomenon of water layering in different temperature bands) do occur, my opinion is that the areas where they occur are productive because of the afore-mentioned oxygen/cloud/food combination, not because of the temperatures. Early in the season, if water temperatures are still low i.e. in the low fifties, carp may well move very little. I believe this is due to those temperatures holding back spawning; spawning areas can be highly productive for up to a fortnight after spawning takes place. The carp at this time show cannibalistic tendencies, feeding hard on their own spawn. Again, it can be very frustrating fishing at this time, with the fish being preoccupied on one form of food. But as stated earlier, a feeding carp is one that can be caught.

To summarise this chapter briefly, I would say, to find the fish, first find the food. To find the food, observe water flow, wind direction and other factors which help to create an environment in which living food matter will prosper.

A note on natural food supplies

You don't need a degree in freshwater biology in order to catch carp, of course, but it's useful to have a basic knowledge of what's going on at the bottom of your swim. If you can determine the location of the carp's natural food larders and put your baits there, you'll increase your number of runs.

Generally speaking the abundance of food items, and the variety of species, increases as the water gets shallower due to increased penetration of light and greater oxygenation, among other things. Within a given water there are a number of different types of habitat for the smaller food items. The poorest black sludge is found in the deepest holes and trenches, and here only bloodworms are likely to be found. Where the water is not so deep, mud-bottomed stretches will have a more varied selection of snails and mussels. In areas where silt (rotting animal and plant material) is deposited, a range of shrimps, water lice and caddis larvae are found. Finally, a great diversity of insect life, bugs, beetles, snails, and flies, occurs in the richly-weeded shallows. Provided that they are not unduly disturbed by the activity of anglers, carp will feed in the silted and weedy areas.

Not only do the type of habitats and the species of food items vary between different places in the same pond, but even greater variations may occur between different types of water. On the one hand, for example, you have small, mud-bottomed clay pits, often shallow and weeded, and on the other, wide open gravel pits with great variations in depths. Different approaches to these types of water are required, and are discussed in detail later on. Basically the mud-bottomed clay pit will have extensive weeded shallows near the bank, whereas gravel pits often have steeply sloping banks with deep water close in. In addition, while carp in the smaller clay pit may have nowhere else to feed if frightened from the bank by anglers, carp in the big pits can often find alternative food areas well away from the bank, around the margins of islands and gravel bars. It's important to note the occurrence of silt deposits here, which tend to collect at the foot of the marginal slopes "behind" the prevailing wind direction. Here the carp find an abundance of the larger items (shrimps, caddis, snails etc.) on which they feed.

A knowledge of the basis of underwater life-forms is helpful in deciding where to cast your baits and it can also be interesting in its own right, as part of the angler's appreciation of the whole of the natural scene. You'll perhaps find it useful to have one of the little illustrated pocket books to help identify different species.

Chapter 2

Location and Behaviour of Carp '88

Looking back on that chapter, I'm surprised to find that there is nothing which I would basically disagree with today. Location always has been and always will be the key to successful carp fishing. The one thing that the chapter lacked and which had not become evident at that time was the effect upon the carp of intense angling pressure. I still believe the areas I suggested anglers look for, i.e the areas containing natural food, to be the ones to go for in a quiet environment or lightly fished waters but in heavily fished waters even the very best natural larders will get fished out. As more and more anglers learn the places to fish, so more and more fish get caught, to such an extent that there are now areas in some waters where it is virtually impossible to get a fish to pick up a bait. Many hot spots are now no go areas, places associated with danger. However I am now sure that the carp are never far away and drift back into that area when there are no lines in the water. I can think of three classic instances of this happening in three different countries. All of the waters in question being under intense angling pressure and each area formerly produced prodigious bags of fish.

The first of those waters is Savay Lake at Denham, Berkshire in England. This is my favourite lake of all, despite the fact that, in recent years, circumstances have been such that I've been able to spend little time there. My favourite swim on the lake was what became known as "The Birches". This swim was a natural larder, a bottleneck for food, driven down by strong north winds. Many gravel bars exist in this swim, along with two or more mushroom like mounds which rise up about four feet from the bottom. It also had when I first fished the swim, a snag tree either side of the swim. Snag tree is a term given to trees which hang way over the water and also have many branches below water level. Consequently many hooked fish would make for these branches and often would become snagged and lost. However that part is irrelevant because snag trees actually help create a good swim, as they are areas where the carp can go when the sun is too hot for them, or when they are disturbed either by bankside noise or the continual casting of heavy leads.

The important part is that they keep carp in the close proximity of where it would naturally feed. Amongst those submerged branches the carp feel safe and it is my strong belief that while their removal will increase the ratio of numbers of fish landed to being lost, it will drastically cut down the number of takes an angler will get. A carp hooked but lost for any reason, most times will head for such an area, often just lying up for a day or more, "sulking" as we term it in my neck of woods. The point is it has been frightened and it needs to rest up in a place it feels safe, until it has the confidence to feed again. Once that confidence is regained it will resume its feeding in those close by areas it knows contain plenty of food but, should there be no "safe" area close by, I believe a frightened fish will travel until it finds such a place to lie up in. When the feeding urge returns, it is most likely to feed close by to the new area it regards as being safe. The snags disappeared either side of the Birches, I think in the spring of 84. Before that time, during northerly winds an angler knowing where to place his baits could expect up to six runs a day when conditions were favourable to feeding. Since that time, I think an average of two fish a season have been taken from the swim. Fish now swim through very fast in midwater, not even going down on what are large deposits of natural food. I should add that this behaviour occurs when lines are out in the swim, for I cannot believe fish will not sneak back to such a natural larder when no anglers are present.

I've spent many hours thinking about this swim, such was my love for it and the successes I've had there. The bottleneck I described earlier is a very rare occurrence where two gravel bars actually join up to form a V shape. That V being open to the strong north winds which frequently blow through. The trough beneath the vee and the sides of those two gravel bars, collect all floating debris which has accumulated into an area of silt rich in bloodworms, snails and swan mussels. Also such is the direction of the water currents, I am quite sure that many of the anglers baits which originally may have been spread around the swim, eventually accumulate in that trough within the V of the gravel bars.

Yet at the time of writing the swim rarely produces fish while far inferior swims either side of it now regularly produce. If fish are caught, it is not from the V shaped, old hot spot. Carp location in 1988 and the coming years is no longer just looking for areas of natural food, it is now more a case of trying to think how carp will respond to being caught, where will they go, where will they feed? You cannot give a fish the intelligence of man, yet I think to really get to grips with them today on heavily fished waters, deep theories and too much reasoning will have to go out of the window. Very simplistic thinking will be called for. I find myself thinking more and more "where would I go, if I was a big, frightened but hungry carp?"; but I don't believe a carp can think, only respond to instinct. They are a very hardy, adaptable animal. We may think it's great because we catch big fat carp when they are feeding in rich areas but is being big and fat of any consequence to the carp? If those great food deposits were not there, the carp would survive; admittedly they would not attain large sizes but they would survive none the less. What I am trying to say is that while I believe in a perfect unfished environment, food will be all and everything to the carp and it will take advantage of the best quality food it can find: in the pressurised environments they live in today maybe "fear" is a more contributory factor towards their behaviour than the need for high quality food.

The days when we'd say to ourselves "no point fishing there because there's no food in the area, there's no reason carp should visit here," could be over. Getting away from flying leads and tight lines could easily push carp into relatively barren areas and, make no mistake, if left alone those carp will find food of some source, they will survive. Later on in the book is a small piece which may throw some light on so called "mug" fish. Now while at the time I wrote that piece, I thought there were many so called "mug" fish, today I'm not so sure. Maybe it was just that large fish were more readily recognised. Be that as it may we all know of fish which for a period get caught and caught again and most times (providing they have not suffered tissue damage), their weight goes up and up. Or let me say it used to. In the past couple of seasons, I can think of quite a few fish like that which disappeared for a season or more, only to be caught again at weights far below those they held when they were being caught regularly. The reason for their previous growth and capture was obviously down to the fact that they were feeding on anglers' baits, many of which are of a higher food value than their natural food.

Now the reason those carp were not caught for quite a period I believe to be because those individual fish simply were not in areas being fished and those areas where they were, were not being fished presumably because they were not rated by the anglers. The fish had simply moved to areas they regarded as being safe irrespective of the amount of food present, hence the reason for their dramatic weight loss. Then maybe a combination of a need for better food plus previous fear had been forgotten, and had taken those carp back into fished areas. I think if the angler really thinks about it even in the smallest lakes he knows, he will recognise places which rarely or never receive a bait.

Yet surely to a carp those places must be the safest areas within a lake.

Back to "The Birches" swim; I believe its decline was due to three contributory factors. Number one was undoubtedly the fact that it produced a great many fish within a relatively short period and also the vast majority of those fish came from one small area within that swim i.e the bottleneck created by the joining of the two gravel bars, so much so that despite its natural food resources the area became associated with danger. Secondly the removal of the snags took away the refuge the carp sought when under pressure and a third contributory factor was the opening up of a new swim, approximately 80 yards north of the Birches. During periods of southerly winds and flat calm conditions, also when the Birches had been under pressure and quite a few fish taken, the carp would move up into this area, which became known as "The Gravelly". The lake is extremely wide at this point, and the carp generally hugged the relative safety of the far bank. Yet by 1984 rods had improved so much that coupled with five pound mainline and strong fifteen pound leaders, the carp could now be reached. This particular swim also has many underwater obstacles and quite a few fish were lost there for that reason.

I think a situation developed where many of the carp entering "The Birches" were frightened already, either from being hooked, or just finding lines or bombs hitting the surface in an area they had previously regarded as being safe. Added to the fact a great many had already been hooked in "The Birches", and so treated the area with caution, and I believe suspicious or frightened fish have the ability to transmit their fears to other fish; with no nearby snag trees for the fish to lay up in, the carp raced straight through. Significantly, the one area along that stretch of bank where now you can confidently expect to find fish is the first area of snag trees to the other side of "The Birches" from the "Gravelly". Fear brought about through angling pressure changed the habits of those carp. The need to feel safe overcame the need to feed.

Whether or not "The Birches" will return once again to its former glories is pure speculation. Personally I doubt it, but hope that I'm wrong. The reason for my pessimism is that though in time the V hotspot will no longer be regarded as dangerous, many of the fish entering the swim will still be moving quickly, having been frightened either in the "Gravelly" or the new "Snagtree" hot spot. Had there been an area where they could lie up undisturbed, I would be much more optimistic.

Lac de St. Cassien, near Cannes in the South of France has only been carp fished by more than a handful since 1985, yet despite the huge expanse of the lake, enormous angling pressure in a short space of time has moved the carp from their natural haunts. In 1985 it was carp fishing in its purest form. Find areas with plenty of food and you found plenty of carp. Carp which were still growing, hungry carp which would readily take a bait. Any area with weed growth held carp, all of the points on entrances into bays, were good areas to fish. Any narrow area linking large expanses of water, where fish could be easily intercepted would virtually guarantee fish. The best places were simply where the natural food was but it was all too easy and the obvious spots got fished over and over again. The same fish were getting caught week in, week out and by the second year, even the hungry Cassien carp were moving from their natural feeding areas, simply because of angling pressure. By 1987 the only area you could guarantee carp moving into was during the month of May, when fish would enter the shallow water at the end of the west arm, in readiness to spawn, and not even angling pressure I don't believe will ever change that. Of course the carp still get caught, they are growing fish in need of plenty of food but the hotspots of 85 and early 86 are no longer the places to catch them; but have no doubt the carp know where the food is and they will move in and feed on natural food when times are quiet. So don't expect them to be far away from previous hotspots. Now is the time to look for quiet, little fished areas, in the vicinity of known food holding areas.

You can also forget the rule books that suggest that carp will only be caught in shallow water. The term shallow is obviously relative to what depths the rest of the lake will attain. In the case of Cassien with depths in some places down to at least 120 feet, thirty or forty feet can be regarded as being relatively shallow and a great many fish were caught at these depths during 1985 and 1986. During 1987, I think mainly out of desperation brought on by lack of takes, some anglers tried fishing at depths of 60 feet or more and much to their surprise were rewarded on occasions with some good sized fish.

Now it is very unlikely that at those depths that there will be much in the line of food and to my mind those fish caught were simply lying up away from angling pressure. When food presented itself, it was taken readily because the carp felt perfectly safe, not having been put under pressure (i.e fished for or caught) at those depths before.

An aspect of carp behaviour which really surprised me occurred during the summer of 1987. During previous years we had been surprised to catch the same fish, at the very beginning of the south arm of Lake Cassien and at the end of the western arm, two points which are very far apart indeed; I would imagine nearly two miles. Now although this showed that carp move very great distances either in search of food, or because of angling pressure, we presumed that carp which could be seen at the very top of the North Arm, close to the dam, were different fish from those caught in the other arms. The North Arm it should be explained is a vast area of water, probably as large as the rest of the lake together but the vast majority of it is of immense depth, with there being no shallow margins to speak of, banks dropping down cliff-like, preventing the growth of weed and the accumulation of food. The small area of shallowish water and only weed that there is, being up by the dam. It seemed unlikely that carp would travel immense distances over barren feeding grounds just to reach the restricted food areas of the dam when the south and west arms were rich with food. However the surprise came when a thirty pound plus carp was caught at dawn on the last point before the dam and was caught again in the evening in the shallows of the west arm by the same angler! Indeed it became apparent that during the height of summer, when there were vast numbers of anglers, holiday makers, boats, windsurfers etc, that during the day apart from the weed beds at the tip of the west arm, most of it and the south arm were devoid of fish. The fish had simply moved under the bridge to the comparative safety of the depths in the north arm. As evening fell and the holiday makers departed, so they would return, back onto the feeding areas of the other arms!

It was a far cry from the summer of 85 when during the course of an afternoon on the bends in the west arm, you would expect to see upwards of fifty carp roll. Friends who fished the area in 87, have gone as long as a week without seeing a carp roll during the day time. Sheer angling pressure again has changed the carp's natural habits.

Yet while 60 feet of water may represent the deeps in the South and West arms, 60 feet is relatively shallow in parts of the North arm. I once found a quite large gravel bar close to the bay in which the dam is situated. At the time I dismissed it because even the top of the bar was 60 feet down! Yet thinking about it now, what food there was in the area should have been on that bar as surrounding depths went down to almost 100 feet! True the feeding would not be anything like as rich as that in the other arms, but there would be food none the less in an otherwise barren area. Add to this the fact that any surface activity, i.e, boats, windsurfers, large leads and baits hitting the surface are not going to disturb them at this depth, then the prospect of such areas becoming relative hotspots at times when fish are driven out by pressure from the other arms, looks very likely.

One interesting point here is that I have seen fish leap and roll in these areas, and I have always maintained that such fish are feeding fish. Yet for the life of me I cannot believe that they were coming up from those great depths, rolling, then going back down to feed again. I believe that they must have been feeding on some food source either in midwater or just below the surface. If they were, this would go some way towards explaining the behaviour of certain carp in some English waters, which seem pretty much impossible to catch in some areas in which they roll. I now believe that those fish are simply not bottom feeding at such times. Sort out the correct technique and they will become catchable.

That same pressure talked about has made fish react in the same way, on some areas of the profilic Twente Canal in Holland. At Hengelo is the famous "hot water" stretch, where a salt factory pumps out hot water into the canal.

Now this stretch has been heavily carp fished for a number of years, but up until 1986 the areas above and below the lock gates were very lightly fished, particularly the stretch around the caravan site. Twenty carp a day was nothing unusual, maybe twelve being the norm, and there were many big carp amongst them. One of the old regulars on the caravan site once even caught sixty five carp in twenty four hours! I must admit that would be too much for me, I'm pretty sure I'd have wound the rods in after twenty or so, but it does show just how profilic the area of water was. Imagine my surprise when I arrived the first week of September 1987, and was informed by a friend of mine who has a caravan there, that he had not had a run for a month! Admittedly this was just fishing Saturdays and Sundays but all the same it was astonishing. Then he explained that during June, and for the best part of the summer, most days had seen at least a hundred rods out in the area. Only a year before most people on the camp fished for small fish, but on seeing so many carp caught that season, everyone cast out at least one rod for carp. The opposite tow path also being packed with carp anglers.

Now within the confines of a lake, carp when under that sort of pressure, can only move from one area to another, but the canal has no such barriers; besides its own great length, there are the countless other small canals and rivers which join it. All in all, this accounts for over a hundred miles of waterway. The canal along its whole length is rich in mussels, so the carp have no reason, other than winter when the high water temperatures are to their suiting and during the spawning period, to remain in the area. Put them under pressure and they will drift off to quieter places. This was later proved when another friend informed me that he had been fishing an area about five kilometres away during the same period. On the stretch he fished, he never saw another carp angler, which he was very pleased about because he was doing very well, one night taking three fish over twenty pounds plus a number of double figure carp.

The message now is very clear. Carp location on all popular waters is about how carp will behave when under pressure. The questions now are, how many fish can you expect to catch before the fish move on? You can't expect them to stay in the one area continually being caught. When they do move, where will they go?

To give an example of a situation which happens many times, there are maybe three anglers on a water. All bait with about the same number of baits, boilies but of different flavours, none of which is a "blown-out" bait. "Blown-out" being a bait that has caught so many fish on that lake that it is no longer successful, ie, it is regarded as dangerous. After a couple of hours, angler A catches a fish. Anglers B and C get no takes. During the next few hours, angler A catches more fish. Angler B on still having no takes and seeing no sign of carp within his area, moves swims, going as close to angler A, and fishing as close to A's baited patch as he can, without getting a crack in the ear. Soon angler B starts catching as well, while angler C still has no action. More anglers arrive and not unnaturally on learning what has happened, move close by anglers A and B. The action slows a bit, but odd fish are taken amongst those anglers fishing what is more or less the same area. As you arrive, anglers A, B, and C are all packing up at the end of their sessions. A and B have both taken a good number of fish, and the anglers either side of them have also caught. C, although fishing in a decent swim, one known to produce at times, has caught nothing. B's original swim was also known to be a good area, although during the time he fished it, no takes had been forthcoming. It's Friday evening and you know that other anglers will be arriving at any moment, you have to make your choice quickly. You know that if you don't jump into one of the swims vacated by A and B, then pretty soon someone else will.

Nowadays on popular waters you are forced into this sort of situation regularly. You are never going to make the right choice every time, but the times you do will either make a poor season or a very successful one.

Now obviously the situation has been laid out very simplistically and there are many other variables, ie, the direction of the wind at the times of the captures, and the expected winds for the coming weekend. So to keep things simple we will say that an area of high pressure with little or no wind has been in progress and is likely to continue. Here is how I would review the situation. The area A and B have just left has produced a lot of fish. I cannot see that situation going on much longer, although there is a good chance of picking up one, maybe two fish, but they have got to be on the move soon.

Now B's original swim and the one fished by the whole session by C, have to all intents and purposes been left quiet. By that I mean although they were fished, there were no carp there. I make that presumption because the carp were on the feed, shown by the captures in the area of A's swim. Now to fish either B or C's swim would for me be a better choice. Those fish moving from one area to another are to a degree, frightened. In both of those swims, there is bait out on the bottom. The action is slowing in A's pitch, so it could be that some fish have crept in already. With the free baits of B and C out, there is no need to bait up, a process which could push the already frightened fish further down the lake. I would happily fish both those swims with hook baits only. The fact that my baits were different to B and C's free baits, would not influence me in the slightest because I do not believe carp will feed on just one bait to the exclusion of others. The boilie over particle method discounts that theory. Besides which, my baits being fresher into the water will hold more flavour and hopefully be more attractive.

The choice between swims B and C would be down to their distance from swim A. Sometimes carp just shuffle fifty yards or so up the lake. At other times after taking a hammering they will travel from one end of a lake to the other. Another influencing factor would be which swim out of B and C was the last to produce a significant catch of fish and how long ago. For example, if a large number of fish had been taken from swim B within the past week or so, is it likely to produce again so soon? If C had not produced for a few weeks, I would be inclined to go for that swim. That is of course providing that C is not one of those swims that only produce in set weather conditions. I mention this because there are swims which only come alive in big blows from one direction or another and fishing them in anything but those conditions is a waste of time.

There are so many imponderables but piecing the parts together and getting it right, is as much fun, gives as much satisfaction as the actual catching of the fish. There is also the influence of the individual angler to be taken into consideration. Without being rude to anyone, all anglers do not have the same ability and when trying to get an idea of how a lake is fishing and what swims to go for, you need to have some idea of the ability of the anglers fishing particular swims. I remember when I used to fish Savay regularly, where the syndicate is run on a one week on, one week off basis, I used to ring a member of the opposite rota to find out how things had gone and what swims had produced. Often when I showed surprise at a certain swim not producing in good conditions, I'd be told "but don't take too much notice of that because so and so was fishing there and he can't cast more than sixty yards. If they were there, he would not have reached them." Likewise you know when a really competent angler has been in a swim, that he would have caught carp, if they were in his area.

Then there are swims which when fish do move in, they do so in great numbers. You have to learn just how many fish you can expect to get caught before they move on. It may be that the angler before you has taken three or four fish, yet you know the swim is good for a dozen before the shoal is on the move. At the opposite end of the spectrum there are swims which no matter what you do, you never catch more than one fish.

One lake in particular comes to mind here, where in a spot in the margins beneath an overhanging bush I can confidently expect to get a take every night but try as I might I cannot get two takes. The surprising thing is though, that I have yet to catch the same fish twice, which would indicate to me that a shoal of fish patrol that margin. I can only presume that because the takes come in shallow water, in this case about 3 feet, the disturbance frightens off other members of the shoal. Be that as it may it just shows the difference in behaviour of carp from one swim to another. The likely explanation being that those swims which will produce the most fish are in fact areas with a great deal of natural food. Areas into which lots of carp move, irrespective of anglers baits.

I should add here that I think you are much more likely to catch a number of fish in a relatively short period of time in open swims well away from the bank, rather than shallow marginal swims.

Anglers have to be aware of this fact that some swims produce lots more fish than others. If an angler elsewhere catches say six or more fish, don't necessarily expect the swim that you are fishing to produce the same. Maybe it has the capability, maybe not and you have to learn those facts about your own individual waters; but if you've caught a fish or two from a swim which never produces more than that, you could waste a lot of valuable time sitting it out in the belief you will catch more. Carp know their environment, lots of fish move in one area because they know that area has food for them all. Only one or two fish move in another area because that is all that area is capable of naturally feeding. Even if food stocks were equal, more than two fish caught has been rare for me in margin swims and I think it is simply because of vibrations. The vibrations of a panicking hooked fish bouncing off the margin side in shallow water must I think be more intense than out in open water of good depth and more likely to scare other members of the shoal. As I said earlier, the behaviour of carp is very much down to what is happening at a certain time. Latch on to how they are behaving and use it to your advantage.

Back in 1980 a lot of anglers credited the success I was having on a number of waters, down to the fact that I used tiny yet heavy tungsten carbide leger weights and looking back I know their use did in fact increase my chances of catching. At that time many waters had still not seen boilies. On those that had, no one had yet fished them after mass baiting. Most waters had yet to be put under real angling pressure and consequently fish were still behaving naturally, moving with the wind and feeding in areas of high natural food stocks. Even if fish were at long range I could present a bait to them with the very minimum of surface splash and disturbance through the water, by using the tungsten carbide legers and very small baits. I was able to catch lots of bubbling fish by casting directly to them, while other anglers not having the legers either scared the fish off, by casting directly at them or they had to cast their baits into areas they hoped the bubblers would move into. Fish at that time were simply not used to the sound of large heavy leads hitting the surface above them and consequently were very easily scared. Yet within two years, mass baiting of boilies became the vogue. Anglers catapulted out anything from five hundred to two thousand boilies in some cases before they started fishing. The carp quickly learnt that these large splashes, just like the rain-like sound of particle baits in past years, meant food. They came to the sound of it hitting the surface. A few anglers, myself included cottoned on to this fact and used it to their advantage. The method then was to fire out about 100 baits, enough to get the carp homing in and then cast into them with the heaviest lead you had, deliberately making a disturbance because you knew the fish would investigate expecting to find food. Which indeed it did, only it was attached to your hook. I should add that the heavy lead was used at all distances even close in. It had nothing to do with casting, or being balanced with your rod, it was simply to create disturbance. Should the reader be thinking that this has nothing to do with location, I should point out that in this case, you made the carp locate you, or rather your baits. I should add though that while you did not need to be precisely on the carp, so to speak, you did have to be in the vacinity of them, for them to hear the sound of the boilies going in. If the carp were not close enough, you either had to simply sit and wait, hoping a shoal would eventually move in and find the baits, or you kept moving, repeating the method in swims until you found the fish. Fortunately enough for me, a great many times I made the correct choice first time but I do remember one occasion when I moved swims five times in a day. During that period of time I had so much faith in the method and the bait that I knew that it was just a question of find them and catch them.

But like all good things they come to an end. More and more anglers mass baited. Not all of them could be on the fish and consequently you had great areas of lake bottoms, laced with boilies. Often those areas would be quite safe to feed in, as the anglers who had baited them had long since departed. Carp no longer needed to come to the sound of food hitting the water, they know their environment, they knew there would be plenty of food elsewhere. They also began to associate the sound of baits hitting the surface with danger, as many had been caught during such baiting onslaughts. As the carp changed, so the method had to change. The bait simply had to be in the swim, before the fish arrived, for it to be regarded as safe.

This association with danger is very much a question of fact as far as I'm concerned. It is what makes the carp learn and change its habits. Over the years their attitude towards lines has changed remarkably. Back in the 60's and 70's, I did everything I could to keep my lines on the bottom, and I would also camouflage them so they were not seen. However it often had a drawback. Should a fish unintentionally pick up the line on any part of body or fins i.e. a line bite, they would panic and belt from the swim as if shot from a gun. They couldn't see it, didn't at that stage know what it was and it scared them to death. So we set about eradicating line bites. This was done simply by showing them the line. Anything they could see, they were not afraid of and line had yet to be guilty by association. So very tight lines coming straight off the bottom to the rod tip, comprising a thick black leader were the order of the day. The difference in behaviour was remarkable. At Savay and other lakes, we could see fish swimming towards the lines, on seeing them, they simply swam under or over them. There was no panic whatsoever. The beauty also being that the thick leader helped you cast further and decreased losses on gravel bars, while the tight line helped the bolt rigs we used function perfectly.

Two years on the picture had changed completely. In those two years it seemed that practically everyone had gone onto tight lines. At my local lake and at Savay I was able to observe carp coming up against the lines and actually turning back. They simply would not enter the swim. I'm not saying that this happens all the time because fish simply would no longer get caught tight line fishing, but certainly when the carp are finicky, on edge so to speak, tight lines can now destroy all chances of success. Anything that is obvious such as line rising directly from the bottom i.e. tight line fishing, can be associated with the fact a fish was caught close by.

Just the same thing happened with anti tangle tubing. It is obviously something to associate with. When few people used it, its effects were entirely beneficial. Besides stopping tangles it virtually eliminated cut outs on gravel bars, but from becoming just another twig or weed stem rising to the surface, it became something that was there each time a carp was hooked. It became on pressurised waters, something that could not be used on a tight line. However its benefits are so obvious, it became a case of learning how best to use it again, the solution being at this moment in time, to make sure that it is well and truly flat to the bottom. I have friends who even go to the length of camouflaging it with paint to blend in with whatever bottom they are fishing.

Enough of this, I think I have shown how carp will react once under pressure and hopefully guides on how to control it. Whilst many English waters are at pressure point, more and more anglers are travelling to enjoy the relative quiet of the host of carp lakes, rivers and canals available on the continent. Over the last couple of seasons I have had the opportunity to fish waters throughout France, Belgium and Holland and, touch wood, with only one exception have caught carp at all of them within a couple of days. The method used will be described later in the book but I think more importantly it shows that the location was right. The time when I didn't catch, after leaving, another carp angler took over the swim and caught a number of fish the following day, so I don't think I was far out on that one, just that bad weather conditions had put the carp off feeding.

The approach to every water be it a ten mile long lake, or a 2 acre pool has been the same. The beliefs set out in the original book hold true, find the food. If it's a river or canal, find somewhere quiet away from boat traffic, although that statement can be reversed when a water is under pressure from anglers, carp will often then find refuge beneath boats, but food is the real answer. Shallows offer food, weed does the same, reeds trap food. Points jutting out into lakes trap food and make perfect interception areas. The farther south I've travelled and the hotter the water temperatures have become, so does the need for a steady supply of oxygen become recognised. All of the very big lakes I've fished have had rivers or small streams feeding them at some point,

'Night stalking' can produce . . . this time a 24 Redmire leather

the mouths of which offer areas rich in oxygen. I have found that in these warmer waters it is most likely that there will be different areas in which the carp will feed during daytime and night. Most French lakes have night bans on fishing but during the hour before dusk and the first two hours after dawn you can expect carp to be in their night time feeding areas.

Shallow water is ideal for these periods simply because there is plenty of easy food and the carp know it. At Lake Cassien I caught a fish of 46lb 8oz in only three feet of water, while two fish of over 50lbs were taken in only 8 feet. Back in 1985 during early summer there was little or no bankside disturbance, yet the carp left the shallows within two hours of dawn. I can only presume that this was because the shallow water became too warm for the carp, plus the fact that their main natural diet there, the crayfish, also went deeper in an effort to hide, the lower light intensity of deeper water enabling this. The higher the sun rose in the sky and the hotter the water became the greater the depth the carp fed at. Before angling pressure affected them, 30 to 35 feet, was the most likely depth to find them feeding in during the hottest part of the day. The carp in St Genez D'olt, another very large lake in southern France, behaved in exactly the same manner.

Obviously to keep in touch with the fish around the clock it is essential to know the contours of the lake bottom and the corresponding depths. While many people use boats and echo sounders to do this, I much prefer to find out by plumbing from the shore. Whilst in a boat it is very difficult to know precisely just how far you are from the bank. By marking your line with Tippex (a milky substance used to eradicate mistakes on type-written letters) every five or ten feet, you can know exactly how far out your plumbing float is.

The rig up I use to find the depths is shown in the diagram. The float wants to be very buoyant and the lead heavy enough to take the float down quickly. I use the same rod all of the time for plumbing, a rod on which I have positioned the butt ring precisely 3 feet from the rim of the spool. First of all cast the plumbing tackle as far out in the swim as you intend to fish and let it sink on a tight line. This ensures that the float and lead will sink together. I then release three feet of line at a time, simply by taking it from the spool up to the butt ring. The float obviously will then rise three feet in the water. The process is then repeated until the float breaks the surface, each time counting the number of feet of line you have taken from the spool, which by checking the Tippex marks on your line, your will also know at what distance it is from the bank. Slowly wind down the float to the lead, then wind in another five feet of line and release the float again, counting off the number of feet from spool to butt ring, it has taken for the float to hit surface. It is just a question of repeating the process every few feet until the float is retrieved and you will know the exact depths throughout the direction on which you cast, in your swim.

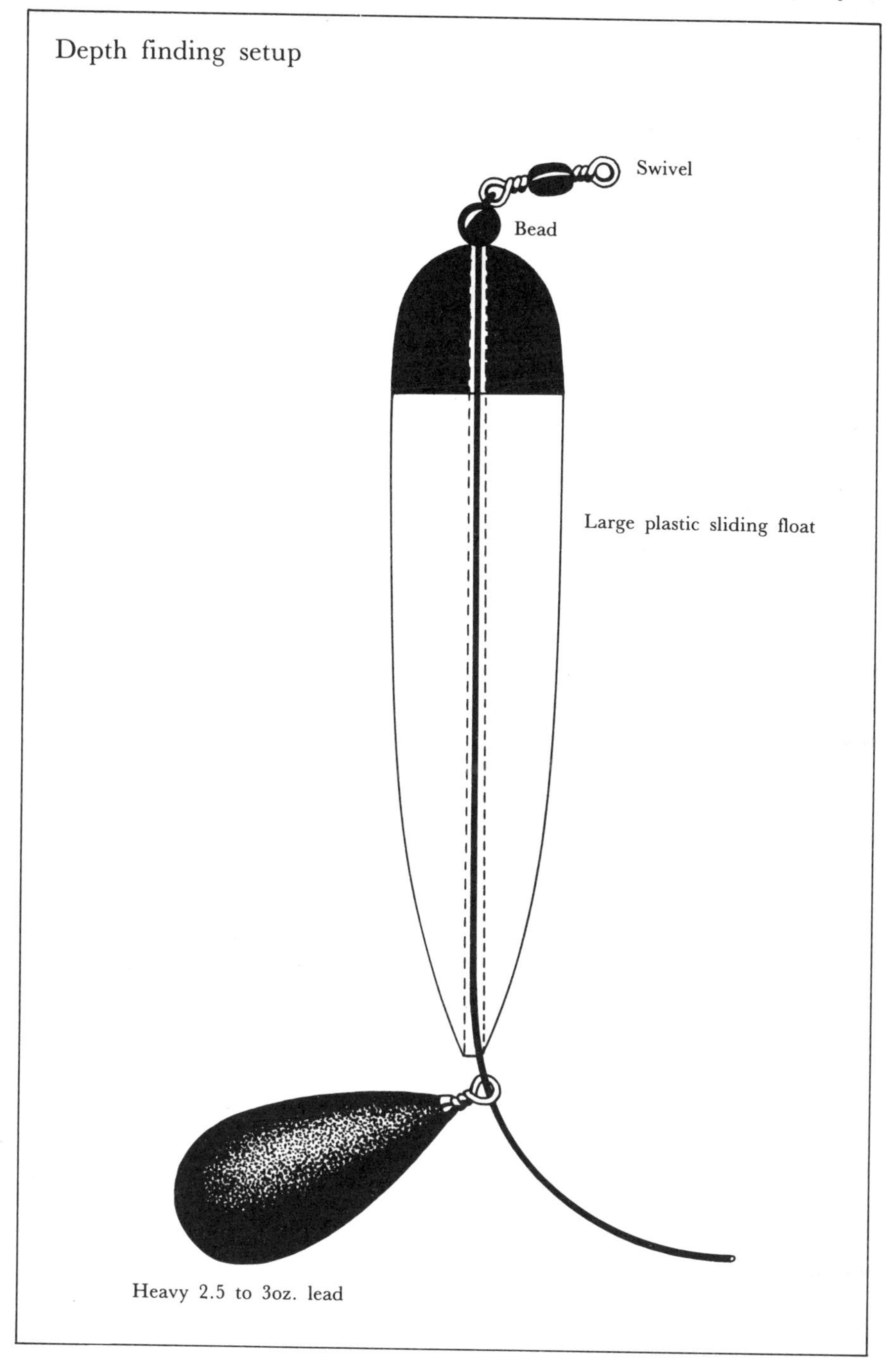
Depth finding setup
Swivel
Bead
Large plastic sliding float
Heavy 2.5 to 3oz. lead

Every time you fish a new lake or even a swim in your local lake you have not fished before you should go through this procedure. It is all the more relevant in waters that are muddy and fish rarely show themselves, or any water where observation is difficult. Knowing the precise depths will give a good indication of where food is more likely to be. On the set up I use, comprising a 12' Horizon 2 1/2lb TC rod, a large streamlined sliding float and a 3oz lead, you can plumb effectively up to a 100 yards range. To do this, tie the antenna of the float back to the line above the lead, using P.V.A. String. A leader of 15lbs breaking strain is used, the leader being just long enough to have 4 turns on the reel at the point of casting. I generally use 7 lbs breaking strain for the main line but a poor caster or one with a poor casting rod will find the distance easier to come by, by going down to 5 or 6 lb breaking strain main line. The float must be extremely buoyant for long distance, the one I find best takes 70 grams of lead to sink it. In these long range circumstances, do not use a lead that incorporates a swivel, or you may have difficulties getting the leader knot through the eye of the swivel. After a while, when you have used this plumbing method many times, you will learn to feel the difference in the different types of bottom, as you retrieve your lead. Large stones will feel like a series of jolts. Gravel will give a scratching sensation up the line, while sand will give a sensation like moving your fingers over sand paper. In thick silt or mud you will really have to pull on the lead, besides which if you have actually landed in it, you will have great difficulty in making the float rise. However this is easy to overcome by putting the lead on a link, with some buoyant material such as cork, polystyrene or the Kevin Nash rig foam at the top of the link. I really do believe that after the countless times I have performed this process I can tell the nature of a bottom just by the feel but for anyone who has yet to gain that experience, further indication can be gained by painting the lead in Tippex. It gives a rubber like coating which is easily scratched by gravel and becomes discoloured in silt and mud.

Carp fishing tackle, methods and baits have moved a long way since 1980, so get the location right and you are three quarters along the way to being a successful carp angler. Your eyes and ears are still the best tools you possess when locating carp. Some, in fact there are many, simply follow other anglers and let them do the location for them but in the long term this gets you nowhere. There comes a time when you will be faced with a big water and no one else to count on, so the art of locating carp is the one thing above all else you should seek to improve.

Finally, as you start to recognise where the food is and the carp are likely to be, you will realise that there are many such spots in most lakes. Which one do you choose? The answer is simple enough really. The one nearest to the pub.

Chapter 3

Tackle and Tactics '80

YOU'LL see from the this chapter that I'm no tackle fanatic – I don't follow fashions, and I prefer to use what time and energy I've got catching carp, rather than getting immersed in technical gadgets. Too many people seem to expend their energy fussing over the visual aspect of what's on the bank, and as long as there's a bait in the water somewhere, they think they're fishing for carp. Well so they are, but I'd rather be putting all my effort into catching them. As Dick Walker said a long time ago, tackle needs to do only two things: to put the bait where the fish can find it, and to hook and land it if it takes the bait.

There is no such article as the perfect all round carp rod, the requirements needed in such a rod being so diverse, as many different situations are encountered. Rather, there are rods that are suited to different situations. Likewise there is no such thing as the perfect all round line or hook, again different situations require different attributes from both these articles. Let us look at a series of situations and the tackle required to meet the problems encountered.

Close range fishing

Close range fishing I would class as fishing within about fifteen yards of the bank, perhaps near overhanging trees with roots stretching underwater. Fishing for carp in this situation requires a rod and line that can absorb the initial run of a carp at close range, whilst at the same time having enough backbone to keep a fish out of trailing branches or roots. The rod should therefore be of a slow or compound taper, the test curve of which depends on which technique of playing a fish an angler uses. I prefer to use a rod with a test-curve of around 1¼ lbs, using my hand to support the middle section of the rod should any extra power seem necessary. Anglers who prefer to play a fish just through

What it's all about . . . a 30lb Leather

the rod usually go for a more powerful test-curve between 1½lb to 1¾lbs, the taper being the same.

The line, needing the ability to absorb shock, should therefore not be of the pre-stretched variety, and have a breaking strain of 10 to 15 pounds depending on the size of fish likely to be encountered. At the moment there is a certain amount of debate going on as regards carp and lines. One successful angler has expressed the view that carp are more afraid of lines than hooks. His conclusions come from observing the reactions of carp to different items in the confines of a tank. Taking his observations into account, he advocates the use of a line as fine as possible. My view, however, is that if one's tackle is presented correctly, neither line nor hook should scare carp. Indeed I tend always to go on the safe side as regards line, increasing the strength rather than decreasing it with finer lines. Rarely do I go below 11 lbs breaking strain, only doing so when a finer line is needed to aid long distance casting. Even then my minimum strength is 9.6 lb; I don't go below that because I don't see the need. Despite what other angling writers have advocated, I have yet to find a water where I have needed fine lines to enable me to catch carp.

Back to close range fishing and the type of hook that is needed. Its number one requirement is strength, other requirements being dictated by the type of bait used. Should the bait be a soft paste or par-boiled potato, where the hook is buried within the bait, then a hook which requires the minimum of force to pull it through that bait is needed. The best hook therefore is one with a small surface contact area i.e. the thinnest wire to do the job, and narrow gape. The ideal hook in this situation is not readily available on the market, but a cut down Partridge Salmon hook, solder blobbed to provide a spade end, meets the requirements. If the bait is a hard boiled paste bait (in which case the hook can be left on the outside of the bait), then the hook's only requirements are strength and sharpness. The precise model of hook depends only on the individual angler's preferences. If the bait used is of the particle variety a strong hook, round or crystal bend, with a gape large enough to prevent the point of the hook being masked by the bait on the shank, is needed. A size 2 Mustad Salmon hook meets all these requirements.

Medium to long range fishing

In this example our quarry is feeding at a distance of 60–80 yards. The water is free of snags and of a uniform depth of around 8 feet. There are no bankside snags or tree roots likely to be encountered.

The lack of snags in this case allows the angler to play his hooked fish out in open water before being brought to the net. The rod does not need the ability to absorb shock at close range, the main requirement being the ability to cast a bait and set a hook at the range being fished. The most suitable rod, therefore, has a fast taper with a test-curve of 2 to 2½lbs. Rods made of both glass fibre and carbon fibre are suitable here, which one depending on the extent of the angler's bank balance. If you can afford the extra cost of a carbon rod, then all well and good. Carbon blanks are extremely light and, I find, a joy to use. Whereas a glass blank of the required taper is very thick at the butt and requires two hands to strike and play a fish, the slim handle of a carbon rod enables one handed strikes to be made. Also, being thinner, they cut through the air faster than glass, setting hooks that bit quicker. However, glass will do the job; after all thousands of carp were caught at this distance before carbon rods were on the market.

The line to be used in this situation needs different qualities than that used for close range fishing. There is no need for the line to be able to absorb shock at such range. Its main requirement is to transmit the power of the strike to the hook. Also a more direct feel of the fish at this range is beneficial. Bearing this in mind, a pre-stretched line would seem in order, my personal preference being "Abulon Extra" of 9.6 lbs breaking strain. Although this line is no longer manufactured many shops still stock it, and the fact that it is sold in a light-proof plastic case appears to stop any marked deterioration whilst on the shelf. It does however need dyeing, as it is bright blue in the original state. However, if stocks cannot be obtained a reliable alterative can be found in "Sylcast Bronze", again a prestretched line, which is available from most good tackle shops.

The shape of the hook needed is again determined by the type of bait being used, only in this case as less power will be transmitted to it, a hook of finer gauge wire can be used. For example, "Au Lion D'Or" hooks are excellent here for soft paste baits. The angler should also consider barbless hooks in the situation where few or no snags are likely to be encountered. At long range they undoubtedly penetrate far more easily than a conventional barbed hook.

A true hat-trick . . . 20lb Common, Mirror and Leather carp, caught in the same session

Extreme long-range fishing

The problems of long-range fishing are magnified at extreme distances over 80 yards, which are sometimes necessary in order to put your bait amongst feeding carp. The type of lake in which this style of fishing may be necessary is often a gravel pit, with a hard bottom consisting of gulleys and gravel bars formed when it was dug out. To reach the feeding carp, the angler has to cast over literally dozens of gravel bars which reach to within a couple of feet of the surface. The tops of the gravel bars are colonised by pea and zebra mussels, and their sides covered with thick lush weed growth. The margins of the lake may be well landscaped, again with plenty of overhanging trees with trailing roots.

The situation, which is encountered on many of the large southern counties gravel pits, is in my opinion the most difficult there is to deal with. It presents a whole series of problems: (1) setting a hook at 100 yards; (2) having hooked a fish, being able to keep your line off the mussel-colonised gravel bars, to stop it being cut; (3) having set the hook and prevented the line cutting on the gravel bars, the rod has to be powerful enough to stop a fish reaching bankside snags, yet able to absorb close range runs and not be so powerful that the hook will be torn out. (I must also add here that it is my opinion that more fish are lost through the hook being torn out by too powerful a rod or too much pressure being applied whilst playing fish, than by a hook not being set in by the strike. I believe a hook is rarely set deeply in by the strike, but just nicks the skin, working its way in by continual pressure during the fight.)

On hooking a fish the angler has to hold his rod as high as possible in order to lift as much line as possible off the sand and gravel bars. With this in mind, the rod must be as light as possible, otherwise the angler's arms will soon be aching. Yet that same rod must also have power to set the hook and be of sufficient length to keep the line high out of the water. This is where, in my opinion, carbon comes to the fore, being basically a much stiffer yet far lighter material than glass fibre. Again the rod also has to have the ability to absorb shock close in, so the ideal is a compound taper carbon rod. In order to have sufficient power to set the hook, the rod should be longer than general carp rods, by increasing the length to 12 feet. Although compound taper, with its real power between the middle to ⅔ sections of the rod, the increased length pushes that power to a higher level, increasing hooking penetration.

Line

Having decided just what is required of the rod, we must now look at what we require in the line. A plain pre-stretched monofil line, although suitable for long-range fishing in normal circumstances, is unfortunately liable to snap on the first graze from gravel. An ordinary non-stretched line appears to be much more durable, and so a compromise is called for. The line also has to be fine enough to assist long distance casting, but again the finer the line the less the margin for error. We must also look for ways of keeping as much of the line as possible off the bottom. In my opinion, this situation calls for the use of a shock leader. At the extreme range being fished, the angle between rod and

BASIC PARTICLE SHOCK RIG '80

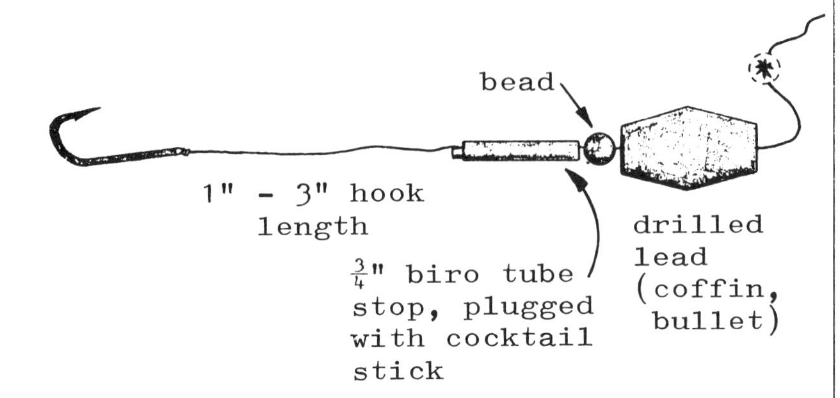

* If baits are taken well down, or bite-offs occur, pinch a swanshot on the line about 1" behind the leger weight.

SHOCK RIG WITH BREAKOFF LEAD

Useful when fishing snaggy areas

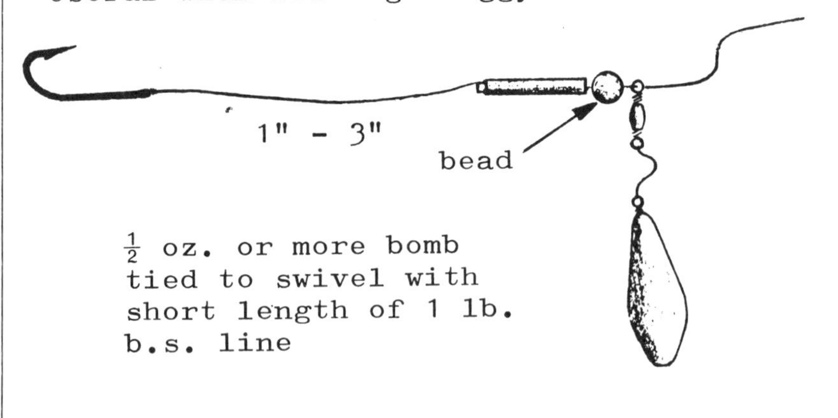

bait will mean in the region of 15 to 20 feet of line lying on the bottom, presuming the gravel bars in the region of the hook bait are within a couple of feet of the surface. The shock leader should take this into account, being of the same length (i.e. 15 to 20 feet). The use of a floatant such as "Mucilin" on the shock leader will also help to keep it off the bottom. To improve things still further, by using a braided material such as dacron or terylene for the leader greater quantities of floatant can be used, as the braided material will absorb the floatant, whereas monofil can only be coated. The braided leader ensures there is no stretch in the last 20 feet, thereby helping hook penetration. Secured to the leader by an "Abu" barrel knot, I would use a main line of "Sylcast Bronze" of 9½ or 10 lbs breaking strain. Although this is pre-stretched, it is not stretched to its limit, and still has a certain amount of elasticity. At this range, I'd go for a barbless hook every time, for easier penetration. The model I use is a "Mustad" hook, supplied by Dons of Edmonton, although I'm not sure if they are still stocked.

Baits and Rigs

The purpose of using these examples is to show that it's not just a case of casting out a carp bait, on a carp rod, on a strong line. Thought must be given to each single item of the tackle, in each different situation. The same rules apply to terminal rigs. The rig to be used again depends on the type of bait, the nature of the lake bottom, the amount of snags present, the relative awareness of the carp, and also the length of time of the fishing session undertaken. As with the rods, lines and hooks discussed above, the angler should be asking himself "Will this terminal set-up do the job I want it to?".

With regard to baits, in this respect they can be divided into three groups: particles, pastes and floaters. All need a different presentation to fulfil their maximum potential, the reason being the different types of feeding associated with each bait.

Particles

When particles are being used as a bottom bait, the carp respond with a feeding method reminiscent of a vacuum cleaner, moving slowly over the baited patch taking in great mouthfuls of seeds and mud, often dwelling on the same spot for many minutes. This can lead the carp into swallowing the hook bait, which in turn usually results in the angler's line being cut on the teeth in the carp's throat. To prevent this happening, the angler has somehow to shock the carp into running before the bait is swallowed. This is done by intentionally creating resistance on the line, once the bait has been picked up, by using a leger weight situated as close to the hook bait as bottom weed will allow. Snags and the nature of the bottom also dictate whether or not the leger weight is put directly on the reel line, or attached by means of a short link. Either way the important point is that resistance must be felt by the carp. Heavy butt indicators will also help some way in achieving this aim.

There is a certain amount of debate over what the length should be between hook and leger stop. Many anglers say that they only get good runs on long hook lengths. If this is the case, my opinion is that the carp is already afraid of the bait. It is being inspected individually like a conventional bait and only taken if there is no resistance. The tackle is not wrong, but the bait. I have been told that bite offs (when the fish swallows the bait) don't occur with these long hook lengths. Again, I believe this only adds more weight to my point. The carp is still suspicious of the bait, holding it in the front of its mouth when it moves off, as it would with a paste bait it was afraid of. Luckily for the angler, with much of the hook lying bare, there is a good chance of hooking the fish.

I always try to get the bait right in the first place, and having done that expect heavy preoccupied feeding, in which many bait samples may be eaten at the same time. With a long hook length and no resistance, bite offs would occur regularly. So with particles I always go for the "shock" rig described earlier in the book. I did at one time use hook lengths of nine inches with some success. However I have now gone down to three inch lengths, losing no fish through bite offs, with less chance of tangles on casting, and with no decrease in the amount of runs. I now use far heavier leads than I used to, half and three quarter ounce leads being used even in margin swims. I believe they help achieve the shock effect I want better than a light lead. Heavy, stiffish line also helps. It may sound crude, but the point is that it has been thought out and it works.

A theory put round by some carp anglers is that an extra sharp hook will help achieve a shock effect i.e. the fish will bolt on being pricked by the hook point. As far as I'm concerned, this is a complete fallacy. For a start, regardless of whatever method is used, the hook should be honed to perfect sharpness, but that apart, the theory to my mind shows a complete lack of thought. The natural diet of a carp involves eating molluscs, crustacea, caddis etc. It is unthinkable that in the crushing and eating of these food items a carp never pricks itself on a shell fragment. So at all times keep your hooks sharp, but don't go thinking they will make a fish bolt – lead and resistance should achieve that.

Paste Baits

The feeding response to paste baits is completely opposite to that of particles, by the very fact that each bait is inspected and taken individually. The bait should therefore behave the same as any free offerings that are picked up. With that in mind, the angler should do everything possible to rule out any resistance which a carp could feel on picking up the hook bait. Free-lining, the use of long link-legers, and fixed paternosters, are all ways of achieving this, in different circumstance.

The various merits of free-lining as opposed to legering are well documented, so I'll just add that I myself would not free-line a bait at a distance of more than 25 yards. After that I believe its disadvantages outnumber its advantages. The main disadvantages are: (1) lack of a sufficiently tight line to the bait, preventing the angler from adequately interpreting what is going on; (2) continual tightening up, to try to keep a tight line, moves the bait, often out of the baited swim; (3) relative lack of weight at the bait end often results in currents and water pressure on the line moving the bait; (4) little indication is given when a fish moves with the bait towards the angler, resulting in a slack line bite.

The choice of link leger or fixed paternoster depends a lot on the length of the fishing session undertaken. If the hook length and tail to the leger bomb were the same length

A typical tackle box of the time

in both cases, then I believe the fixed paternoster would be both more sensitive and provide less resistance to a feeding carp in the initial stages of a run, since the tail to the leger weight must be straightened out directly to the fish before any resistance is felt. Until this line is taken up the method has the advantages of free lining, plus some of the advantages of link legering i.e. direct indication, and little movement of bait. However, once the tail has straightened out the full weight of the leger is felt by the fish, probably resulting in the dropping of the bait. Therefore, for the angler fishing over his rods on a short session, where he can hit the bites before the lead is felt, I believe the fixed paternoster is the most efficient method for paste fishing.

The link leger, involving the line running through some sort of eye, be it a swivel or split ring, must create some resistance, however slight. The eye is also prone to clogging by weed, or being buried by its own weight, both creating extra resistance. However, if that resistance can be kept to the absolute minimum and a fish induced to take the bait, then that slight resistance will be constant and the carp should carry on running with the bait. On a long session, which could involve night fishing, where the angler becomes tired and correspondingly reacts slower to a run, link legering would seem the method to use.

Float fishing

Within the context of terminal rigs, we should also look at the relative merits of float fishing. Its merits are: (1) quick indication of a bite, due to its proximity to the bait; (2) lack of resistance to a taking fish; (3) it shows well the direction and depth of a hooked fish; (4) it is less open to line bites from bottom feeding fish. On the other hand: (1) to take full advantage of its ability to indicate bites quickly, only one rod can be used; (2) the bait is more liable to move due to wind and current pressure on the float; (3) casting distance is cut down; (4) in shallow water, the sight of a float may alarm fish; (5) in extremely clear water, with only bottom weed growth, the line coming perpendicularly from the float could alarm fish; (6) eye strain may result on a long session. Taking all this into consideration, I believe float fishing to be a useful arrow in the angler's armoury, but because of its limitations, the most suitable times are when fish are behaving cautiously at close range and mouthing baits but not running off with them, or when fishing in close proximity to snags, and quick indication of a bite is needed.

Dick Walker has advocated the use of a float in conjunction with particles fished at close-range in order to prevent bite-offs. Many years ago when first presented with this problem, I too thought float fishing was the answer. In fact I suffered more bite-offs as a result, due I believe to the lack of resistance. I also suffered a number of false bites due to the bottom shot being picked up in mistake for a bait; this problem arises when using any of the small pea baits. It can be overcome I'm told, by the use of mouse-dropping or Olliveti leads, but to be honest, with particles the method is not for me. Which only goes to prove that I'm a lousy float fisherman: its just a matter of paying your money, and making your choice.

Floating Baits

The choice of tackle when using floating baits is basically decided by whether one wishes

Buoyant baits produced even before 'the hair'

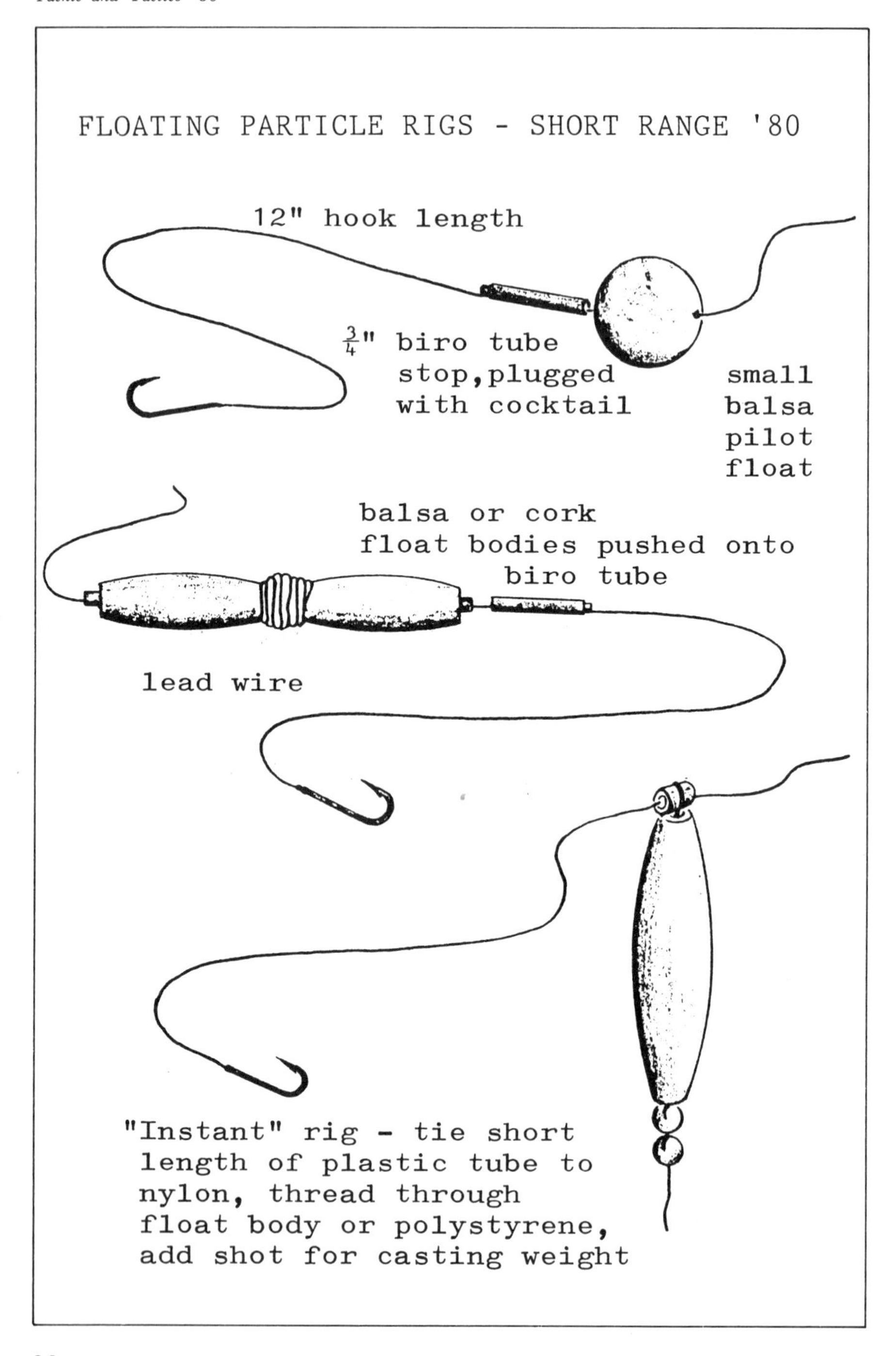
FLOATING PARTICLE RIGS - SHORT RANGE '80
12" hook length
¾" biro tube
stop, plugged
with cocktail
small
balsa
pilot
float
balsa or cork
float bodies pushed onto
biro tube
lead wire
"Instant" rig - tie short
length of plastic tube to
nylon, thread through
float body or polystyrene,
add shot for casting weight

the bait to remain static or float along with the surface current. A static bait is achieved by the simple use of a link leger rig. The bait is allowed to float to the surface, whilst a heavy indicator is used at the rod to counterbalance the bait. In the case of a free-floating surface bait there are several options open to us. At close range a completely free-lined buoyant bait, using either a greased line, or with the line held off the surface by the rod, fits the bill admirably. Once the bait is used at a distance of more than 20 yards, however, problems start. With a straight free-lined bait, it is very difficult to make the bait float at the same speed as other material floating on the surface current. The mere weight of line is enough to slow down the bait. The angler is faced with the constant necessity to mend his line in order to try to keep up with the surface flow, and also to keep the bait floating in a straight line, otherwise any drag causes the bait to move in an arc across the current.

There are several ways of improving this situation, each involving the use of some other buoyant material upon the line. These materials also add weight, which in itself helps casting, should extra distance be necessary. I'll list these aids in no particular order of merit, as each does the job to a certain degree (that is, efficient enough to catch some fish), whilst at the same time admitting that I do not think the perfect solution has yet been found: (1) the time honoured use of a partially-filled bubble float, attached above the bait. This method went out of fashion for many years, but does its job as well as methods that have evolved in recent years. Its sheer bulk provides air and water resistance against the bait being speeded up in the surface current. Its disadvantage, however, is that if a taking fish is not hooked before the resistance of the float is felt, then the bait is liable to be spat out; (2) the use of a non-leaded zoomer float, attached top and bottom to the line. With its slender shape, little resistance is felt by a taking fish. Its shape also creates little air resistance and so helps in casting light baits, such as floating particles. However that lack of air resistance does not help in keeping the line straight, although the buoyancy of the float helps line to be fed out; (3) the use of small balsa surface floats. These do the same job as a bubble float, but lack the weight and so are not such an aid to casting. They do however have an advantage in that they can be shaped and painted in the same colour as other floating materials, such as leaves, feathers, or twig fragments; (4) the use of a cigar-shaped balsa float containing a lead insert, the shape of which aids distance casting. Size can be varied to carry sufficient lead to achieve the required distance; (5) the use of a length of fly line. This again adds casting weight and is very buoyant, making the main line very easy to mend. The only real disadvantage is that an extra two knots are incorporated into the tackle where the fly line is joined to the reel line and hook length. Any extra knots of course make weak links in the tackle. Carp are very quick to wise up to any visible article found in close proximity to a bait they've been caught on. It takes time but eventually they seem to add two and two together. So when takes slow down to one of the listed methods, it pays to switch to one of the others.

Twitch bites

Whilst on the subject of tackle and terminal rigs, it seems to me that the topic of twitch bites might be relevant. When an angler comes across this problem, he usually either changes

FIXED PATERNOSTER
FOR ANCHORED FLOATING BAITS '80

This method is more efficient at hooking than the standard link-leger rig, as the strike is directly at the bait, not first through the bomb.

LONG RANGE BALSA
"SAUSAGE"

"Sausage" made from 6" plus length of shaped balsa; insert barrel lead for weight.

his terminal set-up, and also probably changes down to a finer line, or he adjusts his indicators to a short drop, with his pick-ups on, and strikes at the merest movement of the indicator. This to my mind is a case of just trying to live with a problem, not solving it. I believe the angler should be thinking "Why are the carp twitching on the bait?"

"Twitchers" can be divided in two groups; the confident twitcher, and the cautious twitcher. The confident twitcher picks the bait up, eating it on the spot, instead of moving off and giving a conventional run. This is often the effect of over-heavy ground baiting with bait samples. The fish has probably eaten many samples already, gaining confidence that the bait is safe. The fact that the next sample which it moves to is very close at hand prevents any major movement or run from the fish. The angler can alter his terminal tackle so that it provides a shock effect but this, as I said earlier, is a case of just living with the problem. If the bait is a paste, the fact that a carp might associate that shock with an individual food item, can easily make it suspicious of that bait in the future. It is far better to avoid the problem in the first place. This can be achieved by ground baiting two areas approximately four yards apart. Hook baits are then cast midway between the two areas. When a fish picks up the hook bait, it then has to move at least two yards to its next bait sample, giving the angler a conventional run.

The cautious twitcher is a different creature altogether. It is afraid of the bait, yet at the same time wants it. The fact that the fish is mouthing the bait (giving the actual twitch), means that it wants that food item. However for some reason it is also afraid

"The business end"

of the bait. Its fear may derive from many things: the bait being used may be reminiscent of a bait on which the carp has been caught before, either in appearance, smell or texture, or the particular fish may have been hooked in precisely the same spot making it afraid of confident feeding in that area. In one case, I know of a lake where fish twitched on one particular make of line! A local specimen group leased the lake, every member using the same make of line, in the same breaking strain. The carp eventually learned that a food item attached to a certain coloured line of a certain diameter meant trouble. It was not until a guest angler fished the lake and had success on the same bait as the syndicate members, but on a different line of greater breaking strain, that the anglers were able to put two and two together. Whilst admitting that this shows awareness to an extreme on the carp's part, it also illustrates how carp can associate different materials with danger.

It is said that carp in certain lakes are more clever than carp in others. This I don't believe. A carp's awareness grows the more times it is caught, and the greater the fishing intensity on a particular water. However on some waters, through over-stocking or a natural lack of food, caution is thrown to the wind. On many waters, anglers' baits have to be eaten in order for fish to survive. Early this season I fished a small one-acre lake, where the fishing is really intensive from the season's beginning till its end. No ground baiting is allowed on the lake whatsoever, which in turn means that every bait has a hook in it. In such a small lake every carp has been hooked a number of times, and so naturally they have developed caution. Within five minutes of casting out a bait, you get a good six inch twitch. Although all the anglers fishing were expecting this twitch, being tuned up for it and striking accordingly, not once did I see a fish hooked. After observing this situation for a full day, I decided to leave the twitches completely alone. What happened was that after five minutes came the first 6 inch twitch. If no strike was made, five minutes or so later came another good lift of nine inches to a foot. Hitting these also proved futile. If that second twitch was also left alone, then a couple of minutes later a full confident run developed.

My thinking on the situation was this. The carp were well aware that each new bait they came across had a hook in it. After being hooked many times the carp started behaving cautiously, picking up the bait and moving off a short distance with it held on the very outside of their lips. In this position resulting strikes missed the fish. After performing this procedure a couple of times, the carp found the baits which had been struck off the hook safe to eat. It was not a thought process in the carp, but a gradual development of awareness built up by fear of being hooked. The answer to it all again is for the angler to think, "Is the carp suspicious of the bait, the area being fished, or some item of tackle? Or are they really aware and are "trying" the bait out, to see if it is safe?" The angler has to decide just what that item is which causes suspicion and find an alternative to it.

Hooks

I'd like to go back to that most important item of the tackle, the hook, and describe two different theories. This I hope will help the angler decide just what make of a certain pattern he should choose. Theory (1) is that the shorter the distance between point and

HOOKS & BAITS '80

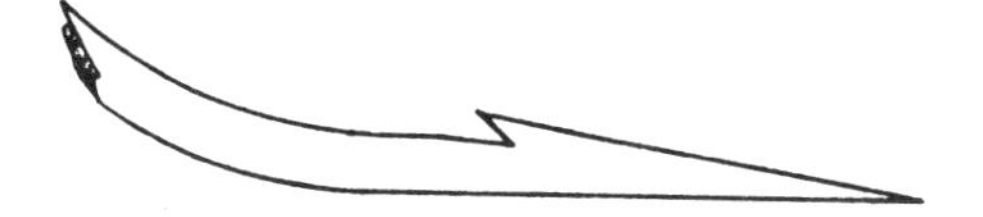

Long needle point - good penetration

Short wedge point, blunt angle, and
poor penetration.
When your hooks look like this,
chuck them out!

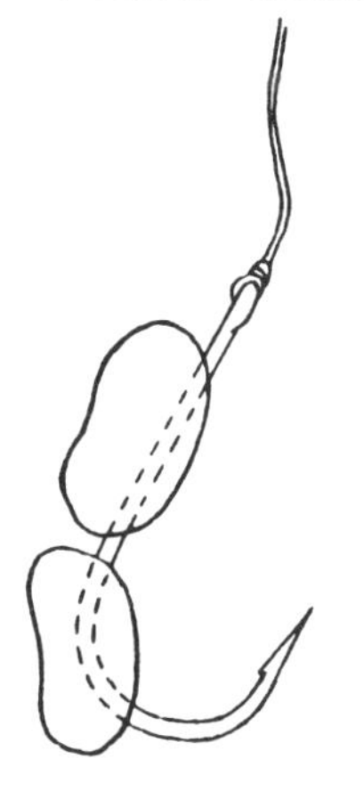

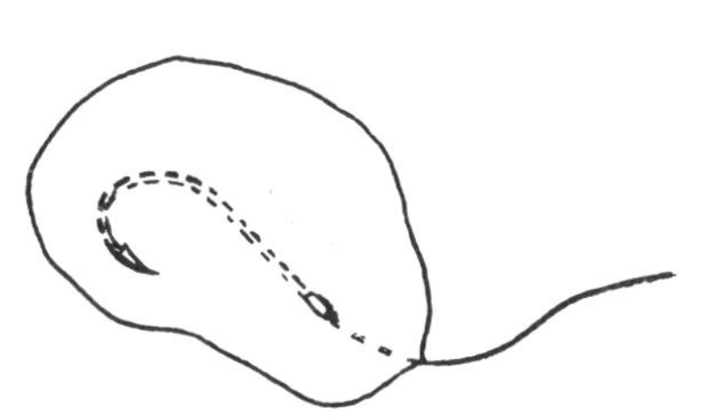

Hook with narrow gape,
thin wire and inturned
point to pull through
paste bait

For a given size of particle, make
sure the hook gape is wide enough
to keep the point clear if the bait
swivels round.

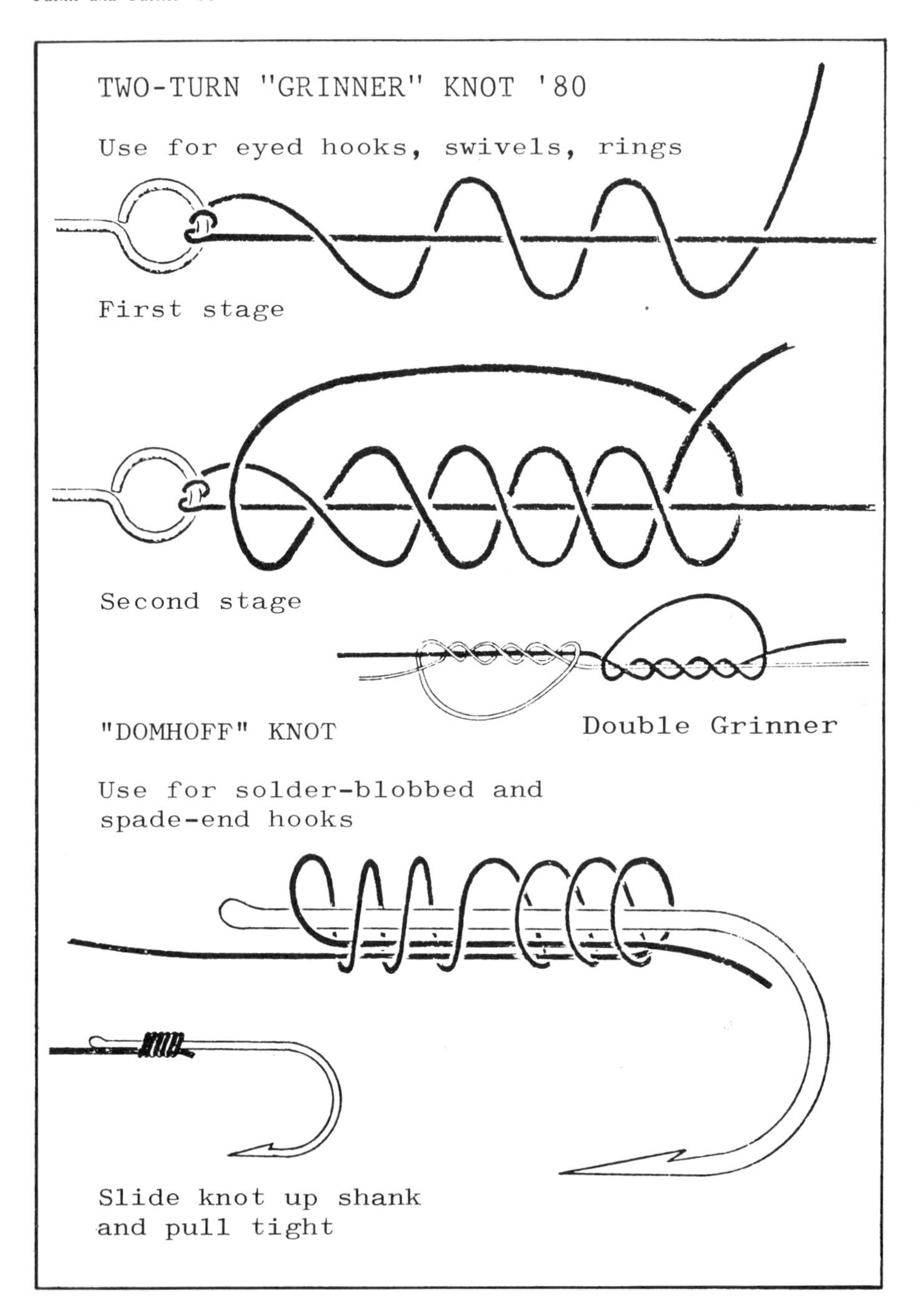
TWO-TURN "GRINNER" KNOT '80
Use for eyed hooks, swivels, rings
First stage
Second stage
"DOMHOFF" KNOT
Double Grinner
Use for solder-blobbed and spade-end hooks
Slide knot up shank and pull tight

hook barb, the easier it is to set the hook home over the barb on the strike. Theory (2) is that the longer the distance between point and barb, the greater the chance of a successful hook hold. At first glance, theory (1) would seem the most credible. But go into it more deeply and theory (2) comes out on top. Let me explain. The closer the point is to the barb, the greater the angle formed at the point of the hook. As the barb is moved down the hook, so that angle decreases. With the barb close to the point, what we are left with is a wedge-shape, while the further the barb is moved down, the more a needle shape is formed. What would you rather hammer into a piece of wood, a wedge or a needle? The angler may decide that he can punch the short barb in on the strike. If that strike is not successful, however, there is very little of the point in the fish and that point is at a very blunt angle. The chance of the hook then falling out is great. With a long barb, which I prefer, I don't expect to pull the hook in over the barb on the strike. I do however expect to have enough point in the fish to hook it. The needle shape works its way in over the barb by continuous pressure, while the fish is being played. Again the choice is up to the angler as to which theory seems most practical and logical to him.

Where the tackle for carp fishing is concerned the hook and the line must be 100 per cent. Hooks must be stronger than any force they will have to bear, and as sharp as is possible. Line should be of a constant diameter, and break consistently at or above the given wet strength for that line. Due to the state of your bank balance, you may have to compromise on the rod issue. There can however be no compromise with hooks and lines. Rather do without some other item of tackle than settle for the cheapest or second best hooks and lines. It is they that land fish, other items being mere aids by comparison.

Having stressed that hooks and lines are the two most important items of tackle, obviously the joining of the two, the knot, is critical. All anglers have their favourites, my own preferences being the Domhoff knot (as recommended by Jack Hilton) on all spade end or solder blob hooks, while for all eyed hooks, or for joining swivels or split rings, I use the Two-turn Grinner knot. In the case of the Domhoff knot, I use as many turns around the shank as I can get on – I believe this evens out the pressure on the line underneath the turns.

Other tackle items

Although not essential, another item of tackle which I myself would be lost without is the catapult. There is still no ideal weapon on the market, but by adapting present ones a passable compromise can be achieved. I use the American "sling shot" type which uses tubular silicone rubber. This rubber is far more powerful and longer-lasting than the conventional square rubber. Two models, the "Hunter Sharp Shooter" and "Barnett Diablo" can be obtained through the advertisements in "Exchange and Mart". The pouches or slings on both models are suitable for paste baits, but for particles your own pouches have to be put on. The velocity of the rubber is such that pouches only last a short time, so they must be very strong. They should have a number of holes in them to allow air to escape, otherwise the speed built up by the silicone rubber is slowed down by an air pocket, and the advantage over conventional rubber lost.

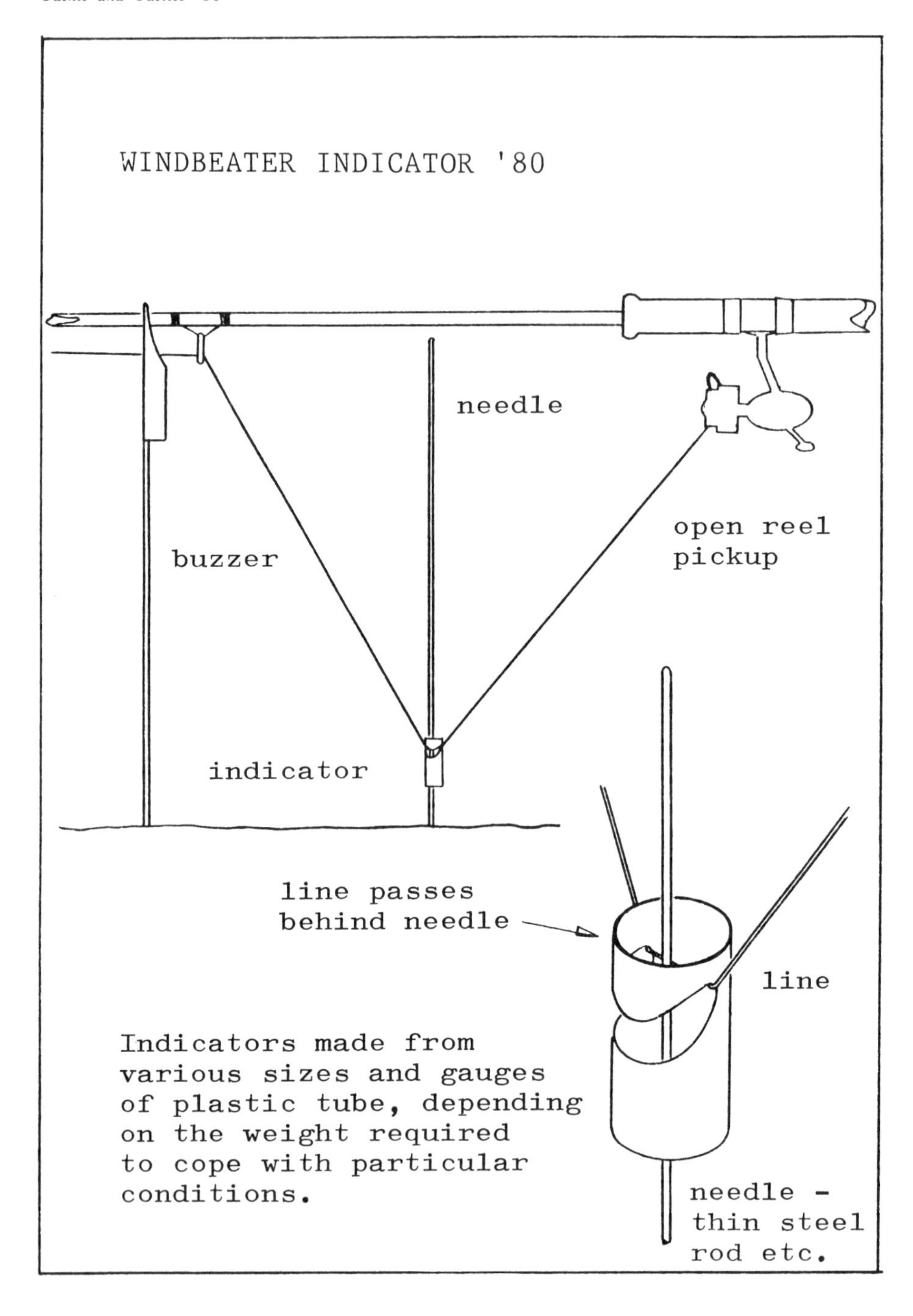
WINDBEATER INDICATOR '80
needle
open reel
pickup
buzzer
indicator
line passes
behind needle
line
Indicators made from
various sizes and gauges
of plastic tube, depending
on the weight required
to cope with particular
conditions.
needle -
thin steel
rod etc.

It is always handy to have a good pair of binoculars. These can be used for scanning the water looking for signs of feeding fish, such as swirling, bubbling etc. Even if the fish never show or bubble on your local water, they still come in handy for watching the local crumpet.

Striking

I don't think striking technique can be taught; the physique of the angler and the amount of room available in each swim determines how you strike. The important thing is always to strike on a tight line. One angling author I read advocated striking as soon as the line moves; this I believe the worst advice possible. My own striking technique is something like this: with particle baits and soft rods, I pick up the rod and wait until the rod is virtually pulling in my hands before I bend the rod into the fish (whilst at the same time usually depositing a cup of steaming hot coffee into my lap. If the reader wishes to copy, the coffee is optional.)

With paste baits, or when fishing at any distance over thirty yards, I pick up the rod, wait for the line to pull tight, step two paces back and strike high and sideways over my right shoulder, usually (but not always) falling over my bedchair in the same movement. Again the last part is optional. If I'm really on form, I can also manage to cut off all the overhanging branches of nearby trees in the same striking movement.

Indicators

Although buzzers are not an essential item, I do believe they are beneficial. Contrary to most opinions, I find the buzzer of most help in the day. Having audible indication allows me to survey the water looking for signs of feeding fish. I can't do this if my eyes are glued to a pair of bobbins. Any item which allows the angler more time for observation should help put more fish on the bank. There are lots of good buzzers on the market today, the most popular perhaps being the "Optonic" system. While excellent for small waters where drag is often non existent, for large pits, where the majority of my fishing is done, I prefer the "A.J.S." system. These are really a refined version of the old antenna design and as such are not as susceptible to false bleeps.

The majority of carp anglers also use some sort of visual indicator on the line. The one employed by my friends and I is the windbeater system, the brainchild of Ricky Gibbinson of Essex. This method keeps the indicator on a needle until a strike is made, at which point it falls off the line. Its biggest advantage to me is that one is not continually getting up and down to replace an indicator on a needle, should wind, drag or twitches be troublesome. The actual indicators can be made from a variety of materials, their individual weights being used to combat the prevailing conditions. I have made them from thin plastic obtained from vending machine cups, plastic salt cellars, rod corks and, for really windy weather, gun cartridge cases.

Retaining fish

One final and important point is that of retaining fish. If a fish must be kept for

Gary using a modern weighing sling, much preferable to a net one which can damage scales and fins

The result of an hour's action when it all comes right

photographing, handle it in the safest way possible. Sacks made from soft nylon or "Courtelle", with holes punched or burned in them are the best. Fish should be left in these for the shortest possible time. Remember that if any damage is done to a fish, no growth will take place until that damage has healed. In the case of big fish, many will have finished their growing years, and damaged cell tissue takes a very long time to heal; sometimes healing will not take place and then infection sets in. So at all times, take care, not only to preserve your own fish and enjoyment, but also that of others.

Chapter 4

Tackle and Tactics '80 to '88

This chapter will probably give an overriding picture of a time when the greatest changes were made in carp fishing, yet to me it represents a period when nothing really new was found out about carp. It was simply a period when old ideas and theories were endorsed. It was a weird period when everyone seemed to be taking up angling. Whether it was down to growing unemployment, the mounting pressures of life, or a combination of both and a thousand other things, who can say? The fact was, every day another fisherman seemed to be born. Really big carp were now being caught regularly, and they captured the public's imagination. They appeared in the weeklies with the actual bait recipes used and diagrams of the terminal tackle you would need to use to catch such fish. The angling weeklies' circulation leapt. Each month new periodicals appeared on the local newsagent's shelf. I remember reading a letter along the lines of "I subscribe to two weeklies and three monthly magazines just in the hope of reading the occasional article on the one thing that occupies my mind, carp fishing. I know there are thousands of anglers just like me, why can't we have a publication just devoted to carp?" The fact was, angling and carp angling more particularly, had become big news.

The hair and the boilie had arrived during the writing of the original chapter, and was no longer the asset of just a privileged few. It was now as common knowledge to the average angler as the swim feeder or stick float. Suddenly, silly but innovative ideas spoken of over a few pints by groups of anglers started hitting the press, before they had even been put to the test by their innovators. Some ideas just weren't getting the chance to be brought to their rightful conclusions. While at the same time, it has be be admitted that lots of different minds looking from the outside at problems which confronted but a few, soon turned up new ideas, just by having a fresh point of view.

Almost overnight I think, Kevin Maddocks transformed the face of carp fishing. Before I suppose, us so called name carp anglers liked to think of ourselves as some sort of cult figure, unspoilt by the taint of commercialism. It is true Jim Gibbinson had his name on the occasional rod, but then again Jim did only endorse tackle he actually used; besides which he was a schoolteacher, and anyone who can face a classroom of kids every morning, let alone try to teach them, deserves every penny he gets in my book. But by and large most name carp anglers, would just drop the occasional good fish in the papers, just to let others know we were still about and probably write a once a year article for the monthlies, I suppose to show off about what we had caught over the season. But we always kept our cards close to our chest. Show off your catch but don't give too much away. If you named the water, everyone would be descending on you. Can't name the bait, maybe one day you will be able to fish that lake you've been trying to get in for twenty years. You know you would have it off if you were first in with the bait. Can't name the rod, if they all had the same blanks they would all be able to cast as far as you. Carp fishing had been very much secret society stuff. It was as if you had to earn the right, to serve your apprenticeship before certain secrets would be passed on to you.

As I said previously, suddenly Kevin changed the whole picture. He started appearing regularly in the weeklies with big fish, and not only did he name the water, he also mentioned the rod used, the bait and many times even the actual terminal rig. The papers were not slow to grasp the commercial aspects of this new openness. People would want to buy the rods, baits and bits of tackle they had read about, that meant advertising, that meant revenue. Companies sprang up as if from nowhere to meet the new demand. It was funny really, I had spent years trying to get blank manufacturers to make a twelve foot carp rod, without ever persuading one. They always said that there was no demand. Then the picture changed, they saw there was a demand and they came asking me to design one. As I said at the outset, the idea was not new, the advantages of such a rod were outlined in the original chapter. It was the same with everything. There were now simply enough carp anglers around to make the manufacture of specialist items a viable proposition. Within a short time, everything a carp angler might use was available, be it a custom made bedchair, a ready tied hook rig or a ready made boilie. If he had enough money a newcomer could walk into any decent tackle shop, buy all his rods, tackle and baits and be carp fishing in an hour. Once the market place had been established and the vast majority of ideas had been turned into actual products, there was only one way forward and that was to produce better products utilising the latest materials, technology had given us – and this is how tackle will progress in the future. The state of the art rod for instance will only change in its composition of material, not in its action. To my mind the perfect curve was achieved long ago. What can be improved on is the speed at which a rod moves from the bent position back to the straight. It is this speed that flings a lead out. The faster that speed, the further the cast will go. At this moment in time I believe this is best achieved with a combination of Kevlar and IM7 carbon fibres as utilised in the Sabre range of rods made by my own company, but in years to come I would even expect these to be improved as stiffer materials become available. The beauty of all carbon fibre rods is that they can be designed to actually work at close range by having an action that works all the way through from tip to butt, yet at the same time the stiffness of the material ensures that such a rod will also cast well.

To achieve true long distance casting, the right reel must be used. Whatever the rod, really long casts cannot be achieved if a narrow spooled reel is used. The longer the spool, the better the cast. Every time a layer of line goes over the spool, there is a point of friction. With a narrow spool a great many layers will have to go over the spool to get any sort of distance. As each layer hits the spool, so the cast is slowed down and the distance of the cast minimised. At this moment in time, Shimano reels with their deep spools are far and away the best for distance fishing. The Carbomatic 4000 and the Triton Baitrunner 4500 being the best of their range for this situation.

When it comes to lines, what we are looking for above all else is reliability. I view such things as invisibility and extra fine diameters as no more than sales gimmicks. If a so-called 8lb BS line for instance has the diameter of a 4lb line, then it will only have the ability to withstand abrasion as a 4lb line. I am not saying such lines have no use, maybe there is a case to be made out for them, used as hook lengths, but as far as the main line is concerned stick to a good reliable, tough line that will not break below its given breaking strain. The diameter of the main line will make no difference whatsoever to the amount of fish hooked apart from when really long casts are needed to get to the fish, in which case it pays to use a heavy leader anyway. I believe the best lines around for general carp fishing to be Sylcast Sorrel, Maxima, my own Rod Hutchinson Specimen Line and Brent Monofil. The last of those just mentioned is quite thick for its breaking strain, but at the same time is very reliable and relatively cheap. Sylcast and Maxima have both been around a long time. While Maxima is slightly finer than Sylcast it does not withstand abrasions as well and where dense weed or gravel is likely to be encountered, Sylcast is the better choice. In my own line I tried to bring together the best points of both lines, i.e. the easy spool lay and casting ability of Maxima combined with the resilience of Sylcast. I am happy to say that to a fair degree, this was achieved. Certainly I can't think of a line more suited to the general needs of the carp angler.

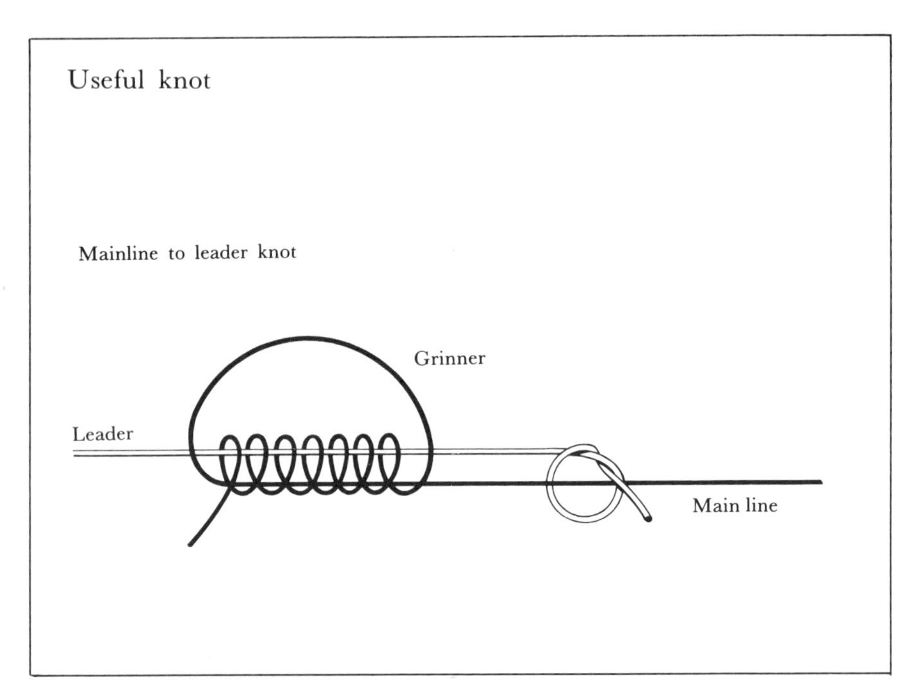

Where the hook length is concerned, I doubt very much if there has now been a material that has not been tried. Suppleness is the thing which everyone seems to be aiming for. A limp line that has good knot strength. The basic idea being that the more supple the line, the more naturally a bait will behave. Dacron is probably the most used material, closely followed by braided nylon. One thing I have been pleased to see arrive in recent months has been the multi-coloured braided lines. They are supposed to be camouflaged which I doubt very much, after all every lake bottom is to certain degrees different, but I like the fact that the line in appearance at least is broken up. I am sure that the standard black braid did in many waters get sussed out so to speak. Fear comes in fish when it can associate some items with danger.

There must have been lots of lakes where each time a fish was caught, a black line had been lying close to the bait. I remember the first time I used dental floss as a hook length in my local water. I had an incredible amount of takes, yet I doubt if it was really any more supple than dacron. The fact it was light green in colour just made it different. It was something the carp had not seen before and so was not something with which they could associate danger. Yet within a few short weeks, after many fish has been caught on it, it produced no more runs than a standard black braided hook link would have done. I have caught carp on everything from lengths of Bri-nylon, to wool, to surgical sutures, to three strands of one pound monofil and while I do appreciate it if the length is supple, I thing it more important that it just be different to an average set up used on a given water. Not just different in the way it has been set up, but also different in appearance.

It was not until the use of braided lines became widespread that silicone anti-tangle tubing was needed. Before, when monofil lines were the accepted materials to use for hook lengths, tangles were far fewer, simply because monofil being relatively stiff compared to braid, stood out well on the cast, rarely tangling back around the lead. But as it became realised that more supple lines did produce more takes, then the use of tube to prevent tangles became all the more necessary. The first anti tangle set ups had the lead coming off the tube via a swivel, I suppose just following traditional running lead techniques. However once it was realised that the majority of anglers were using them fixed in line with bolt rig theories, it became evident that it was much more practical to have the tube running through the centre of the lead. Not only did this minimise tangles even further, it also led to longer casts. Kevin Nash with his Cruise leads and E.T. products with their Comet leads took up this idea, refining it to the products they produce today. It was not a new idea though, in principle it is the same as the basic particle shock rig, incorporating a drilled bullet, as shown in the diagram in the original book. Today because of the changing behaviour of carp, these anti-tangle tube set ups have become even more refined and now incorporate a drilled bullet at the back of the tube; ensuring that the tube lies flat along the bottom, not rising up due to the air within the tube, something which could scare fish off.

The use of fixed leads was really an extension of the bolt rig principle. Once bare hook fishing, (all types of hair rig) became the standard method, it was easy to see that by jolting the hook against the lead, the method really became self hooking. The other advantage of having a fixed lead was that once a fish ran off with the bait, it had to carry the lead with it as it did so. By doing this, the lead was far less likely to get caught up in any snags on the bottom. The main worry amongst many anglers was that should a break occur above the lead, then the fish would be left towing the whole lot around, lead and all. This should not be the case though if the rig has been tied up correctly, incorporating a small diameter bead behind the tube, with a sliding knot above that. Should the tackle get caught up in anything i.e. weed, gravel or snag, the knot will pull off the line followed by the bead, tube and lead. In most cases it does not even need to be caught up, as the weight of the lead is usually enough to slide the knot down and off the line.

As modern day techniques do rely very much on the fish hooking, or at least pricking itself it is essential that the right choice of hook be made, especially now when many anglers are turning towards smaller and smaller hooks. An interesting fact regarding carp hooks is that when the original book came out, the two most popular sizes were 2s and 4s. Some anglers side hooking boilies at that time even used hooks down to size 2/0. Today the most popular size of hook used in England for carp is a size 8. The main reason for this turnabout is that carp anglers have realised like match anglers did long ago, that the weight of the hook will inhibit the movement of a bait.

Everyone seems to have their own favourites when it comes to the pattern of hook they use. The old saying of if you have confidence in something then use it, I suppose is true to a degree, but from experiments I was able to do last year, I know that some patterns are far less likely to come out of a hooked fish than others. I was fortunate enough to fish a lake in France where the carp were not at all tackle conscious and 25 to 30 runs per day could be expected. Four different patterns of hook were used. My own which is a beak pointed hook with a turned up eye, based on the old Sealey Speedbarb pattern, one called a carp special; a very in-turned hook almost 'S' shaped based on patterns used by longshore fishermen for long lining for cod; a standard straight shank round bend hook; and the Kevin Nash Outpoint Hook which is the same as the S.S. stainless steel hook my own firm has sold for a number of years for snag fishing. All of the hooks were fished tight line to fixed lead set-ups. The rod tips being very high in the air so indication could be seen on whether a bait was being mouthed at all. From a total of over 120 runs the following pattern emerged. The straight shank, round bend hooks appeared to prick fish the quickest but they also were far and away the pattern most likely to come out during the ensuing fight. This point was reinforced when a friend moved into the swim for a day the following week; using this pattern of hook, he hooked 18 fish but only landed 8. I might add that at this lake the fish lost ratio is the highest I have ever known. The fish only average around ten pounds, but fight like crazy and a ten minute battle is nothing unusual, even though the fish are small.

My beak point hooks and the Nash Outpoint hooks came out about equal, with the fewest fish lost. If a fish was lost on either hook it was very quickly after the strike, leading me to believe that on those occasions the hook had not been set against the lead. However, if a fish was still on thirty seconds after the strike then there was very little likelihood of it coming out. The beak point ones on many occasions went through the flesh and hooked again. Incidentally my beak point hooks worked best with the hair being tied from the offset eye, while the outpoint hooks performed best with the hair coming off the shank half way down the hook.

The carp specials based on the long line fishermans pattern, I am afraid did not perform at all. Rod tops would often be knocking for minutes on end without the fish hooking themselves and charging off. While it is true that some were hooked by striking hard when there was a lot of indication being shown at the rod top, it was rare indeed for one to hook itself against the lead. Now this may be excusable when fishing in daytime, tight line fishing and striking at each movement or indication, but the hooks have no place when you have to slack line fish and you are dependent on the fish hooking itself against the lead. Their only virtue that I can see is that if a fish is hooked, then there is very little likelihood of it being able to shed that hook. After all this is why longshore fishermen use them, but it has to be remembered that a sea fish only sees a hook once, then it is dead. It simply finds food and eats it on the spot. There is no comparison between a cod and carp which are fished for day after day and which have to learn if they are to survive.

I mentioned earlier about smaller hooks being used nowadays so as not to inhibit the movement of a bait. It should be said that they also go in much easier as well because of the fineness of the wire and the sharpness you can achieve. Having said that though, there is a disadvantage in that only a small piece of flesh will be picked up which can easily tear during a long or hard fight. Should you be able to still get takes with a larger hook, then your chances of landing a fish are better. All hooks can be made to float whatever their size and so not inhibit a bait's movement, after all what is a dry fly, but a floating hook. Likewise they can be made to a neutral buoyancy. In years gone by I used a fly-tyer to make me up floating hooks. Today there is no need, as you can push your hook through a piece of Kevin Nash Rig Foam, and then whittle the foam down until you have the buoyancy you require.

Floating hooks really come into their own when surface fishing. Every carp angler knows the days when every surface bait is inspected. If the hook hangs down, you get no takes. Even if the hook comes out of the top of the bait it won't guarantee a take as it is nothing unusual to see a carp's head come out of the water as it approaches the floater. I'm pretty sure when this happens that the fish is seeing if the bait is attached from above. When this behaviour occurs, even the many variations of the beachcaster rig are likely to fail. It is then that a bait attached by a longish 1'' very fine hair (½lb bs) to a floating hook is most likely to score, and once the bait has been taken there is little likelihood of the hook coming out, as it will naturally fight against its own buoyancy and end up in the top of the mouth or the top lip.

I mentioned the beachcaster rig, as shown in the diagram and this has without a doubt far increased the amount of fish caught on floating particle baits, by the simple virtue that no line is left lying on the surface. Providing the carp are not in one of their heads up out of the water moods, it can be a killer method. On many shallow surface feeding orientated lakes, such as Cuttle Mill Fishery in Staffordshire, it is common to see anglers with their rods up in the air on sea spikes, just letting the tackle fish for itself. This is made easier when Shimano Baitrunner reels are used, takes being indicated by the sound of the running clutch.

However, I have found it far more efficient just to fish one rod and hold it up high. When fished from the rest, the floating bait, which is generally

Standard "beachcaster" technique incorporating a large standard pikefloat

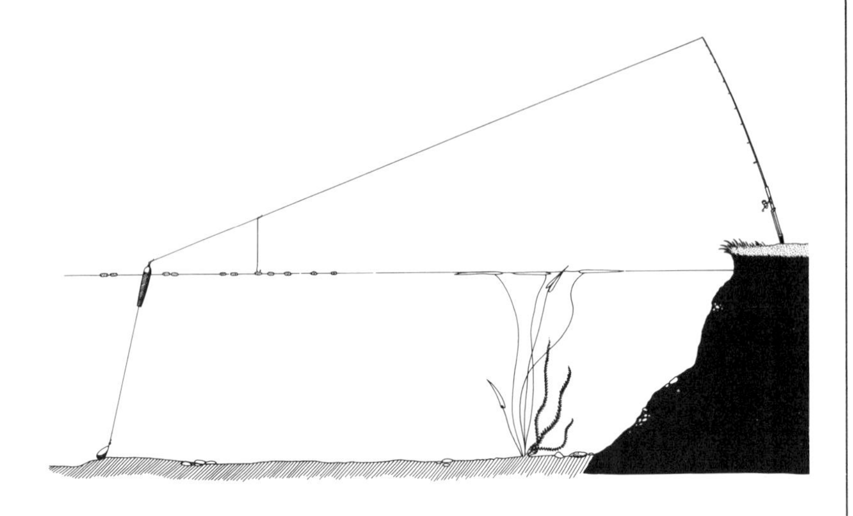

Mobile "beachcaster" rig.
with this there is no leger tail to get snagged up.

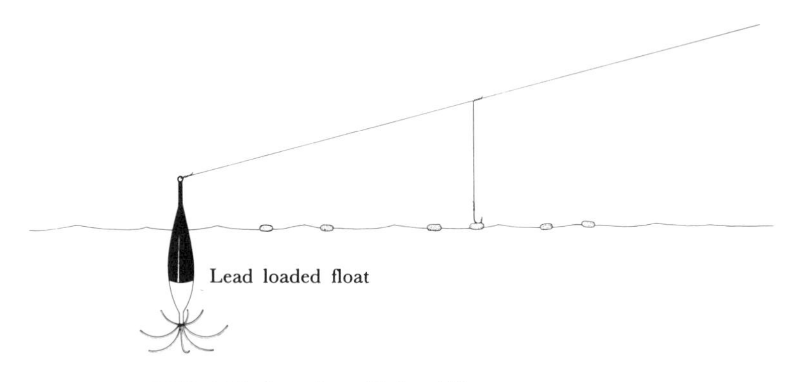

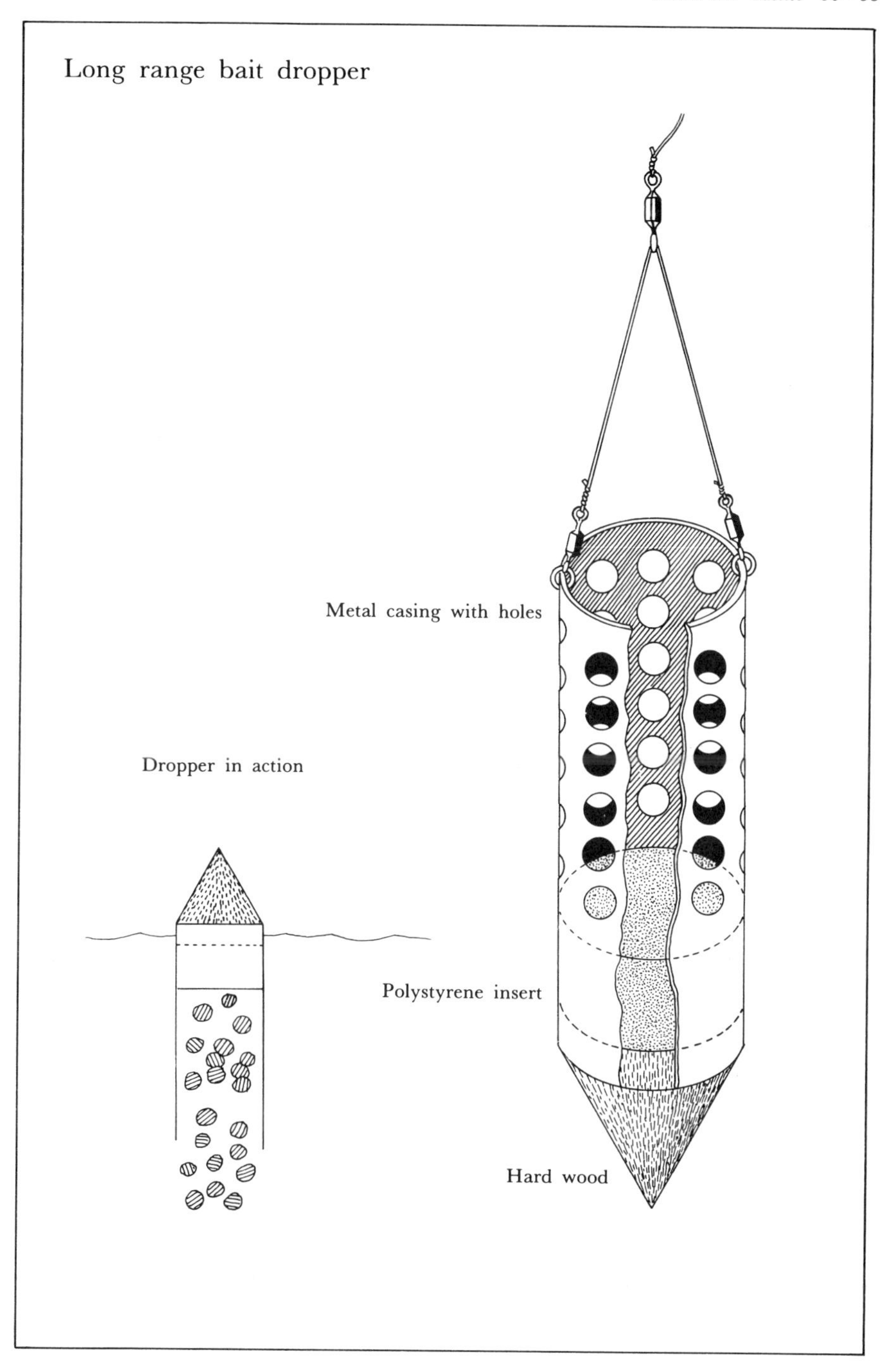
Long range bait dropper
Metal casing with holes
Dropper in action
Polystyrene insert
Hard wood

Chum Mixer or the same, dyed and flavoured and put out under someone else's name, is still tethered although no line can be seen on the surface. Freebaits however, and it is often necessary to put hundreds in before the fish start taking them, will move around with the surface drift even on a calm day. On a windy day they move very quickly indeed and the tethered hookbait stands out like a sore thumb. Because of this, I don't cast out at all, until the fish are taking the free samples really well. I then cast out well over the fish, wait until I can make out one moving in a certain direction, then I simply lower the bait in front of it. In such circumstances it is rarely refused. The beauty of the method is that you don't have to fish a long tail and a heavy lead, which can easily become snagged up. The bait is not left on the surface to be inspected, it is only dropped in front of feeding fish. You can fish direct to a large self cocking float, or cast a lead onto any islands there might be and then lower the bait. There are many variations as can be seen in the diagrams. Fishing just the one rod, watching for fish feeding and then lowering a bait into them is very active and exciting and far more preferable to my mind than just waiting for the sound of a slipping clutch.

One of the difficulties with surface particles such as Chum Mixer is that they are very light and so very difficult to catapult out any distance. The best method I know is to use a large baitdropper, the mark II version I use today

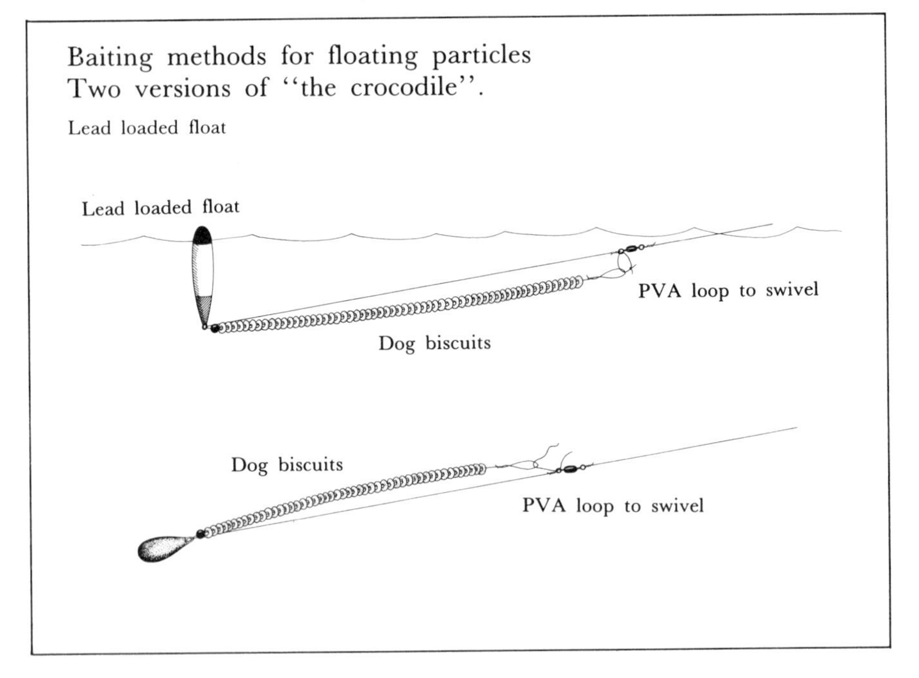

Baiting methods for floating particles
Two versions of "the crocodile".

is illustrated in the diagram. There are many other floating biscuits which are just as good such as Munchies, Purina etc., many of which have a hole through them. When I use these, I bait up with what we christened "the crocodile". Basically it comprises of a swivel then a two foot length of line terminating in a large lead loaded float. Another piece of line is attached to the float upon which are then threaded an 18" to 24" line of biscuits. A loop is then tied to the free end of the line, which is then tied back to the swivel with PVA string. With the right rod, this set up can be cast quite a distance. Within a minute the PVA will melt, you pull back the float a yard, and all the biscuits are free to float away. Even longer casts can be achieved by dispensing with the float, replacing it with a heavy lead.

I have deliberately left the subject of terminal rigs until last. Maybe because I couldn't face it because there is a lot of bull talked about rigs. The fact is I doubt very much indeed whether anything will ever make the impact, or improve so much the hooking of carp as the hair rig as pioneered by Kevin Maddocks and Lenny Middleton. Everything that has come since has simply been a refinement around the basic concept. Not that I believe the original theories were correct, the basic fact of having a free hook that did not have to be pulled through a bait is why the method was and still is so effective. Anything sharp entering the mouth is likely to prick or take hold, add that to the jolt effect given by a bolt rig or fixed lead set up and it is easy to see why the method is so effective. I think all hair rigs work best when tight line fishing can be used, everything from the lead, to high rod tops, to tight line clips to heavy bobbins work towards ensuring that the hook is driven in.

I say without any doubt in my mind that if fish in any water still accept tight lines, that the more you can do to ensure everything is solid, then the better all rigs will work. Unfortunately that is not the case in a great many waters now and there are some where you will not get a take if the line is not lying directly on the bottom. A certain degree of tightness can still be achieved by incorporating another lead into the set up, dropped directly from the rod top, but it is nothing like the cheese wire effect obtained by rod tips up high, bent into the terminal lead.

There are two lines of thinking on how best to achieve self hooking when you have to slack line fish. The most used technique is to fish a very short hooklink between 3 to 6 inches, counting on the weight of the lead to set the hook. Yet with the D rig and the sliding rig I like, we are counting to a certain extent on the fish not knowing it has a hook in its mouth, and moving away thinking it has rejected the bait. I think we can use this to our advantage by using a very long hooklink, either coiled or one on the sliding hooklink principle, incorporating two rings as shown in the diagram. This allows a fish to swim away without any resistance. In doing this it builds up speed until all the line runs out, then there is a sudden jolt against the lead. I am sure that this would

Using two leads to keep the line on the bottom

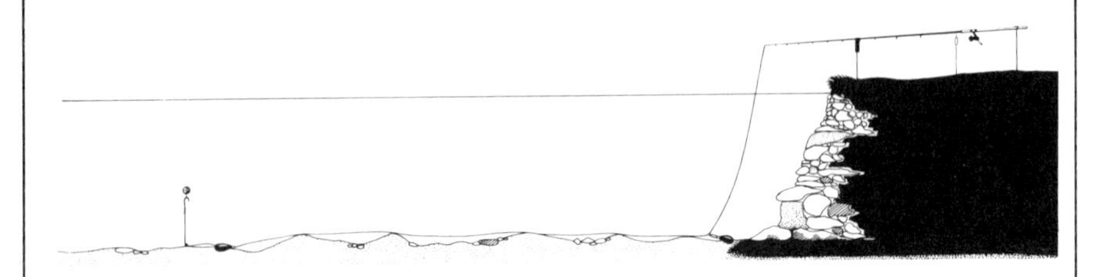

The second lead is clipped on via a snap link at the rod top after casting.

PVA tube is very useful in that it can cover up any rig likely to tangle on the cast. For example, really long hooklengths can be coiled up so that there is no resistance to a taking fish.

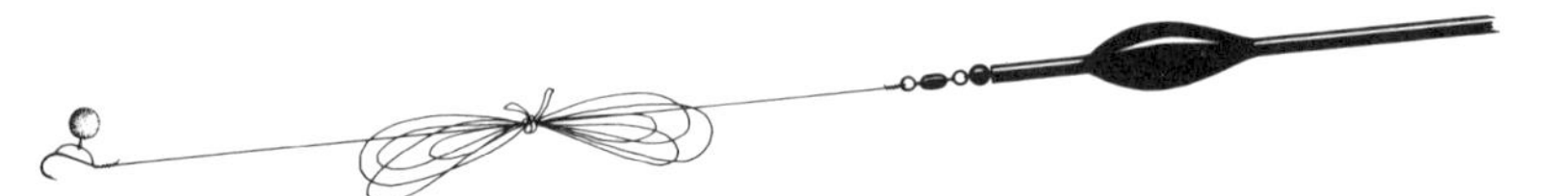

Tied in the middle with PVA microthread.

This rig would be covered in a PVA tube.

have far greater impact on the hook, than just the weight of the lead alone, thereby increasing the chances of a pricked fish turning into one that is actually hooked. The hooklength can be coiled to any length you desire, and cast out without fear of tangling, if a PVA tube is used to encase the whole terminal tackle.

So all in all, we now have to do our utmost to ensure that the hook is set itself either by the fish or against the lead. This requires that we try to make sure each time that the hook enters the mouth in a position where it is most likely to take hold on entry or more frequently on ejection. The original hair rig worked so

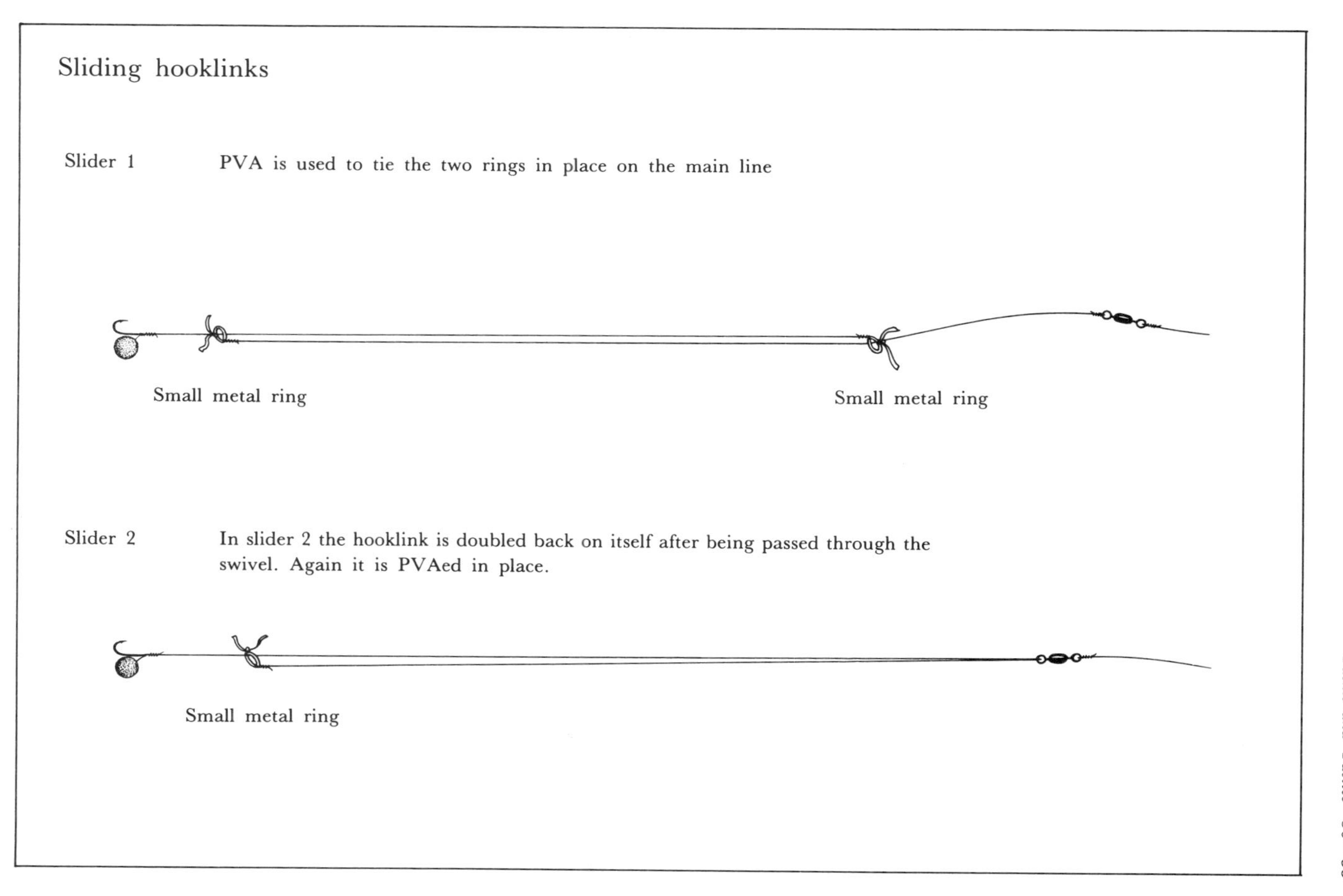
Sliding hooklinks
Slider 1
PVA is used to tie the two rings in place on the main line
Small metal ring
Small metal ring
Slider 2
In slider 2 the hooklink is doubled back on itself after being passed through the swivel. Again it is PVAed in place.
Small metal ring

well because of the carp's natural tendency to suck and blow its food. If you watch them in a natural environment where they are unfished for, it is rare for them to swallow a piece of food first time. Most times it will be taken in the mouth and blown out: this may occur two or three times before it is taken back and swallowed and I am convinced that it is on the blow out when most fish get hooked. Maybe I should say got hooked, because now there are many waters where carp can be observed just staying in one spot with their mouths over a bait, but not sucking and blowing. They must have learnt that to do so was dangerous. Once in and either swallowed or just one rejection seems to be the form on hard fished waters now. If it does manage to eject the bait, then it does not get picked up again.

Roger Smith's D rig is still very likely to work because the bait can be blown up the line whilst the hook remains in the mouth. The fish thinking it has got rid of the bait, moves off therefore jolting against the lead, hopefully setting the hook (see diagram).

Similar in principle is a sliding set up I use a lot. I am told some people call it the revolving hair although I arrived at the set up myself with no knowledge that it was used by others. It entails putting the bait on a short hair, tied to a tiny ring. So that the ring cannot pass over the eye of the hook, a small piece of eye-silicon is jammed over the eye. Two inches up the line from the eye is another piece of plugged silicon. The bait therefore slides on this two inch length of line. My own hooks with their turned up eye work best with this rig as the eye ensures that the hook stands out at an angle as it enters the mouth. The idea around the rig is that the bait can once again be ejected and blown up the line without the fish realising it still has the hook in its mouth. Obviously this is not the case with any standard rig when the bait is attached to the hook. In that case if the bait is ejected, then the hook will be as well. This rig also works well when a buoyant bait is used. The bait being tied as close to the ring as possible. A small weight either just behind the hook, or pushed into the end of the silicon is used to counteract the weight of the buoyant boilie, so that it lies more or less on the bottom with the hook underneath, at an angle. If picked up this pretty well ensures that the hook will end in the bottom lip, as the hook is weighted, yet at the same time the bait can be ejected with very little force getting applied to the hook.

Buoyant boilies are being used more and more as bottom baits rather than pop-ups simply because once sucked in they will naturally rise higher in the throat and so be more difficult to eject. The standard popped up bait, a couple of inches off the bottom was incredibly successful in hundreds of waters, but now in many they simply do not work anymore. Before they worked because they stood out, today they have stopped working because they stand out.

If a bait has to be on the bottom the same as freebaits to stand a chance of being picked up, then it makes sense to use one that can have its movements

Variations of the D Rig

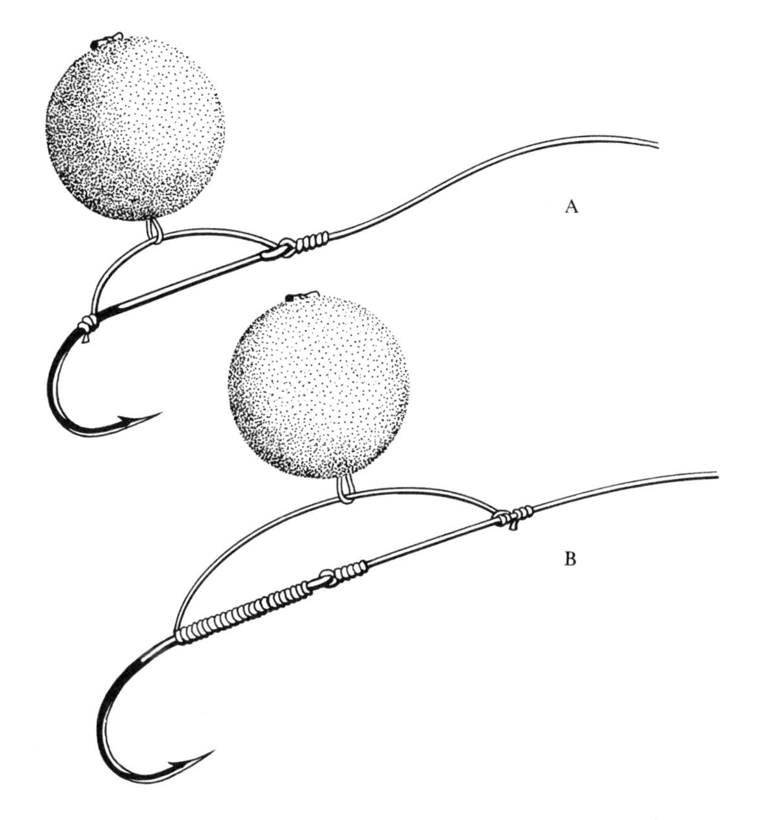

In diagram A the D is tied from the eye of the hook to the bottom of the shank

In diagram B the line is whipped down the shank of the hook, and the loose end brought back and tied on the line above the hook

made to order, i.e. a buoyant one. The only problem with buoyant baits is that once water can get inside, the texture and the buoyancy will slowly change. Obviously, just putting a needle through the bait to attach a hair, will create a passage into which water can seep. This can be overcome by tying around the bait, rather than putting the hair through it. Braided lines are far better than monofil when attaching a bait in this way. Better still is dental floss which goes quite flat when tightened, squeezing into the bait rather than cutting in. A bait attached in this way will remain fully buoyant even after 24 hours in

Sliding boilie rig

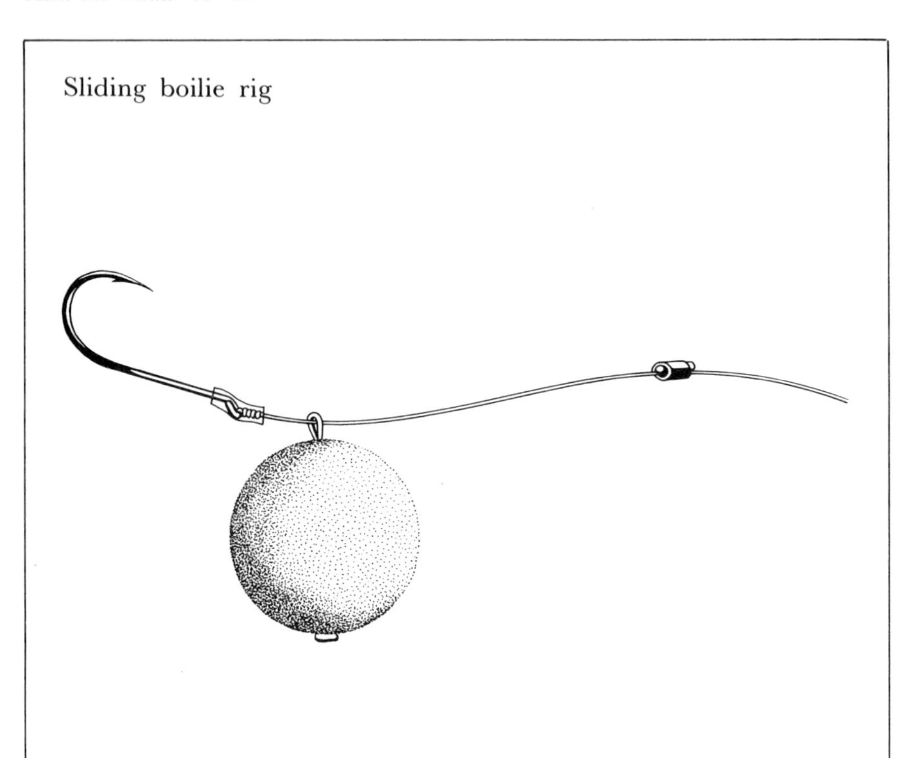

Rig tube is forced over the eye and another piece plugged up the line. The boilie slides between the two. This rig is useful for both bottom and buoyant baits. It is best fished with a hook that has an offset eye. The distance between the tubes is determined by the size of fish likely to be encountered, i.e. the larger the fish, the greater the distance.

the water. Large baits will obviously need weight near the hook to anchor them, but often with small baits, the correct choice of hook will hold it down. The bait can be pulled really tight to the hook and very importantly the hook held in the position that the angler wants by pushing a length of line through the ring of dental floss holding the boilie and by then taking the two loose ends of the line through the eye of the hook. The boilie is then pulled tight to the hook which is positioned at whatever angle you require, and the two ends tied back above the hook. (see diagram)

Another version of this is to pass a piece of heavy nylon through the side of a piece of Kevin Nash Rig Tube. The line is made to form a loop out of the side of the tube, and is then superglued in position. The tube is then generally slipped down the line over the eye of the hook, but also can be slid down the shank of the hook if it is so required. Dental floss is then passed through the loop and tied tight around the bait. Although both versions work

Variations of the looped rig for buoyant baits

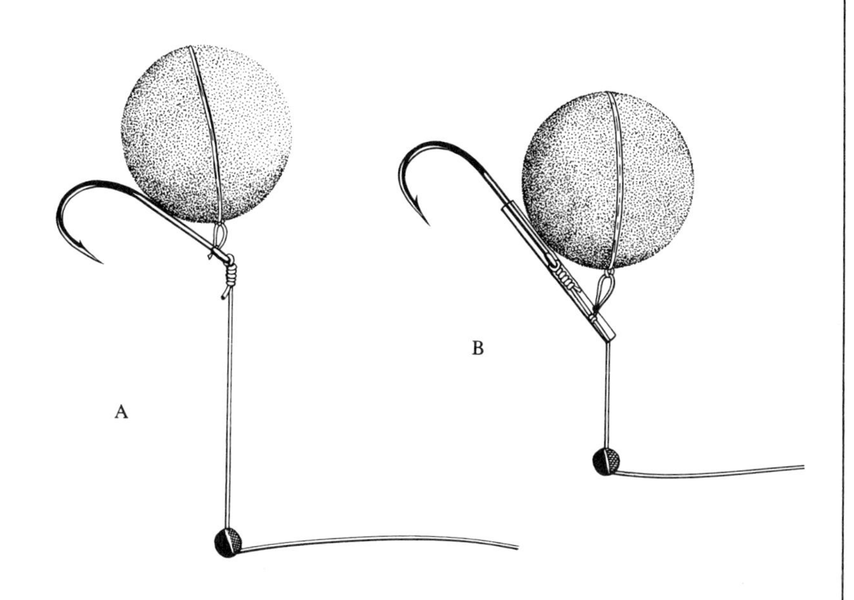

In diagram A the loop is tied through the eye of the hook.

In diagram B rig tube is used to make an extension to the shank, the loop being created through the side of the tube, above the hook.
In both cases dental floss is used to tie on the bait.
Please note that in both cases the weight may be pushed close to the hook so that the bait fishes close to the bottom, the hook can then be positioned to come out the side.

very well indeed they are miles away from the original hair rig theories and are in fact refined versions of side hooking i.e. see the original diagram showing the semi-buoyant bait. (see diagram)

A very simple rig that works particularly well in winter when I think it very beneficial to put up a good visual display of the hook bait, is a multistranded hair, also incorporating a couple of short stringers. Should you fear tangles with this set up, the whole lot can be enclosed within a PVA tube before casting. It is essential to use mini 8 to 10 ml boilies for this, one hair being

Modern side hooking techniques

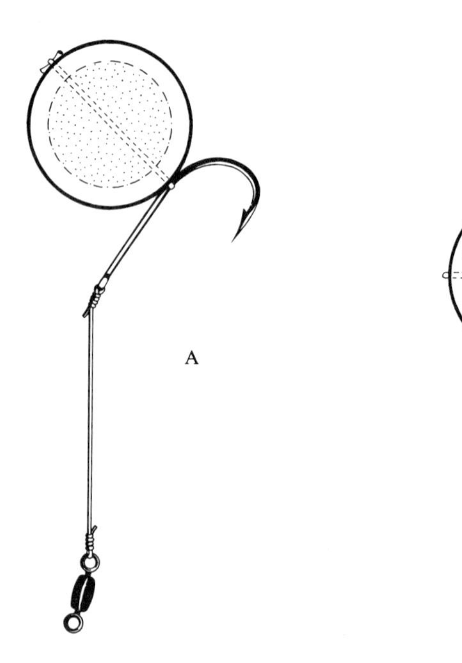

In diagram A, which is an aeriel view, the dotted centre circle represents rig foam within the bait which makes sure that the baits lies in this position, so that the hook is not hidden. This is best fished on a short hooklength. See diagram B for side view of the bait. This rig will also work with a fully buoyant boilie.

tied off the eye of the hook, one being tied off the shank. Two small boilies are placed on both hairs, the outside one in each case being a standard dense boilie, while the inside one is buoyant. Two small disposable PVA hairs, tied on micro thread are also used. One being tied off the bend of the hook and another off the eye again. This presents a very nice looking pile of bait lying on the bottom, with the hook bait having a great deal of buoyancy. It has been observed by a number of anglers that if there are a number of baits in a small area, that it is rare for a carp to eat them one at a time. Depending on the size of bait, two, three, even four may be taken in the mouth before they are crunched up in the throat. If a fish goes down on this multi hair set up and sucks up, the four being attached to the hook should be, because of the buoyancy, the ones that end up in the mouth. Multi hairs are also very hard to eject because no one bait takes the full force of the ejection blow.

Just how far can we go with rigs? I doubt very much if a new concept will arrive. There have been literally thousands of anglers looking for something better than the hair for at least eight years now. Like rods I think the method will just get more and more refined as new materials come up. Eight pound line with the diameter of 1/4lb line and the suppleness of dental floss would be handy, just as hooks made of finest wire like a tiny match hook, but having the strength of the strongest carp hook, would also help catch a few. Kevin Nash suggests the best rig would be one where the hook ends up in the mouth at the slightest suck from a fish, even if the bait does not move. In fact it would be so much the better if the bait did not move, as the carp would then move off as the bait would be regarded as suspicious, yet the fish would not realise it had a hook in its mouth. Now there is one to ponder about!

I have deliberately skipped over many items of tackle just because they are only improved versions of what we already had. PTFE or nylon composite monkey climbers with a central hole, going up and down a stainless steel needle are far superior to our old home made jobs, while I don't think anyone would now argue about Optonics being the best electronic audible alarm. The recently introduced Super Optonics are just that, while line clips or butt foam have eradicated the line drag problem.

Just like the old chapter, I will finish on the handling and retention of carp. Today, with fish often being caught several times during the course of the season, it is vitally important that they are returned in the same condition that they were landed. We don't have to make our own sacks any more because the ones developed by Kevin Nash are as close as you can come to being perfect. The materials he uses are both soft and have excellent water exchange qualities. There are several excellent weigh slings available, some by the same firm. Always wet one first, and please stay clear of ones made from net, these are always likely to split fins and remove scales. Always try to stake sacks out in deep water and please keep the time spent in the sack to the minimum, particularly in high temperatures. If the banks are hard, gravel, or rocky, always lay the fish on some sort of cushion, such as lilo, sponge, or one of the unhooking mats now available. When photographing a fish, for years I thought it best to cradle one like a baby. I never understood why my fish leapt around more than other people's did, until I realised I was putting pressure on the stomach and organs which have no protection. The best way to hold a fish I am sure is with one hand just behind the gills, and one just in front of the tail. Please treat all fish with the same regard, the small ones of today are the big fish of tomorrow.

Chapter 5

Introduction to Baits '80

THE consistently successful carp angler must have many attributes. He should be a naturalist, a keen observer of what goes on above and below the water line. He must be able to interpret what he sees, and be able to apply the appropriate measures in each circumstance. While on the one hand he must have the patience to see his own ideas through to their logical conclusions, not being swayed from them by other people's views or performances, he must always remain alert to any opportunity that comes his way, and take advantage of it. Conduct around a water, plus the above attributes, are all part of what is generally termed watercraft. Armed with just that skill and a modest collection of simple baits, the angler will catch carp.

He will not however reap the same rewards as the angler who sets about discovering the fishes' dietary requirements, why they should feed in a certain manner, and why different lakes require different approaches. Consistent success comes to the angler who never stops learning. His aim should be to increase his knowledge of carp to the extent that he knows just what bait to use in any situation. The carp is a simple creature which must feed to survive, but it also has the ability to associate baits, tackle and specific places with danger. This being so, no bait will provide positive results for an indefinite period. So the angler should always try to be one step ahead of the fish. As it is essential to use a bait of some description in order to catch fish, an extensive knowledge of the subject is required. Now it is a sad but true fact that the larger the number of anglers using a given bait, the fewer fish the individual angler can expect to catch before that bait is associated with danger. This does not mean to say that I am advocating downright secrecy. By all means anglers should pass around ideas on baits, improving everyone's knowledge. But within the confines of a given water an angler should go his own way, working on

Happy particle times at Waveney Valley

his own ideas, and at the most should only confide in close friends.

However there are those who go bait crazy and forget the essential skills of watercraft. The consistently successful angler has both watercraft and a wide knowledge of baits at his disposal.

The following two chapters are about my own thoughts on the subject and the directions I have taken; I don't expect you to agree with everything, but I hope they will provide food for thought and maybe lead you into new avenues to explore.

Chapter 6

Particles

In the Beginning '75

By the time the old book came out particles had already been established for a decade. To show just what had been done I include the following, which is an article I had published in the magazine Angling in 1975; the magazine unfortunately went out of existence long ago. I think that most of what I thought at the time is still relevant, although I must admit it was a period when I drew very quick conclusions. A whole new world opened up before my eyes and baits which did not perform quickly were quickly dismissed.

The concept of particle bait fishing was first thought of by Dick Walker and the Carp Catchers Club, the theory being that carp could become pre-occupied not only with baits of the same type, but also of the same size, though I believe their baits were usually pieces of flake, or potato, or paste. The Taylor brothers experimented further with potato-chips and butter-beans, the thinking being the same as the original Carp Catchers' theory.

The first signs that big carp could be caught on small baits of the same size came with the fine catches made at Redmire Pool by Roger Bowskill, the bait in this case being maggots. This gave food for thought to all dedicated carp anglers; the seeds of particle bait fishing as we know it were sown.

Shortly after Roger's efforts a water I fished in Lincolnshire, where it was considered at the time to be well-nigh impossible to catch carp, produced an

18 pounder to an angler who had groundbaited very heavily with maggots and used a hookbait of a hundred maggots threaded on cotton. The few carp anglers around my area at the time (1967) became very excited. At last, here was the answer to Heartbreak Lake! How wrong we were. What we didn't take into account was that the water held only seven carp and most of these had, at some time or other, been hooked on maggots by tench anglers using tackle unsuited for the big carp.

Just one more fish was taken that year on maggot bait; hardly an astounding success rate but two more fish caught than ever before. Small baits, it appeared, were the answer, but what to use was the problem.

One night at home I was browsing through my old *Fishing* magazines and came across an article about the hemp ban at Throop. The article made it clear that the barbel on that famous fishery had become preoccupied with hemp to the exclusion of all other baits. It hit me then that if it could happen to barbel then why not carp? It had to be the answer!

Hemp had its own problems, though mainly in its presentation. In those days I believed that a hook had to be hidden. Experience since has proved this not to be necessary but, as I have stated, at the time I couldn't believe that any carp would pick up a bait with half the hook showing. To overcome this worry a very fine wire hook was used, enabling hemp to be put on the shank. From the eye of the hook several lengths of cotton were tied and onto this cotton – which was always green, supposedly imitating blanket-weed – were threaded several more seeds of hemp.The thinking behind this was that if a carp should take in the hemp on the cotton, the hook would be taken in as well. I thought that with all these tiny baits about, instead of bothering about individual seeds the fish were more likely to go across the bottom vacuum-cleaning up, as it were. With all the lengths of cotton about I reckoned one was bound to be picked up.

(Comment – 1988. This, to all intents and purposes, was a hair rig and I was not the only one to use similar rigs at that time. When I sent a drawing of it to Jack Hilton back in 1969 he replied by sending me one very similar which he used for perch fishing: it consisted of a size 4 main hook off which was tied a 1½ piece of 2lb line with a size 20 hook at the end (see diagrams). However, neither Jack nor I would claim to have first thought of the hair rig concept, I'm sure. My reason for using such a set-up was simply because hemp was so small; I could not at that time see any other alternative when presenting it for carp. Jack's rig was designed so that a fish would still be hooked if a worm was only picked up by the tail. Neither of us ever realised the potential of using it with other baits. It was simply practical to do so and in no way detracts from the work and originality displayed by Kevin Maddocks and Lennie Middleton whom we have to thank for the hair rig and its concept.)

My original hemp rig
Jack Hilton's worm rig

It was three sessions before a run occurred and up to then three gallons of hemp had gone in. Hemp was a darn sight cheaper in those days! The hemp, by way of interest, was the Chilean variety, which I find is unobtainable these days. Well, that first run on the bait didn't produce a fish on the bank – the hook straightened. Two more runs that night produced tench.

The following weekend I arrived with what I thought to be strong hooks – Speedbarbs – which had never let me down on other waters and which were still fine enough in the shank to enable hemp to be put on. That night produced two runs, both at short range on 15lb line. It is hardly surprising that with 20lb-plus carp on the other end of the line the hook snapped on both occasions. By the time the season was over I had connected with seven carp and lost the lot, and in doing so had made them very frightened of hemp.

The winter was spent searching for another bait. The most obvious answer was peas, but close season observation showed that, in this lake at least, the carp were just not interested in them. An alternative was found at work – by accident. I was a fork-truck driver in a cold store at the time and on one night shift, when I was more tired than usual, I knocked over a full row of pallets. The cold room was absolutely covered with sweetcorn.

Knowing the success sweetcorn has had since I have to laugh when I look back at my first season using the stuff. The main thing about it at the time seemed to be that the hook could be covered, so a strong hook could be used. This time I had to have the answer. That season produced eight fish hooked – and none landed. Six times I thought I had smashed on the fish but now know that the line had been severed by the carp's throat-teeth. Gorging is a problem with sweetcorn. I wonder now if I should write to the line manufacturers and apologise for all the nasty letters I sent them in 1969! The carp anglers of today will nod their heads sagely at what was going wrong then, but at that time I had never *heard* of such a thing happening, let alone experienced it.

So, after two seasons using particle baits I had caught no carp. But things were beginning to piece together. I did know that carp would take tiny baits if enough of the bait was put in to educate them, and my mind kept going back to that Throop barbel article. If enough bait was used then preoccupation was a strong possibility, and although I had caught no fish, the amount of runs I had had at this very hard water was nothing short of amazing compared to past seasons.

In the 1970 close season I took a job in Wales and the waters I fished there were only just seeing 'specials'. Admittedly none of the waters I fished could be called hard, but at the same time, armed with my specials, I had a very successful year's fishing. In this period I landed my best two fish up to that time – mirrors of 19½lb and 19¼lb. Particles had been forgotten for the time being, mainly because I didn't need them. The cold winter nights in my little, grubby, Swansea bed-sitter were spent corresponding with Jack Hilton and generally begging for a place in the Redmire syndicate, apart from one night when I was visited by BCSG Midlands regional organiser Alan Cubley: he took me out for the evening and got me so drunk I didn't wake up for three days and he never found his way back to his digs. Still, that's another story.

On New Year's day 1972 I received the letter I had been waiting for; I had a place in Redmire. Time to start thinking about particles again.

From what I had read in the press at the time it seemed that with all the members using maggots the fish would be preoccupied with this bait; but there were enough subtle hints in Jack's articles to make me think that other particle-baits were being used. The best thing seemed to be to start the season off with an open mind.

So the Sunday of the second week of the season found me on the banks of that Mecca of carp fishing. I remember now how I sat down on the dam for a solid hour; I was completely overawed by this beautiful lake – it was too much to take in. It wasn't until a battered motorcycle coasted down the hill behind the lake that I was awoken from my reverie. The rider was Chris Yates, a new member, like myself. Chris was equally taken aback with this, the lake we had read about and dreamed about since our youth. To cut a long story short the first four days were spent flogging maggots, mussels, snails, caddis, artificial moths, all to no avail, although I did come unstuck on a good fish one morning when I presented a bunch of brandlings to a bubbler. We had fished our hearts out for nothing, and we were very tired, so we decided to retire to the local pub and have a re-appraisal of the week so far. One thing we were sure of: the Redmire carp that had already been caught that season didn't come out on maggots. Small particle-type baits again had to be the answer.

The outcome of the discussion was that Chris, without any prompting from me, was going to try two small vegetables he had with him for his own consumption, namely, sweetcorn and bamboo shoots. I opted to try baked beans and continue with tiny worms on the other rod.

I didn't use corn because it seemed logical to assume that now we knew that small baits other than maggots were taking carp, then the obvious (to me) alternatives, corn and hemp, would have been used already. As things turned out I was wrong and to my knowledge only one bait, sultanas, had been used with any success.

The reader will have to understand that the Redmire syndicate, being split into rota groups, is ultra secretive. Nobody knows what bait the other rota groups are using. So we were starting at the beginning and had to learn by our own mistakes or successes; very much a case of trial and error. Still, our discussion had given us renewed confidence and we set off back to the lake full of expectancy.

We didn't have long to wait. Chris caught a fish first cast on the sweetcorn, while I had a run after a couple of hours on the baked beans. By the time we had to leave on Sunday we had had eleven fish, none of them large, and eight falling to Chris on the sweetcorn.

The following week the press was full of a massive catch of fish from 22lb to 40lb taken by John Macleod and Bill Walkden from the pool. To me at home reading the story it seemed that Chris and I were going wrong somewhere. We had caught fish all right, but small ones. How come John, Bill and Jack – who had caught a 36½ pounder on opening night – were getting all the big ones? It struck me at the time, though I know now it to be wrong, that we had got in at the tail-end of a bait, that sweetcorn had been thrashed in the previous seasons. I decided to go ahead with the baked beans and also take a vast range of particle-type baits to the lake on the next visit. I also decided to make my own baked beans as those straight from the can were very soft and inclined to fly off when casting. This was done by getting a supply of haricot beans and boiling them up in tomato soup. They were left to simmer until I thought they were soft enough to be attractive but firm enough to withstand the casting. The other baits taken were hemp, blackcurrants, red kidney beans, very small seedless grapes and canned peas.

That next week at the lake produced several small doubles, an 18 pounder, a 19 pounder and three twenty pounders between three of us – for Bob Jones, free from his teaching activities, had joined us now. Two of those 20 pounders fell to baked beans. All of the other fish, apart from a small double which took a seedless grape, came on sweetcorn. Fish of 18, 19 and 21 pounds are good fish but still, it seemed to me, small by Redmire standards: I was still convinced that sweetcorn wasn't **THE** bait.

The other baits I had taken I'd thrown in the shallows where, from the top of a tree, I'd been able to observe the fishes' reaction to them. This procedure was carried out every day. I thought a week was a fair trial for a bait.

The blackcurrants were never seen to be picked up by fish, though they did disappear in the night. I put this down to either coots or eels and they were crossed off my list as a prospective bait. The kidney-beans and seedless grapes were picked up only by very small fish – big fish didn't seem at all interested. It seemed to be that they were too large, too much like a conventional bait to interest the big carp. The canned peas remained on the bottom to rot – I never once saw them picked up by carp, either large or small. It seemed obvious to me that there was no future in peas. The hemp, being so small, was never actually seen to be picked up, but I had seen some good fish feeding in the areas where it had been thrown in. Often small fish would swim over these areas as they charged about the shallows, whilst the large fish, generally moving more slowly, would browse along the bottom spending a longer time in a given area, searching out areas more methodically. I came to the conclusion that the younger fish up to about 20lb were sight feeders in the main, whilst the older, larger fish depended more on their senses of touch and smell to feed. Therefore it would seem that a bright bait such as sweetcorn was more likely to catch small fish. It wasn't that the big ones didn't like the bright baits, or were afraid of them, it was just that the small ones would often beat them to the bait.

It seemed likely that the smaller fish would overlook a small, dark bait, which was more likely to be found by the bigger carp as they made their way slowly along the bottom. I seemed to have found the answer for sorting out the big ones, for Redmire is unlike other lakes in that an 18lb fish is a nuisance fish! With this theory in mind I tried out an experiment. I bought ten packets of children's sweets – Jelly-Tots – which I had been considering as a particle bait, whilst not being too sure that they complied with the normal particle idea; namely that the bait should all be of the same size and colour. As it happened, the results when the sweets were thrown in were what I had been looking for. The bright coloured white, yellow and red ones were soon gobbled up by the smaller fish, whilst many of the darker ones were missed. But odd dark ones were picked up, which proved to me that it wasn't the flavour the carp didn't like but merely the fact that the baits were insignificant-looking on the bottom. All of the bright coloured baits had been eaten by the smaller carp within an hour of being thrown in.

All of the baits mentioned so far were thrown in local waters near my home in the following weeks, the carp's reaction to those baits being very similar to those of the Redmire fish.

Another idea that came to me was that if a particle-bait was more natural to a water than the vegetable baits so far used then it was more likely to succeed. With this thought in mind I made arrangements to pick up five stones of fresh shrimps for my next visit to the pool. I never realised how much this volume of shrimps would cost, or the amount of room they would take up! Suffice to say I was left broke for a fortnight and the journey down to Redmire was cramped to say the least! All the gear for a week's stay, four stones of assorted baits, five stones of shrimps and myself in a Morris Traveller! The shrimps were packed in ice and by the time I reached the pool water was half-way up my legs. The shrimps failed completely: no carp were taken, only eels. That week Chris caught a 43¾lb common carp – the second largest carp ever caught in this country. I landed a couple of doubles on sweetcorn; I didn't want to go home having blanked. I had also tried a couple of other natural particles that week, namely preserved bees and caddis grubs: although runs did come I came to the conclusion that one natural is no better than another, the old fishing-for-a-cow-with-a-blade-of-grass-in-a-field theory. The naturals will work but have to be put bang on the fish's nose, otherwise there is nothing to attract the fish. It will help of course if a concentrated area of a particular

Sunny Redmire days

natural can be made, and this can be done with the aid of PVA bags filled with that natural. I had been side-tracked with the shrimp and other natural particles but the next time I was back to my little dark baits.

Thinking about the next visit I decided not to use the hemp as I still hadn't, at that time, sorted out the hook problem. I'm fortunate in living in Grimsby in that we have one of the largest grain and seed wholesalers in the country. I not only have a vast range of baits at my disposal but can also buy them a darn sight cheaper than people in other areas. From this vast range a bait was chosen – Tasmanian mini-maples, a kind of very small, dark pea. I was able to use a salmon hook with them. This bait was used for the rest of the season, vast amounts being thrown in. Results were quite slow: I wasn't catching many fish but what I did catch were generally good sized fish. It seemed that the small fish were being cut out. I also continued baiting with hemp every week, but not using it. That season I finished up with five fish over 20lb.

I believed I was on the right lines with my baits; that a small, dark bait was more likely to catch the bigger fish. The bigger the bait was the more visual it was, cutting down on the length of time it remainded effective. The idea behind this thinking was that if a fish had been caught on a large bait, and it came into an area containing such baits, it was liable to be alarmed as the bait would be clearly seen. But with very small baits that were found by senses of touch and smell they would be hardly likely to be seen on a muddy bottom; so a carp wouldn't be alarmed if it moved into an area littered with small baits on which it had previously been caught.

The close season of 1973 saw me constantly going over the different baits in my mind. It occurred to me that I could have gone too far too soon in going on to very small baits. That is to say, where do you go when a bait becomes impractical to use because of its size? Once I got down to the smallest baits that could be presented on a hook large enough and strong enough to land a prospective record carp, where would I go from there? I decided to try to prolong the sequence by putting out some baits which were slightly larger than those with which I had ended the season, but I would keep up the groundbaiting on the smaller baits in case I had to go back to them. One very large, almost conventional bait was chosen – broad beans. I didn't expect great things from them but thought that they might pick up the odd fish or two as we would be at the pool for the first week of the season.

One medium sized bait, Lobia (black-eyed beans), naturally white, but cooked in gravy salt to brown them and make them less visual, was also chosen. The normal size maple peas were also taken but again I didn't have much faith in them as I believed the carp might be wary after the baiting I had done the previous season with the smaller mini-maples. I also thought they might take the fish off the mini-maples should I need to go back to that bait. I was lucky in that I was able to arrive at the lake three days before the off and by opening night all the baits were well established. Indeed, I had fish of record size feeding on the baits before the sixteenth!

That first week of the season produced six twenties for us; Chris and I had three each. Three came to broad beans, two to black-eyed beans and one came to sweetcorn. This last fish I believe to be the last twenty pounder to come out on sweetcorn. I can't swear to that as I only know what goes on within my own rota group, but that is what I believe; observations in the shallows showed that now even the very small fish were afraid of sweetcorn. Big fish coming across that bait were so alarmed that they were seen to bow-wave off in a very frightened state. The success of the broad beans was very short-lived; only one more fish came to this bait to my knowledge.

From this point onwards all opinions and results are completely my own as Chris and Bob joined together on their own project. Chris and Bob had great success with a bait mentioned earlier* that I had dismissed, although I will not name it as I had nothing to do with its success.

With the life of the broad beans seemingly ended I decided to replace this bait with macaroni, again cooked in gravy salt to make it less visible.

The second week of the season found me back at the very hard local lake where friends assured me that the carp were taking sweetcorn again; in fact they had been practically feeding the carp with it in the close season. I found it hard to believe they would come back onto a bait of which they had once been frightened. It proved to be true. I hooked three fish in that week (unfortunately landing only one, but that was my first twenty from the water) and the loss of the other two seemed to kill the bait. I baited up heavily with maple peas and the following week I returned to take another 20 pounder from the water.

Back at Redmire I had my best ever season, all the previously mentioned baits catching carp. Indeed twenty pounders fell to all of them but by the back-end of the season these baits seemed to be going off and a switch to the smaller, very heavily ground-baited mini-maples produced two more fish.

During this season several experiments were carried out. One was to see if the maggots theme had been exhausted. Maggots were dyed dark brown and ground-baited. The idea was that the carp liked maggots but were afraid of the way in which they were presented i.e. plain white ones. Unfortunately this experiment was completely unsuccessful, only eels being caught. Squatts (tiny maggots) were tried, but again with the same result. The same can be said of wasp-grubs, although this bait did catch carp up to 12lb. Another experiment along these lines was with paste baits. The idea was the same – carp weren't frightened of the ingredients of a paste bait but the plain fact that it was a ball of paste. It didn't matter what was in the paste, if it looked like a ball of bait the Redmire carp were frightened of it. It came to me that

*Red kidney beans

the carp liked specials but in Redmire they were afraid of them. Carp weren't afraid of particle-baits, but some wouldn't be taken because it seemed the carp just didn't like them. The answer seemed simple: present a bait which carp in general like i.e. Kit-e-Kat, sausage, PYM in a manner they are not afraid of i.e. particles. The first trial on these lines was done by rolling out sausage meat on a floured table. Eggs were mixed with the meat to make the mixture more binding; yeast was also put in, but only as an added attractor. The mixture was then stamped out into particle shape using a heart-shaped cutter used for cake decorations. The meat-based particles were then put in a plastic bag and left in the fridge until needed. They were carried to the lake in an insulated box.

The experiment was successful; good numbers of carp were caught. I am still working on different baits with this theme in mind. The possibilities are endless; hundreds of different shapes to go at, hundreds of different special ingredients. Along these lines I found a special bait already marketed in particle form – Go-Cat. This tends to float but the problem is easily solved. One problem with the bait I didn't really solve was its hardness and I had many runs which came unstuck because the bait didn't soften enough. I tried making a paste from the Go-Cat pellets but if the hookbait wasn't picked up quickly the paste would disintegrate on the hook.

I have since learnt how to overcome this problem, by making the paste at home, mixing it with eggs, and then scalding the moulded pellets: at the time I was doing so well with my other baits I didn't get round to solving this problem.

Another experiment carried out during the first two seasons was the use of what I termed weed baits. Into this category come sliced green beans, cut beans, bamboo shoots etc. These baits were not widely successful but did catch fish up to 15lb. Now while this is no proof of their capabilities, as the Redmire carp up to 18lb will take nearly anything, I feel they worked because in those first two seasons there was a lot of weed about and on various occasions the carp were seen merrily noshing at the weed. It is on such occasions as these, I feel, that these baits come into their own. I also wonder if these conditions have arisen when people have claimed to have caught on green peas: I think that's quite possible, although I myself have never caught on green peas.

Carp can, of course, be caught on pieces of weed, as I proved at the Woldale fishery in 1973 when I presented a piece of weed bang on the head of a 15½lb mirror which was quite preoccupied eating away at a margin weed-bed.

The second week of the 1974 season found me again at Redmire. The previous week had fished very poorly; no 20lb cap had been taken. Jack Hilton mentioned that it seemed the carp had gone off particle-baits. The following week I tried most of the conventional size particles, including all those which had given me success the previous season. By the Thursday I had had no fish although a couple of missed runs seemed to be from the smaller fish. I decided to go back to the mini-maples with which I had continued ground-baiting. This produced just one run – an upper twenty. My following week at the pool produced two good fish to the same bait. After that I had no more runs to that bait, although several times I had my hookbait amongst feeding fish. It seemed the time had come to go onto the hemp I had been baiting up with for more than two years. The groundbaiting was stepped up, a mixture of Manchurian hemp and tares being used to cut down on the expense. The result of this mass groundbaiting – four stones of the stuff was nothing unusual – was that on occasions I believe that full preoccupation was achieved. The times when this happened came after days of cold, windy conditions, followed by a short spell of ideal weather. What happened I believe was as follows:

The cold conditions kept the fish off the feed for four days. During this time I was groundbaiting three times a day. After that period there was such a build-up of baits that it out-numbered the natural food in the area groundbaited. It probably didn't out-number the sum total of natural food items but I believe that carp will feed on that natural food which exceeds in quantity the others at a given time, and I also believe my bait outnumbered the most prolific natural food item. When conditions changed to put the fish on the feed my bait was the most abundant food item – and until conditions changed again the carp were preoccupied with it. On the occasions when conditions have fallen right results have been fantastic. Three times I had large bags of fish containing three twenty pounders and other doubles. On the last occasion it all happened in a couple of hours.

I never expected results like this. I expected to catch the odd fish because the carp simply weren't afraid of the bait; when there is that much of it it becomes natural to the water. But with all these seeds lying on the bottom one seed has no more attraction than another, therefore big catches weren't expected. What I didn't foresee was the amount of bait a single carp will eat. The amount regurgitated in the sacks has to be seen to be believed. I have since changed to a tiny cereal bait used on the same principle i.e. vast groundbaiting to achieve preoccupation. This was done for purely economic reasons. A 27 pounder regurgitated enough of this new bait to fill the bottom of a sack.*

Well, there are one man's observations over six years on particle-baits. My conclusions are my own and may differ from those of other anglers using the same type of baits over that period. But for those who have struggled through to the end here are the conclusions I have drawn:

Sweetcorn is definitely the most immediate bait and can often bring instant success, but I don't believe it is the bait to sort the big ones from the little ones. Soya beans, baked beans, black-eye beans could bring the same success

* This was Red Dari Seed

if the water hasn't already been hammered on particles. Meat-based particles and proprietary ones – Go-Cat, Cupboard Love, trout pellets – I would use if a water hasn't yet seen particles; that is, I would start off with them or, alternatively go on to them when the already mentioned particles are no longer catching carp. Red kidney beans, broad beans, chick peas, gunga beans, macaroni and butter beans; if possible use before the smaller of the above named baits but don't expect their success to last very long. Maples, sultanas, currants, tares, syori beans, tic beans; success can be slow and lengthy pre-baiting may be needed but all tend to pick up the bigger fish.

Diced carrots, diced swedes, diced potatoes, small sweets and pasta shapes will catch carp but don't expect startling results. In my opinion green peas are useless. I've never seen them picked up or eaten: I've heard of people catching carp on them but would have to see it with my own eyes to believe it.

Finally, mass pre-baiting with hemp, grass-seed, dari seeds, chilli peppers, small cereals, rice; I would suggest only using them after all other choices have been exhausted. After all, as I said earlier, where do we go from here?

To finish I would just like to repeat that all the conclusions are my own. Obviously in so short a space of time it may be that some of the baits haven't had a fair trial. The conclusions I've drawn may be wrong; I may have put the wrong reasoning to certain catches on certain baits. But one thing is certain and that is this: a great deal of success can be had using particle baits for carp.

You will see that several of the baits on the list at the end have not been mentioned previously in the article. All of these baits work; I have prebaited with them and observed them being eaten but as yet have had no need to use them as a hookbait: I'm keeping those for a rainy day. I would also like to make it clear that Chris Yates deserves the credit for the sweetcorn happening when it did. Left to me it might have taken a full season to realise its potential *(if at all).*

Hutchinson modestly does not mention his catch statistics. He has, however, caught 39 carp over 20lb and 102 over 10lb in the last three years alone! And from many different waters. – Editor (1975).

Chapter 7

Particle Baits '80

IN theory a particle bait is any bait used in numbers, each individual piece being of the same size, colour, flavour and texture. However for the purpose of this chapter the term applies only to baits which have those characteristics, and furthermore are relatively small when compared to a conventional paste bait. The largest bait that comes into this category is the broad bean, and the smallest are some varieties of rape seed which are barely larger than a pin head. Because the smaller sized baits require slightly different ground baiting and presentation methods, all seeds smaller than a tare are referred to as "mass" baits.

Development of the particle approach

A little of the history of particle baits will help the reader get the general idea behind the approach. My own involvement with these baits started in the second half of the sixties. At that time I was presented with a "problem" water. The problem was that I could not catch the carp in it! This water had the most perfect ecological balance I have ever come across, with only a handful of carp, and at all times of the year there was an abundance of natural food in one form or another. I tried to use this to my advantage by fishing with whatever food the carp appeared to be feeding on at the time. This resulted in an average of one fish a year being hooked. The method had no future, for surely the same situation would occur with each new season. If a carp had hundreds of swan mussels before it why should it pick up the one that had a hook in it? Besides, mussels only seemed to form the main part of the diet for a short time in the season. What were the chances when shrimps were on the menu? There were, in all probability, millions of those. At this time, the so called "special", a flavoured paste bait, often containing minced fish or meat, came on the scene. Results with these baits, especially in Kent, were phenomenal.

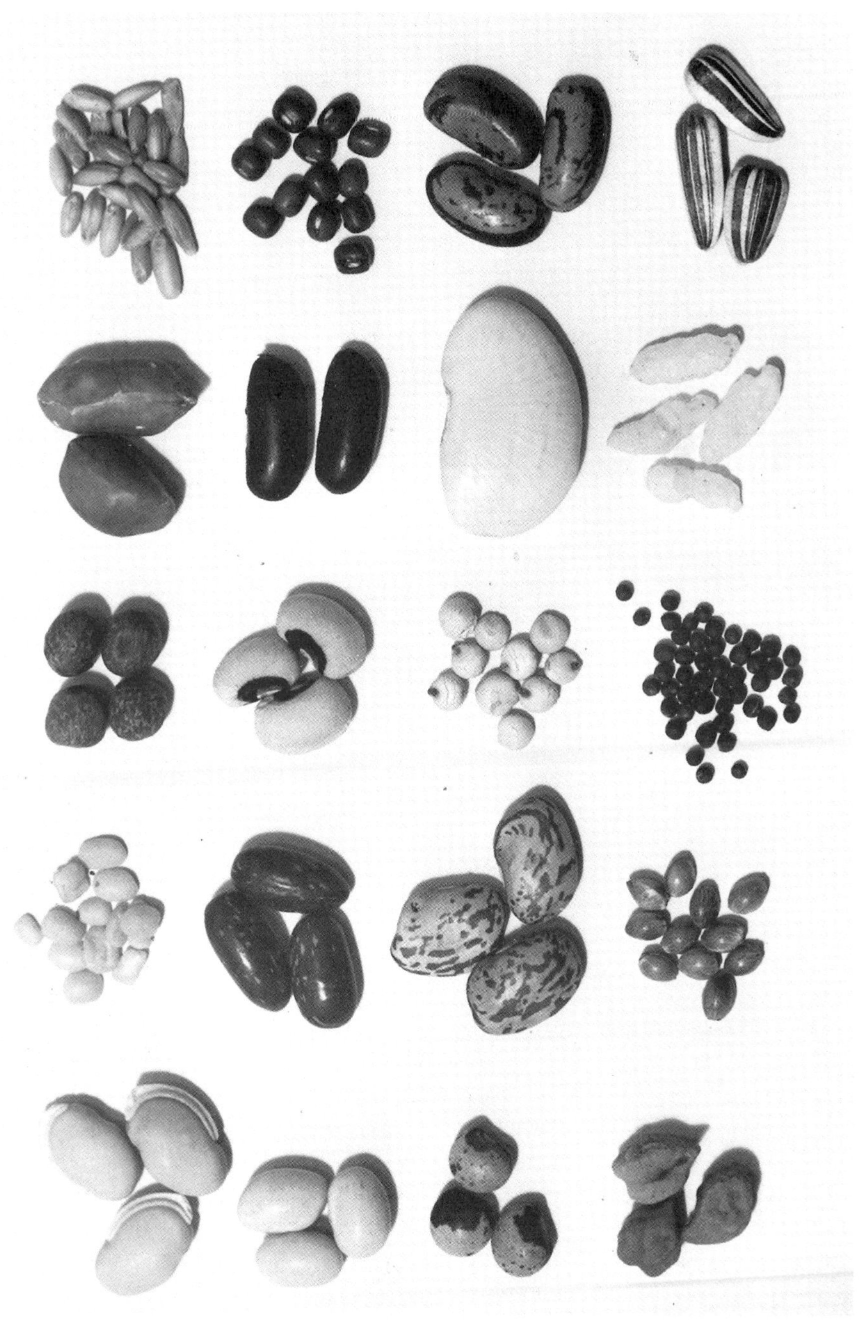

Plenty to go at here in size, colour, shape and flavour

Trips were made to that area and a basic knowledge acquired of the baits and their presentation. I hoped I could apply what I had learnt to my "problem" water. However results were often just as disappointing as before. With hindsight I can see that the environment of the waters where the baits were so successful, and my own "problem" water, were just not comparable.

So it was back to the drawing board once more to find an altogether different approach. It was obvious that for the main part the carp would feed on that food which was in the most abundant supply at a given time. But by fishing with it, I was only offering the old "blade of grass in a field" method. It was also very difficult to know precisely just what the carp were feeding on when engaged in bottom feeding. Slowly pieces fitted together; if I was to introduce something in such quantities that it became the most abundant food available, surely the carp would feed on it in preference to natural items? Also by doing this I would know precisely what the carp were feeding on. It also appeared that the introduced foodstuff should be small, as the carp seemed completely preoccupied when their naturally abundant food was small. At the times when the carp fed almost exclusively on mussels, feeding periods would be extremely short. It seemed logical enough to assume that relatively small numbers of these large food items soon satisfied the carps' appetite, whereas larger quantities, entailing long feeding spells, were needed with smaller items.

It was from these ideas that the particle approach evolved. Although in its original context the "blade of grass in a field" theory still applied, slowly the method was refined until sufficient amounts of bait were introduced to bring about a certain degree of preoccupation within the carp, yet still give the angler a fair chance of catching on the bait. The most suitable foodstuffs that meet the requirements needed to create preoccupation have been found over the years to be various vegetable seeds. All manner of beans, peas, and cereal crops work to some degree. Some work better than others, and different waters (and often different areas within one water) need different properties from a bait. It is being able to decide which of those properties are needed in each new water, that decides the amount of success an angler has with these or any type of bait.

The main requirement of a particle bait is that it should be found in numbers. A carp when feeding on a natural diet of small items feeds where they are in abundance. If that food is shrimp, for example, the carp does not eat one shrimp in one area, and then move off to another for its next. Although the energy output of a carp when swimming is not great, such a method of feeding would hardly replenish that energy expenditure. Therefore the angler should be thinking, "Will this bait be found in abundance at that point at which the carp is feeding?" If the answer is no, then a bait which will be found in numbers must be used. The type of bottom, the kind of weed, the manner in which the carp feed, the amount of natural food available, and the quality of that food, will all help to determine just what the bait should be. I am taking for granted that the angler will have done his work already and will have chosen the correct swim, because the most attractive bait in the world will not catch fish which don't frequent the area you're fishing.

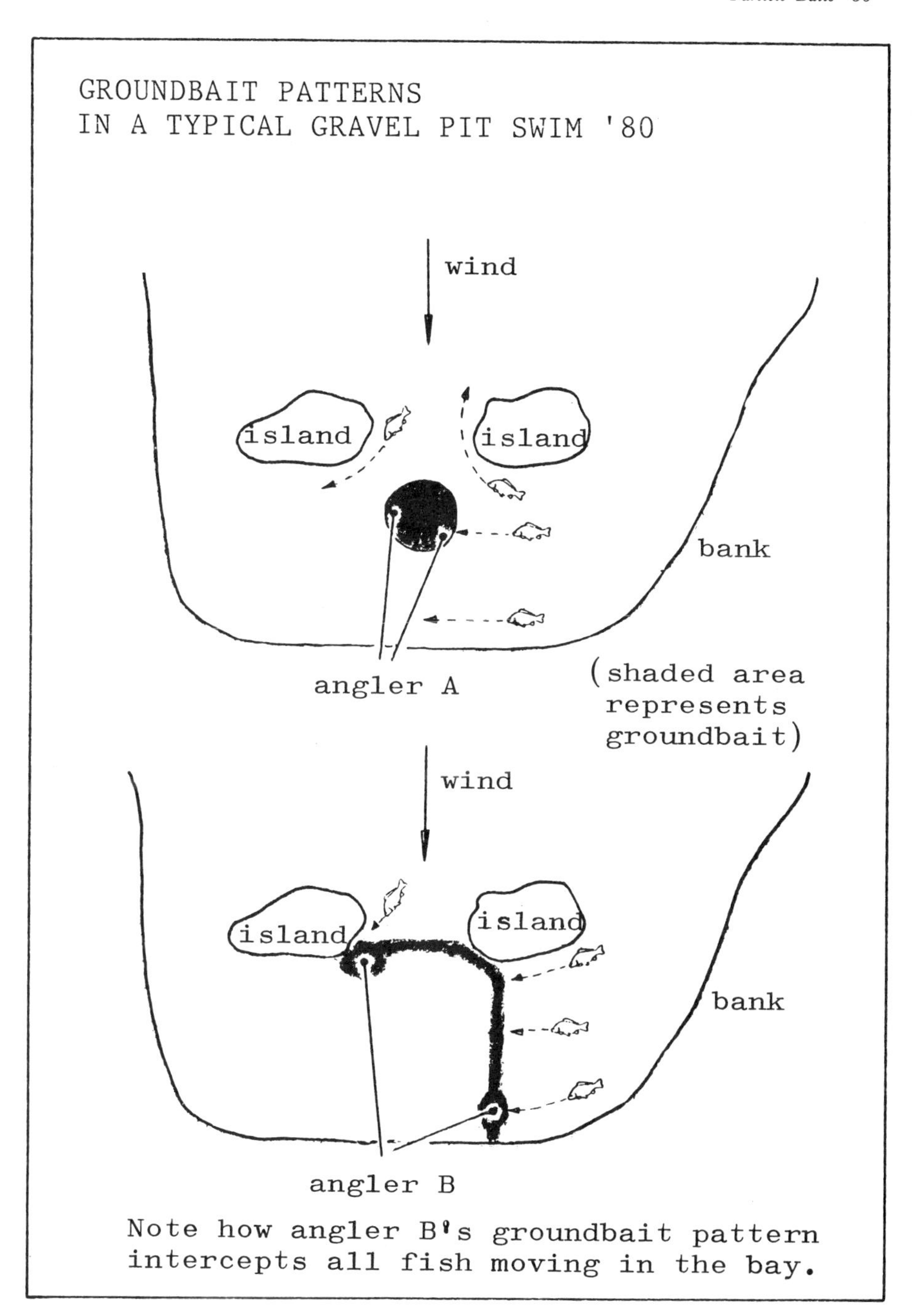
GROUNDBAIT PATTERNS
IN A TYPICAL GRAVEL PIT SWIM '80
wind
island
island
bank
angler A
(shaded area
represents
groundbait)
wind
island
island
bank
angler B
Note how angler B's groundbait pattern
intercepts all fish moving in the bay.

Prebaiting

Although this approach was evolved for very rich waters with small heads of carp, it will work in every kind of water, although baits and methods of presentation may have to be changed to meet each situation. I originally believed that prebaiting was essential for these baits to work, the thought being that a fish had to be weaned onto a new kind of foodstuff. I no longer believe this is necessary or indeed even beneficial. The only exception I would make to this is when dark baits are used in a mud-bottomed water, where it is impossible to observe feeding areas. (I'll deal with this situation later.) My turnabout as regards prebaiting came because I found the reaction to the majority of baits to be instantaneous. Why should a fish have to see a hundred or a thousand baits before it starts feeding on them? One individual bait has to be picked up first, whether that bait is being seen for the first time or the umpteenth. Now I can see that a fish will feel confident, when picking up a food it has eaten many times before without cause for alarm. But it still had to pick up that first bait. If a fish is seeing a new bait either for the first time or the hundredth time, then it has no cause for alarm, since there is nothing frightening for it to associate that bait with. The number of times I've caught carp on a new particle bait with no prebaiting whatsoever now totals over fifty, and from a wide variety of different lakes. The intention here is not to blow my own trumpet but to emphasize that prebaiting is not needed.

Indeed prebaiting has more disadvantages than it has benefits. In my experience carp are the first species to pick up a bait. Other species such as roach, bream and tench do seem to have to be weaned onto a bait. Regular prebaiting does just that, giving the carp angler nuisance fish problems. Once roach or tench are on a bait, it is often a problem to keep a sufficient amount of it available to encourage carp to feed. On top of that, the disturbance created by constantly landing nuisance fish is likely to keep carp out of the swim.

"Mug" fish

Every lake contains some fish that are caught a lot more times than others; in recent years these fish have been termed "mug" fish. Some anglers believe that it is only these fish that will fall to a bait that hasn't been introduced over a prolonged period, and that to get at fish that are rarely caught, the bait must be fed regularly to become almost natural to the water. Again, I disagree, because when no fish have been caught on a new bait, there are no fish to transmit fear or caution of the food, so it is just as likely to be picked up by one fish as another. In many lakes, it also happens that the first fish to investigate a new food is often the largest. Fish grow big because they feed regularly. True, the real monster fish get to their massive sizes because of genetic abnormalities, and probably because they can convert food into weight better than the average fish, but regular food is essential for that conversion to take place. I therefore believe that a new non-prebaited food has a very good chance of sorting the big fellas out.

One aspect of the "mug" fish syndrome that is very hard to fathom is why in some years a particular fish is caught many times, and yet in other seasons hardly gets caught at all. A friend of mine came up with the theory that they may in some years suffer from parasitic outbreaks in the intestines that deprive them of the benefit of the food eaten. Their hunger is not satisfied, causing them to feed excessively, and often without caution. The following year the parasite may have passed through the fish, or lie dormant, so it feeds normally again and stops getting caught so often.

Happiness is my first Redmire carp

Which bait?

Deciding on just what bait to use, entails the angler finding out the nature of the bottom in his swim, and the kind of weed, if any, present. There is no need to know the name of each weed, only to know its characteristics or growth pattern. There are essentially three forms which affect the carp angler. The first is filamentous algae, which grows over the bottom like green candyfloss. The second type grows up from the bottom, spreading out in midwater to form a tree-like shape. The third type grows up straight from the bottom to the surface, where it spreads out like "Deadman's Fingers".

The first type is common over gravel bottoms where there is little silt. This candyfloss type weed holds most of its available food – such as water beetles, snails and shrimp – within and on top of its strands. It is here that the carp expects to find its food, and so feeds accordingly off the top of the weed itself. Any particle bait to be used in this situation should therefore be buoyant enough to rest on top of this weed, in order for it to be found in numbers. Baits suitable for this situation are those with flat, broad sides, such as beans, or those which have a high water content such as sultanas or currants.

Although not acceptable to fish in every water, nuts such as cashew, peanuts and tigernuts, which have a very high oil content, so making them very buoyant and easily found in numbers, can be useful in these circumstances.

The second kind of weed needs a certain amount of silt into which it can root in order to prosper. Although most common in clay or mud-bottomed pits it will also grow in those areas of gravel pits where there are silt pockets. Where this weed is concerned, the majority of the food is found in the mud amongst the roots of the weed. Although a certain amount of food is found amongst the leaves, far more feeding is done amongst the roots. In this case, a bait must be dense enough to get through the mid-water foliage and down to the bottom. Various varieties of peas, such as maple, dun, and chic peas, and tares, are the choice here. Since the bait is at its most dense when uncooked, only minimal cooking is advised. Baits will be eaten uncooked – after all, all natural food a fish comes across is uncooked. However I prefer to cook all baits, with the exception of dried fruits which only need soaking. By cooking a bait, not only are inherent flavours released, which in turn give the carp a scent to home in on, but also the germ of the seed is killed. If an uncooked bait remains on the bottom for any length of time it is liable to germinate and root itself. This is particularly a problem in clear, shallow water. One famous carp water now has a crop of American buck wheat growing in its shallows, thanks to the use of uncooked baits.

The third type of weed is again best suited to mud bottoms. It appears to need a much deeper root base than the others and as such is rarely found in gravel pits of recent origin. Food is again concentrated amongst the roots, which is where the carp feed intensively. Its foliage, which spreads out on the surface, is also a trap for all surface foodstuffs, which promotes a certain amount of surface feeding. Once again, as far as the bottom feeding is concerned, dense baits such as the ones previously mentioned are the order of the day. It may help the angler to mix the groundbait with loose sandy soil in order to get the bait down through the surface foliage.

Surface baits

The surface feeding also lends itself to the use of floating particles. Sunflower seeds, pine nuts or any type of seed where the germ is encased in an outer shell, are all suitable here. There is a large range of small preshaped pet foods and animal food pellets which will also float. My personal preference, however, is for the natural seed floaters. The reason is that the man-made cereal floaters swell up and eventually disintegrate, while the seed floaters get swept back and forwards with the surface drift, staying afloat, and so there is more chance of them being recognised as food. Eventually the seed soaks up so much water that it sinks, though still being in a position for carp to find it.

When using floating particles it is very often necessary to prebait. Although on some waters they are taken instantly, in many waters it is only after prolonged prebaiting that carp seem to recognise the items as food. To cut baiting to a minimum, only bait on days when surface feeding is likely to take place i.e. hot days with a nice ripple on the water. I try to get behind the wind, and then tip a pound of seeds, or some floating petfood, into the start of the ripple. This usually means that the baits will float off, ending in the surface food areas, or scum lanes as I call them. The one drawback with these baits is that they seem to draw every coot and duck from miles around. However, the method doesn't half come in handy around Christmas dinner time.

Come on up . . . it's Munchie time

Different types of water.

Having decided to present our bait in numbers, what other qualities will it require? As well as the location of foodstuffs, the amount of food available to each fish will dictate the way in which it feeds. Many waters nowadays are over-stocked as far as carp are concerned. In these waters, besides the hot spots, every inch of bottom is likely to be visited by carp in search of food. Here every carp, whatever its age, will behave like a young growing fish, moving around quite fast, investigating anything which might mean food. Constant disruption of the bottom usually results in the water carrying a certain amount of colour. With this in mind, in such conditions baits should be made as visual as possible. Visibility can be achieved by either size or colour.

Some baits appear to fill fish up very quickly, not always because of their size, but often due to their food value. Cashew and peanuts are high in protein, as are lupin seeds, dun peas and soya beans. I believe this may be the reason for those baits working well in the hungrier waters, yet being low down the list when used in rich waters. Be that as it may, it pays to bait on the light side with these baits.

In a really hungry, highly coloured water, the bait would do best if it had both size and colour. In such waters, a paste bait will be just as effective as a particle bait. Here a particle bait is not needed to catch fish, but if preoccupation is achieved, large bags of fish are on the cards. Cooking the beans in soups, such as tomato, oxtail or beef, will impart a flavour into the bait, which will aid recognition.

Some of these waters are not exactly what I would term "hungry". Although the natural foodstocks are high, the trouble is that too many carp live in the water. The fish still grow, but not at their full potential rate. The fish get by and grow by feeding constantly, but they are still just as able to be alarmed. So bait size is still limited to the range of particle baits, anything larger being inspected individually like a conventional bait, when reaction is the same as to a conventional bait. Very little weed is likely to be evident, as regular disturbance of the bottom inhibits the rooting process. Therefore all but the densest baits, which may sink deep into the mud, are suitable if visual enough. My own preference is for either sweetcorn or haricot, blackeyed, or lima beans. All are originally white, but I've had greater success when they've been coloured. Yellow, pink and reds are very productive colours, while if the water was exceptionally deep, I'd plump for a blue bait.

Clear waters with high foodstocks fall mostly into two different categories. First there are the gravel pits of recent origin, where the bottom consists of great barren areas of gravel, dispersed with pockets or troughs rich with weed and silt. More often than not they have not been stocked deliberately in any numbers. There is plenty of food to go around, but the carp often have to move around quite a bit to find that food. Small areas soon become "overgrazed". Once again, I'd plump for the visual baits, the aim being to stop the fish in their tracks. Again, strong flavours will help achieve this.

The second type of rich water is the clear, highly weeded clay pit. As often as not they are found where the local soil is on top of chalk. Whereas gravel pits are rich in crustacea, the most abundant food sources in clay pits are much smaller items, i.e. daphnia, bloodworms and waterfleas. Although from time to time larger food items become abundant, a lot of time is spent by the carp feeding up to the gills in mud, on the small food items. For some reason, carp in these waters appear very difficult to catch on the conventional type paste baits. It could be that they are wary of such a bait, but it is more likely that their tiny minds are so tuned to small food items that large baits are not recognised as food, or do not appear appetising enough. Whatever the reason is, this situation of feeding in the mud itself dictates the use of a small, dense bait. In fact, back to the original particle concept, presenting a bait so that it appears natural to the water. I also prefer the bait to be as dark as possible, taking advantage of the carp's natural feeding methods of finding food by touch and taste. Trying to stick as close to the natural as possible, visual aspects of the bait are kept to the very minimum.

Non-visual baits

Success with these baits can last for a very long time. Whereas the visual baits will "blow" once a certain number of fish have been caught, the non-visuals may catch the same fish many times. There seems little with which the fish can associate the experience of being caught. As well as maple peas and dun peas (chic peas being too visual for the job), many small mass baits fall into the dense category. Tares, hemp, dari, millet, rape, and buckwheat all meet the requirements. All will eventually sink into the mud itself.

There are two ways I set about the task of getting the fish feeding on this type of bait. The first method requires that the whole lake is first prebaited. Bait is scattered into every area likely to be visited by carp. This ensures that the carp will recognise that food when it next comes across it; it also means that at some time that food is liable to be the most abundant food available. The fact that the correct clay for brick making is usually found in only small quantities, means that clay pits are for the most part of manageable size, and so vast amounts of bait are not needed for prebaiting. With this method, the smaller seeds are the most suitable. For example, the mass of one maple pea is the same as five or six dari seeds. Therefore more individual seeds can be scattered, whilst only using the same total weight as a large bait. The aim is to ensure that when a carp goes down feeding into one of the ground-baited areas, it gets a mouthful of seeds. Hopefully the fish will eventually recognise (in its primitive way) that when it comes across this food, it is always in abundance. Prebaiting is gradually narrowed down into smaller areas, eventually just to the swim or swims the angler intends fishing. Again it is hoped that by the time the angler intends fishing, the carp will be visiting that swim expecting an abundance of food. Incidentally I would use this method with the larger maple and dun peas only in mud bottomed, coloured waters, of low food content.

The second method, which requires no prebaiting, calls for the water to be so clear that close observation of movements and feeding can be carried out. I will first describe a theory I have, from which the method has arisen. On the water where I first started with particles, I was able to observe carp at all times of the day. Prior to feeding, carp would go down in an area, and browse about for maybe a minute or so. They would then swim off to another area and do the same thing. In all, maybe five or six spots were visited before a carp started feeding in earnest. Observations over several seasons showed that the carp visited precisely the same spots each day. Very occasionally, they would feed hard on one of these spots for a long period, but usually it was just the quick minute or so visit. In later years I was to fish at Redmire pool, where observation showed the carp to carry out this same exercise. Precise spots were visited day after day. Then out of the blue, one day, hard feeding would take place at one of these spots. One of these hard feeding periods corresponded with a daphnia explosion, a huge red band about 10 yards wide stretching from east to west banks. The carp carried on feeding underneath this band, oblivious to the daphnia above. I have often queried in my own mind the value of daphnia to an adult carp's diet; if there was little other food available it would have been eaten, but if larger natural items were available, I was sure these would be preferred. This incident seemed to bear out these doubts. So interested was I in what was happening that I watched this scene for an hour or more, before I realised that the carp were feeding amongst a fly hatch. Later in the week one of the other regularly visited spots became alivé with feeding fish. Interspersed with the bubbles the carp were making, up came flies popping to the surface. A hatch was once again beginning. On subsequent visits to the pool, I again observed that whenever ardent feeding took place at one of the frequently visited spots, fly hatches were in evidence. It was not something that happened every day, but probably occurred once a week. To make sure it was not coincidence, or a behaviour only evident at Redmire, I started making visits again back to the original lake. Sure enough the same events took place.

My interpretation of what was happening is this. The carp is fully aware of what conditions suit a certain kind of food. It knows which kind of bottom a fly needs to lay its eggs. It could be that the large flies, such as sedges, need a looser-textured bottom before they can burrow. Although at all stages of life the growing larva is edible, it is not until it reaches the advanced stages and is about to emerge, that it is considered a substantial food item. By visiting a spot each day the carp is checking if that "larder" is ready. If it is not, the next one is inspected. Should none of the spots be ready, then they commence feeding on the smaller food items.

The reader may not agree with this interpretation; that is fair enough. It does not alter the fact that in mud-bottomed lakes, carp do visit precisely the same spots day after day. If the angler can locate these spots he can bait them, only small amounts being needed. Two pounds of a hemp-sized bait is ample. On checking the area, the carp can't help but get a mouthful of seeds. Hopefully this will be regarded as a substantial enough item to get the fish feeding. Once one fish starts disturbing the mud, others will soon drop in to investigate.

I have found that the best way to put the groundbait into the "larder" areas is on the "little-and-often" principle. After a fish has checked a spot and moved off, I catapult or throw out a couple of handfuls of seeds. This procedure is carried out roughly every three hours during daylight hours, and once again at dawn. The effect of one lot of bait piling on top of another sinks the earlier baitings deeper into the mud and this produces a series of layers into which the carp delve. When this layering is produced, the full preoccupation can be achieved, the fish tearing up the mud in search of every last seed. If there is only a surface layer of bait, the fish soon move off as that superficial layer becomes less abundant.

The method I use to present the hook baits is to take a sample of the lake's mud. This is taken home and heated in an old pan until it is dry enough to make into a powder. This powder can then be stored for future visits. When it is needed, the powder is mixed with a binding agent into a paste of such a consistency that a hook can be pulled through it. Different samples may require a different binding agent, so make up several trial pastes using either gluten, egg white, milk, or gelatine, until the right one is arrived at. The paste itself can be frozen for future use. Once you are ready to fish, merely put the paste onto the hook as you would a conventional bait, and drop the paste into a small bag of seeds. Give the bag a squeeze and you're left with a seed-impregnated mud bait.

Knowing just how much bait to use in any situation is difficult; it's a question of playing it by ear. The amount of bait has to be enough to get the fish feeding hard, but not so much that the fish are satisfied before the hook bait is taken. I always try to keep them wanting more. If more fish enter the swim and start feeding than I have originally catered for, then I fire more baits out over their heads. Knowing your water and how many fish you can expect will determine how much is fired in at the start of a session. As a very rough guide, I would say about a quarter of a pound of bait per carp is required.

In earlier articles of mine I have stated that I do not believe nuts to be good baits. I still hold that opinion where rich waters are concerned, but in waters with low food stocks, particularly those that have any amount of filamentous algae on the bottom, they can be winners. Their buoyancy, because of their oil content, ensures they are found, whilst their attraction (dare I say it) is I believe more to do with the protein content than the fact of being a particle bait.

Other baits I have never rated are green peas, and the majority of soft fruits. I still hold those views. I found out that fish went barmy one year on a certain fruit bait, in a lake I used to fish. What the anglers did not realise was that I had baited that lake hard for three years on that bait, without any fish whatsoever. On that score I prefer to leave soft fruits alone. The length of time they take to work is just too much for me, when there are plenty of instantaneous baits. Dehydrated fruit baits, such as currants and sultanas, work far better, I should think because much of the acid content has been pressed out of them. Even these baits, though, generally take longer to work than most particles. I do not regard them by any stretch of the imagination as "instant" baits.

Flavours

I mentioned earlier about flavouring bean baits with soups to give the carp a scent to home in on. This is because, apart from broad beans, they have very little flavour in themselves. Other baits release flavours once they appear to be going off. Maple peas are a prime example. A day or two after cooking they give off a milky substance and this is when they are at their best. Really hard baits such as plate maize and tic beans seem to be at their best after being allowed to ferment in water. This fermentation produces amino acids, amongst other things, and although to the human nose the water in which the bait has fermented smells to high heaven, it pays to keep this water. If a margin swim is being fished, it should be thrown out in the area of the bait. Freezing this water would enable the angler to direct pieces more precisely, but I feel with amino acids being so unstable freezing could alter their structure. In the chapter on winter fishing I advocate freezing any residue of soup left after cooking beans, but this is different to fermented liquid, being the actual flavour that has been implanted into the bait, not something produced by chemical reaction. Should beans be cooked at the waterside when margin swims are being fished, I again pour in the residue as an attractor.

It took three days to build the swim up . . . then bingo . . . three twenties on red dari seed

Changing the bait

It is all very well talking about the ideal bait in a given situation but the angler may be fishing a lake where every ideal bait has been used. There are several ways of meeting this situation. The first is to ring the changes with a given bait. Say for example haricot beans, dyed red and flavoured in tomato soup, were once a winner on that lake. Try dyeing the beans yellow and flavouring with Marmite. The varieties are limitless. Even the texture of the bait can be changed just by cooking to various degrees, and it is possible to produce a bait at any stage between hard to soft. Baits such as tapioca and sago have a texture all of their own, being practically spawn-like. Eventually, though, success will decrease as the bait is recognised by its shape. The lengthy process of making half-baits may be worth the effort; beans and peas, being in two half segments, are not hard to divide. It usually pays, however, to make a change to an entirely new shape, say from bean to pea. The new bait is then taken through the changes advocated above. It pays to always be on the lookout at seed merchants for anything with an unusual shape.

If you believe that all the vegetable shapes have been exhausted, it is time to produce your own bait. There are plenty of processed foods which can be shaped easily with a knife. All types of cheese, tinned meats, pressed meats like haslet and pressed pork, and things like black puddings and German sausages, will all make good particle baits. Failing those, make a paste bait in which you can determine the flavour, colour and texture yourself. It is then a simple enough process to add eggs to the paste, cut into the desired shape, and boil the bait, so that it keeps its shape. A quick way of producing pellet-like shapes is to turn the paste mixture into a cake bag, having already added the eggs. The mixture is then squeezed out and the tube of paste cut off at any length required.

There is another way of getting prolonged success with particles, without having to ring the changes. This method is particularly useful when the angler is fishing a water for the first time, and where he has a good idea many particle baits have already been used. The method is at its best in the hungrier waters. Its essence is this: the angler baits up with a bait almost certainly used on that lake before. What is generally termed a "blown-out" bait, sweetcorn, is a good example. The fish want that bait because it probably tastes good, and in all probability is actually needed, with natural foodstocks being low. But having previously been caught on that bait, the carp are afraid of it. No preoccupation takes place, but each individual grain is inspected to see if it is safe. If a fish is satisfied all is well, the grain is eaten; if not the bait is spat out. The angler using this as a hookbait will experience a series of twitches, the carp dropping the bait as soon as it feels any resistance. This is exactly how the angler should begin, by using the common baits until he starts getting those twitches. That means the fish are on the groundbait. He should then use a different hookbait that is buoyant enough to be found, and cast this into the baited area. It would appear that all the carp's suspicion is directed at the groundbait, because practically anything else is likely to be picked up and eaten, even some other bait that is equally "blown out" when used in its usual context. Hookbaits of red kidney beans or trout pellets work well over beds of sweetcorn, while hookbaits of sweetcorn, luncheon meat, and cheese work over maple pea beds. The reader should see from these examples

This 23.8 took a maple pea 'on the drop'

that it appears that a bait of opposite colour is most likely to be picked up.

This method will also help the angler introduce a new bait to a water. Take the example where all the visual particles have already been used. The water is highly coloured and the angler not sure of any hot spots. As he is only left with dark, non-visual baits, it may take a long time before these unfamiliar baits are found. He therefore baits up with his new dark bait, but then fires over the top of that bait a layer of corn or beans. The carp come in to investigate the visual bait, and find amongst it a new bait they are not afraid of.

The first time I tried this method on a Midlands day ticket water, I was rewarded with two twenty pound fish. I had walked around the lake talking to those already fishing and had found that the majority were suffering twitch bites on sweetcorn. I used this to my advantage, by using red kidney beans over a bed of corn.

In addition to the floating particles mentioned earlier, there is another off-shoot which, although not strictly particle fishing, may well depend for its success on those baits. It arose out of a conversation I had with Fred Wilton, the protein bait innovator, a few seasons ago. Fred told how he would bait up a lake with a bottom protein bait, and then fish on a floating bait of the same ingredients. Carp used to feeding on the bottom bait would recognise the floating bait as being the same, and would accordingly feed on that. This happened although the cooking involved altered the bait's texture, and different shapes were used. Although I was not in complete agreement with it all, I was able to see that the method worked. This set me thinking. If the shape and texture did not matter, only the smell and make up of a bait, then the same could be applied to particles. Given that fish would feed on a certain particle on the bottom, a floating bait made from those particles was likely to be taken. I then set about having a bag of black eyed beans milled into flour. One pound of flour was mixed with the amount of dry tomato soup flavouring which I would normally use with a pound of beans for bottom use. The mixture was then baked into a floater.

The first time I used the bottom and floating baits together results were very encouraging. Two fish were taken on the bottom bait, and when later in the day fish moved about high in the water, I took my best fish of the day on the floater. On another water in Kent, where I'd been fishing beans for some seasons, reaction to the floater was again very good. Not all waters lend themselves to surface feeding unfortunately, the limitations being such that the method is still in its infancy. However it does work, though whether the idea behind it is correct or not only time will tell. It could be that vegetable-based floating baits are just very attractive.

Particles at long range

Fishing with particles is very simple at ranges that can be covered with a catapult i.e. up to forty yards, but at distances greater than that, problems arise. The two main ones are getting enough bait out to form a carpet to try and create preoccupied feeding, and using a terminal rig that will not tangle on casting. The second problem arises because of the weight of lead needed for distance casting. The speed of a cast with a heavy lead

ANTI-TANGLE SHOCK RIG FOR LONG RANGE '80

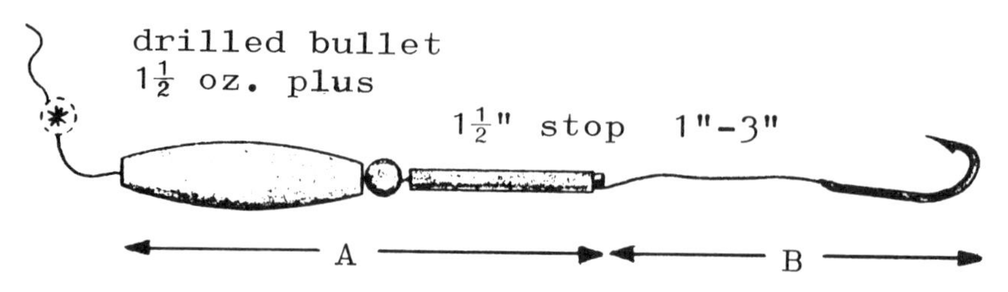

Length B must be less than A, to prevent hook length tangling round main line during cast.

* If baits are taken well down, or bite-offs occur, pinch a swanshot on the line about 1" behind the leger weight.

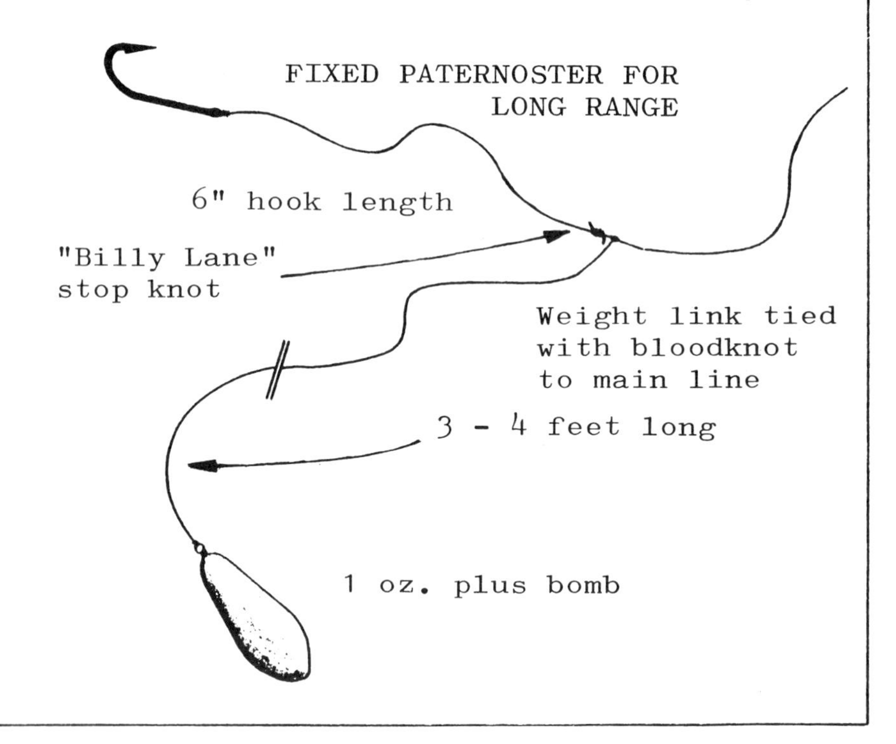

tends to make the light hook bait hang back in the air and tangle with the main line.

There are several ways of going about the first task, although each method does have its drawbacks. The best way involves the use of a boat, merely rowing out and baiting the intended fishing area by hand. Unfortunately none of the clubs of which I am a member will permit this, so other alternatives have had to be found.

The first method tried was the matchman's favourite, using cereal ground bait as a carrier for the bait. Brown cereal was used, and mixed with muddy water to make it as inconspicuous as possible. A number of carp fell to this method, but it had its drawbacks. Distance was limited to around the 50 yard mark (incidentally a throwing stick, made from a fibre-glass blank, with a spoon inserted in the top, proved to be the best way of propelling the ground bait), and the cereal base drew large numbers of unwanted bream into the swim, which would in many cases twitch off the hook baits.

The next method tried was to freeze both ground bait samples and hooks. Beans were cooked up as normal in various soups, and then frozen into blocks complete with the soup. Hook baits were made up on complete traces and dropped into ice lolly containers, which were then topped up with more beans and soup, and the whole lot once more frozen. The groundbait blocks and hook bait containers were then carried to the lake in freezer boxes. At the lake, the blocks were chopped up into cubes about an inch square and fired out by catapult. the hook baits (already on traces) were joined to the reel line by a split ring or swivel. The method worked quite well, in that a number of fish were caught, and greater distances were able to be fished. However, the number caught was not what I would have expected, had I been able to loose feed. I believe this was because the inch blocks of ground bait lay on the bottom in little mounds, rather like a conventional bait, whereas it is preferable to form a carpet of bait. Also even in freezer boxes there is only a certain length of time the baits will keep before melting, and so the method is hardly suitable for a lengthy stay at a water.

The method finally arrived at, after seeing an early prototype used by Rick Gibbinson in Essex, involves the use of a bait dropper. At the moment the droppers I have will enable me to loose feed consistently up to 80 yards, and if needed models could be made to feed up to the magical "ton". The principle behind the dropper is a container that will float, yet tip up and empty its contents (feed) on impact with the water. It is made by inserting polystyrene into the bottom of a plastic tube, and counter-balancing with just enough lead so as not to sink the container when full of baits. The dropper is used on a spare stiff rod, and cast repeatedly until what is considered enough bait to form a carpet has gone in. One big plus for this method is that the dropper will float directly over the area it has groundbaited, so enabling very accurate casting of the hookbaits. The only disadvantage is the amount of disturbance made by repeatedly casting these quite heavy objects. Besides a likelihood of scaring fish from the swim for some time, it does also seem to upset other anglers fishing close by! However if you can put up with their wrath and the occasional rod rest over the back of your head, the fish will eventually return to the swim.

I've experimented with many terminal rigs in an effort to eliminate tangles when fishing at this distance and it must be said that the most consistent is a fixed paternoster rig,

This 22.8 took a maple pea fished over a bed of sweetcorn

using a long tail to the bomb i.e. 3 to 4 feet, in conjunction with a short six inch hook length. Unfortunately it's not as easy as that, as our old enemy the "bite-off" occurs frequently with this rig. It is a fact that on some waters, for reasons I cannot work out, bite-offs are unheard of. If the waters I fished were the same, then this would be the rig I would go for every time.

However, most waters need some kind of non-tangle shock leger set up and I have incorporated an idea from the pike anglers of using a stiff length in the rig, in the terminal set up. Using these rigs, even at distances of 80 yards, the majority of runs experienced are real "flyers", so there is no need for any twitcher hitting set ups.

Chapter 8

Particle Baits '88

In today's carp scene, particles, paste and boilies are no longer apart. The boilie fished over a bed of particles being one of the most popular methods there is, in fact more popular on the whole than basic particle fishing. The reason being that all of the popular particles have been hammered on most waters. Even on a water where particles have not been extensively used, a boilie fished on top can be more effective than seeds on the hook.

This fact was brought home to me when fishing a syndicate water for the first time some four years ago. I had made a swim amongst dense bullrushes, into which was blowing a nice warm south westerly wind. The swim in front of me was for the main part of shallow, three feet depth, every few yards falling into troughs, the deepest of which was about five feet. Observation showed that the carp fed avidly in these troughs, yet rarely fed on the surrounding shallows. Accordingly, I baited heavily with maple peas into three such troughs, a bait in which I had every confidence and was pretty sure had not been used on the lake before.

By 6 pm in the evening I was all settled in and fishing. Within a couple of hours a fish rolled in one of the troughs. From then on, thirty minutes never passed without indication of some sort that there were fish in the baited areas. By dawn I was practically bald, having torn out most of my hair in frustration! I simply could not get a take, yet carp were feeding hard on the baits. I had to try something, so searching through my tackle bag I came across a small bag of floating Ultra Spice boilies I had made the previous year! They still looked in good condition, so I mounted a small one on a size 8 hook, dropped a couple of BB shot two inches behind it, and cast out onto one of the maple pea beds. It took about ten minutes before it roared off. My first fish from the lake proving to be a 20lb 6oz common.

Throughout the day I continued to bait heavily with the maple peas and always within half an hour of baiting, carp would be on them and feeding hard. For the duration of the day I continued with two rods baited with maples and one rod on a pop up boilie. As darkness fell I switched to two rods on pop ups. When I packed up at 8 am the following morning I had hooked sixteen fish, all but one had fallen to the pop up boilies. I could only presume that my maples had been badly presented because the carp had been going crazy on them. One of the problems of fishing a bait like maples on silt is that as fast as a carp roots out one pea, it buries another. The hook bait being the heaviest is the one most likely to get buried the deepest. The pop up boilie on the other hand does not get buried and is too good to leave to a hard feeding fish.

I traipsed off home, very perplexed, planning a trip to another water holding a large head of carp to try out a few things. At home, I found I was out of maples but had stacks of other seeds. Putting some peanuts into soak, I scooped off the top of the water some nuts which were floating. Some of these I grilled, some I dropped into hot oil and fried them. From these I was able to pick out about a dozen very buoyant floating particles. With the gear still stacked in the car I was off to Newark to my new venue.

Picking a swim with a deep mud bottomed margin, I baited up heavily with about five pounds of peanuts. As I was setting up, darkness was falling and as I like to test each pop-up out in the edge first before using it, I decided to leave the floating particles until dawn, fishing the night with two regular peanuts on a size 6. From about midnight onwards, carp rolled on the baits, but there was no action to the rods. Being very tired from my previous trip, I slept late not waking until 7.00 am. I wound in the baits, all of which were intact but discoloured, as if they had been buried in the mud. I baited up again with two pound or so of nuts that I had left before casting out single popped up peanuts on two of the rods. Because these have nothing like the buoyancy of a cooked boilie. I had to scale down to a size 10 Lion D'or hook in order to get the peanuts popped up. A single BB shot two inches behind the hook, anchored the rig.

At 7.30 am I had the first run which incidentally proved to be the biggest fish of the session at 17lb 4oz. By the time I packed up at 11.30 am. I had had an incredible seventeen runs, though unfortunately due to a submerged tree in the swim, only eleven were landed. Of those seventeen runs, every one came to the popped up nuts, and none to the conventionally hooked nuts. It should however be pointed out that peanuts had been used extensively before on this lake. The popped up ones may have been new, they may just have worked on novelty value, but the important thing was as unnatural as they looked, they worked very well.

Driving home, plans were formed for another attack on the syndicate water. Popped up maples had to murder them, didn't they? Back at home, I tried frying, cooking, microwaving, but I could not get the buggers to float! Grinding out the centre and plugging with polystyrene didn't work either. The shell of the pea just not being strong enough to take the stuffing. The only alternative at the time appeared to be using artificial maples, fashioned from polystyrene and painted dark brown.

Back on the water for my next session, in the same swim as before, once again I baited up heavily into the silty troughs. Two rods were baited with a single maple pea popped up underneath by a small brown polyball. Again a small light hook had to be used in order for the bait to float up. Even then it tended to flop over and looked very unnatural. On this occasion, there was only the gentlest of breezes coming into the swim, and certainly there was nothing like the number of carp present as on the previous trip. Results for the twenty four hour session were three fish to the popped up maples, two fish to popped up boilies. So they didn't work any better than the boilie but they worked, catching three fish that I don't believe would have taken on bottom fished particles. It makes sense really when feeding a swim with seeds. If fish are on bait, they're feeding on them. If a hook bait is not taken, it is because it has not been presented correctly.

There are two exceptions to this rule. The first being in heavily fished waters where lots of fish have been caught on a given particle. Often then, the carp move in and take a few mouthfuls before moving off. They are not going to mop the whole lot up, because they know it would be dangerous to do so. In this situation you are lucky to get a take even with a correctly presented bait. Having said that, one popped up would stand the best chance, simply by the fact it would stand out more.

The other exception being on large waters like St Cassien with a population of large nomadic carp, always on the move and for the most part sight feeders. It would not matter how much particle was put in it seems impossible to keep carp in one spot (unless they are there naturally, feeding on some natural food source), for more than two or three hours. The initial blanket of bait on the bottom may stop them in their tracks and get them down, but once they've got to search around a bit for the seeds, they are off. That is why big boilies fished over beds of particles have been far more successful than particles fished on the hook. Big boilies aren't missed, where particles easily can be.

It would be impossible to discuss particle baits in this day and age without talking about tiger nuts. Indeed to some recent carp anglers particles mean tiger nuts. Now I know that a lot of anglers think of them as some sort of wonderbait, yet I honestly believe they are the least attractive of all particles to carp. Their success owing very much to the pressure English carp waters are under. I think it highly significant that of the following particles I have used on the continent, i.e. sweetcorn, hemp, tares, maple peas, maize, chic peas, peanuts and tiger nuts, the last one is the only bait I have yet to catch on! At the same time, I can truthfully say that the most effort was also put into making them work.

On one very lightly fished water in Belgium, my mate Peter baited solidly for two weeks before we fished. Our total return of takes to six rods was nil. In the same swim, a week's baiting with pasta produced two very large fish within an hour of fishing. Two other lakes close by also received the tiger treatment, with the same results, yet sweetcorn fished amongst them produced fish.

I truly believe that the biggest thing tiger nuts have going for them is the fact that they don't break down. They stay on the bottom until they are picked up, and it is very rare indeed for any species other than carp to do this. Even when picked up by a carp, this is not necessarily the end of the story, because on many occasions whole nuts have been seen emerging from the carp's backside! In consequence the carp spreads the nuts around the lake. Even when the nuts have been ground down before passing through the carp's system, when excreted they are still in hard, small nut pieces, which the carp will eat again. It seems they need two or three goes at them before obtaining any nourishment. Maybe there is something in them that carp really like, but for the life of me I can't find it. When the word first got out about them producing numbers of fish, I bought 1cwt of them and had them ground down and natural juice and oil extracted. The results when put into a boilie as an attractor - absolutely nothing! Now while it is fair to say that certain synthetic tiger nut flavours have caught fish, they have caught no more than other nut flavours. Even then the synthetic flavour smells and tastes much better than a natural tiger nut. In fact they have very little to do with the nut itself, just being a nice nutty taste and smell, vaguely reminiscent of a tiger nut.

So why do they work so well in English waters? Number one reason must be their selectivity, nothing else eats them. They don't break down in water, so even if you pick a swim containing no carp at the time of baiting, they will still be there until a carp eventually picks them up. They get scattered around a lake by carp as well as anglers. They are also very importantly hard however long you cook them. They cannot be whittled down, they have to be taken to the back of the throat to be eaten. Considering that in general, large amounts of this nut have to go into a water to get them working, by the time carp do start feeding on them they have probably seen lots lying around the lake. Also considering that many are passed through the system whole, they are likely to be found in any part of the lake and not just in baited swims. As such I think within a given time, they must be regarded as natural food. As fish are caught, the more the nuts go in, further increasing the opinion that they become a natural food.

Once fish are well on them, I know that some anglers don't bother cooking them anymore. I have spoken to lots of anglers who admit to just casting out dry nuts and letting them swell up on the hook. However, no matter how hard a cooked nut might be, an uncooked nut is a damn sight harder and there have been lots of reports of carp bleeding from the vent when excreting them. Now, I have seen all sorts emerging from a carp's backside including a whole swam mussel, but I had never before seen blood as was the case with a fish caught by an angler fishing uncooked tiger nuts. Now there is no way in a million years that this can be good for the fish, so I would plead with all anglers, if you are going to fish tiger nuts, PLEASE cook them first. Uncooked ones catch no more than cooked ones, and they do not require a great deal of preparation. An overnight soak, bring them up to the boil and simmer for half an hour is all that is required. Longer cooking won't get them any softer than a half hour cook.

There is no doubting the success of tiger nuts, which incidentally also work best popped up, but I much prefer the standard, maple, black eye bean, peanut and chic pea baits. They all work instantly, and I feel they are much safer in the knowledge that if the carp don't take them, other species will. With all of these seeds, also hemp and tares, I am now utterly convinced that each one makes a far better bait if it is first left to sprout before it is cooked. I am sure they are much easier to digest, and are also much more visual to fish. While I have known maize was much more effective sprouted, for something like 15 years and chic peas for probably 10, it wasn't until I watched a match angler in Belgium fishing sprouted hemp that I realised the potential with all particles. The sprouted hemp out-fished ordinary cooked split hemp hands down. The great difficulty he explained was obtaining hemp which would sprout. Apparently it is all treated to stop people from growing it into naughty plants! I didn't think of asking him how he had managed to do it, or if it was even legal to do so. I just know when I saw him catching fish after fish (800 in four hours), I couldn't wait to try it out on the carp. Having stated my preference for sprouted particles, please cook them afterwards, to stop them growing in shallow water.

The best way to prepare particles in this way is to leave them out in the sunlight in a long, shallow tray, covered in about half an inch of water. Just soaking in a bucket will only sprout the top seeds.

I must admit that writing this chapter has been very difficult indeed. I first wrote about particle baits back in 1975, and in the thirteen years since that first article I must have written fifty or so articles or chapters for other books on the subject. Finding something new to write on the subject being the most difficult part. When the chapter was written for the original book, particles, boilies and soft paste fishing were viewed as three very different dimensions of fishing. Today boilies are fished in the same way as particles. The terminal tackle for both are practically the same. Any little trick that produces a few more fish with one type of bait, will also work with the other. Even single particle hookbaits fished without a bed of similar samples catch quite a number of fish, which is totally against all my original theories of pre-occupation when feeding on baits of the same size and shape. Today we should simply regard them for what they are, just good baits. Good baits that are relatively cheap and easy to prepare. If they have a drawback, it is that you cannot ring the changes with a given seed, as you could a standard boilie mix. Cooking or soaking in different flavours may bring a few more fish and prolong the life of a seed, but the flavour can never make a particle totally different, which it can a boilie, as it is very difficult indeed to implant a flavour inside a particle. Most flavour is taken up by the skin of a seed, and washes out quickly in water.

I have seen on occasions absolutely vast amounts of particles put into a swim, and then anglers wonder why they don't catch anything for two or three days. Once at St Cassien I saw two hundred weight (101 kilos) of peanuts put into a swim in one go. The swim did not produce for nearly a week. I now very much agree with Roger Smith's opinion that each seed should be regarded as a bait in itself. This is particularly true with things like peanuts, tiger nuts and broad beans, which can be larger than some of the boilies used nowadays. But even sweetcorn must be viewed the same, if you think in your lake each grain would be searched out. You have to look at your fishing from a fresh angle once you regard a couple of cans of corn as not just being one pound of seeds, but as being over two thousand baits! Lots of anglers remark how once tiger nuts are established, it is more successful to fish into six or eight catapult fulls, rather than fill a swim in. Using the previous line of thinking, it would not be just eight pouches, instead, three to four hundred baits, which I think most people would regard as being a substantial amount. We might pursue this angle more by pointing out that particles for the most part are carbohydrate, and while some people may argue that lots of them have to be eaten to provide any form of nourishment, a counter argument would be that carbohydrate is very filling indeed. I wouldn't like to come down on any side with that one, all I am saying is that maybe it is time we looked at particle fishing in a different way.

Looking at particles in the same light as boilies, and not a different concept of fishing, just like boilie recipes and flavours, you have to decide just what are the best ones if you are going to be successful.

In the original chapter I pointed out that some seeds are more suited to different types of bottom, which is the case. However, today we know that the best ones can be used any time by using boilie rig techniques. I explained earlier of all the experimenting I did to try and make some particles float, not knowing as we do today that carp will just as readily pick up seeds supported by a piece of cork or rig foam. I must admit to always shying away from these artificial means because they looked so unnatural. If I did have to use them I would go to great lengths to make them look like a certain seed, i.e. brown painted polystyrene ball with maples, or yellow polystyrene with sweetcorn. There may come a time when a piece of cork or rig foam is looked on with suspicion but that is certainly not the case at this moment. I hooked three carp in an afternoon this past season, fishing what must have looked the biggest abortion of a rig ever seen. It was a surface fished tiger nut, supported at either end with a piece of cork! It looked like a knobbly potato, stood on a box, balancing another box on its head!

The realisation that carp don't mind these buoyancy aids, I think could lead to anglers fully realising the potential of hemp seed for the first time. Hemp for some reason or other has definitely got a lot more going for it than other seeds. By the time a pouchful has descended six feet to the bottom of a lake, it has spread a fair distance between seeds. Imagine how far those seeds would be apart, if the depth of the lake was 60ft as is the case in parts of the north arm of St. Cassien. Yet carp a friend of mine caught in those depths were absolutely stuffed with the seed, so much so that he was convinced every single seed must have been searched out. I know I said treat each single seed as a bait itself, but for such an insignificant sized piece of food to be searched out over quite a large area, has to mean that the food is something special. It's a funny thing really, I and other anglers have always known this, yet apart from fishing it as a bed, with a boilie over the top, I have rarely used it as a hookbait since the middle seventies. I suppose we were intimidated by its size, those tiny seeds close to a big carp hook just didn't look right, while once the full potential of the hair rig was realised, the old mud ball carrier for hemp seed got discarded. Then again with so much going on, on the boilie front, it was probably only human nature to pursue new fields and forget about baits we'd used so much in the past.

I suppose after hempseed, I would have to rate maple peas next on my list of top particles, although they don't have the instant visual appeal of sweetcorn, chic peas, black eyed beans, peanuts or maize. Having said that though, sprouted maples are visual enough. My preference for this seed is because, hemp apart, it has such a long successful life. It can be absolutely hammered on a water, but give it a season's rest, and it will start catching again. Talking to some anglers in my shop, I discovered that they were fishing a lake I had not fished since 1972; the surprising thing was that fifteen years on they were catching the same fish as I had caught in those days, and on the same bait, the old maple peas.

Going back to the original chapter, I mentioned that maples worked superbly, three days after cooking, when they start to emit a milky like substance. I should have also added that they also work really well, hot! On lots of occasions I and other anglers I know, have caught fish very quickly after baiting with peas direct from the saucepan. In fact it's a toss up between them being hot or milky as to which is the best method.

Chapter 9

Paste Baits '80

THERE was a time when I believed that the traditional paste bait would only work on very hungry waters. At that time my fishing was mostly confined to the other extreme i.e. mud-bottomed clay pits rich in natural food. In those waters it was very hard to tempt carp with such baits. Many years have passed since those beginnings, and the type of water I started on is now very rare. There is a vast range of different types of carp waters nowadays, varying between the two extremes of rich and hungry, and in the vast majority of these paste baits are very good baits indeed.

In the years since these new waters have sprung up, baits have developed from early bread-based pastes, through to the present baits which may contain extracts, amino acids or synthetic flavours. Baits can now be made so that they have within them all the dietary requirements any carp could need. (It is only on waters where fish are small-food orientated that these baits have yet to really produce the goods.) On some waters this development has arisen as the angler continually strives to keep one step ahead of the fish. On other waters it has undoubtedly come about through rivalry between anglers, each trying to catch more fish than the next guy. Often this development is far ahead of the fish, many of the older baits not yet arousing caution. But a state arises where an angler believes he will not catch fish unless his bait is more nutritious, contains more convertible protein, and has more and better attractors, than the baits of anglers fishing along the bank.

This type of angler has been more influenced by human behaviour than he has by that of the fish. It should be his own interpretation of reactions to a type of food that dictates what kind of bait he uses, not what is the current fashion. There is so much chopping and changing with baits nowadays that many are discarded before they have had time to yield their true potential. One angler sees another guy on the opposite bank catch half a

Marmite in fish-meal tempted this wild-looking mirror

dozen carp, while he doesn't catch any. Too often he presumes it is because his bait is no good, when the fact is that the other guy has carp in his swim, while his own swim is barren of fish. If a new bait is being tried it must be given a fair length of time amongst feeding fish before any conclusions are drawn. In order to do that, it is back to the basics of first finding the fish, before baits are given a thought.

The intention of this chapter is not to name specifics, which would put everyone at the same stage of development, and probably encourage the rat race situation I've just mentioned, but to show you what I look for in a bait and the reasons why. Hopefully this will lead you into taking your own directions, and not just following the current trends.

22.4 taken on a black-eyed bean, fished over maple peas

Approaching a new water

When I encounter a water for the first time, I try to determine just how far carp have developed in their caution of baits. I ask around other anglers, trying to find out just what baits have been used, and for what length of time the lake has been fished seriously. It is unlikely that I will be told just what baits are being used at the present time, but people will usually tell of baits which have worked in the past and baits which have not worked at all. From this it is possible to get an idea of the type of bait needed.

Knowing how long a lake has been seriously fished will help a great deal. To give an example, a group of lakes I started to fish about three years ago had only been open to the public for the previous four seasons. When the carp anglers fished it for the first time, they not unnaturally started with the fashionable bait of that time, which was trout pellets. All subsequent baits were developments which arose after trout pellets. Within two years, chemical baits were the vogue. Yet none of the fish in that lake had ever seen the simple "specials" of the sixties. All baits used before trout pellets came on the scene were forgotten. The current baits may be good, yet the old fish or meat based baits were also very productive, and still are, when fish have not seen them before.

Another aspect of this following of fashion came when the first angler to have a number of fish baited up with two hundred or so baits. Thereafter, other anglers started baiting with five hundred baits, and soon it became a thousand. I suppose they were hoping that this would correspondingly multiply their success rate. It didn't happen, yet today the same practice is continued. Back in the sixties, my friends and I used to throw out half a dozen free samples amongst our hookbaits. We had a great deal of success by so doing. As carp populations increased so did this number of free baits, nowadays twenty to thirty baits being the norm. For us at least this has been very successful.

Prebaiting

As I have said in the chapter on particles, I don't think prebaiting is needed if the bait is good enough. The only exception here is if one attempts to apply Fred Wilton's principles of High Nutritional Value ("H.N.V.") baits. Fred's basic principle comes from known animal facts. If an animal or fish has access to all its dietary requirements, it will take advantage of them and eat a well-balanced diet. Not only proteins will be eaten, but roughage, minerals and vitamins, in fact everything it needs. This has been proved in many scientifically controlled experiments. Fred believes that if a bait holds all of these requirements it will be preferred to baits which do not. If a lake has any deficiencies, such as lack of minerals, these deficiencies can be made up by eating the bait, and so a fish will naturally take advantage of this supply. For a fish to become aware of the perfectly balanced diet, however, a number of baits must first be eaten. It is not a thinking process in the carp, but probably a feeling of well-being it has after eating the baits. Whatever it is, as scientific experiments have proved, a perfect balanced diet will be eaten if available. In order for many fish to become aware that this meal is available, prebaiting is undertaken, and by adding a scent to the bait the carp can then associate that scent with a highly nutritious meal. Although the baits are very good in themselves, it would appear that heavy prebaiting is essential to get the best out of the baits. On waters which regularly receive large supplies of these baits, it is not unusual to notice a marked improvement in the fishes' health. Many fish show improved growth rates, while damaged tissue such as split fins appears to heal very quickly. Both are attributable to the improved diet.

From the angler's point of view, the H.N.V. baits would seem to offer the best chance of catching carp regularly from a particular water. There are however a number of points which affect the issue. The first one is the cost and availability of the ingredients required. Compared to regular "specials" they are expensive to produce. Also top quality casein, on which many of the baits are based, is not easily obtainable. There is also the amount of time available to the angler to be taken into account. The production of a large number

A chunky mirror on soft bird-food paste

of baits, and the travelling to and from a lake to prebait, is going to require a lot of the angler's free time. For my own part, any time off I have I want to spend fishing and in any case the distance of my favourite lakes puts prebaiting out of the question. Therefore on all but my most local waters I leave the method alone. But for the angler who fishes with a small group of friends, where the cost can be divided, and turns can be taken in bait making and prebaiting, the method can be recommended. I have seen the baits used correctly by Fred and his group, and the results at times have been quite startling. The productive life of an individual bait has also in some cases lasted many seasons. So obviously there is an awful lot to be said for the method.

Attractors

As I've stated, time and the distance of my favourite lakes means that the H.N.V. baits are out for me. So what do I work on, as regards a paste bait? I believe nearly anything edible will be eaten once; after that if no satisfaction is obtained by the fish then the bait is most likely left alone. But as my visits to each lake are few, I just try to make sure my baits are eaten that first time. In order to do that, the baits are made as visually attractive as possible, and appeal to a carp's sense of taste and smell. I use anything which is known to attract carp. Since my time is limited, I may not always be able to fish at times favourable to feeding. Normally when a carp picks up a bait, it doesn't mean that the fish has only just found that bait, but that it is feeding at that precise moment. In the course of a day a fish may move past a bait half a dozen times before conditions dictate that it should feed, at which time the bait is picked up. What I try to do is to trigger a feeding instinct each time a fish comes across the bait. It isn't always possible to achieve this, but I attempt to do so by using attractors. Science has again led the way, experiments showing that a whole host of substances attract carp, although that attraction is usually very brief. But that brief period can be enough to get fish down on to a bait.

Amino Acids

Amino acids have been the most publicised of these attractors, but they are only one of many. Meat and fish extracts, certain groups of vitamins, the juice of many plants, some oils, chemical acetates used for solvents, and many sugar derivatives, have been found to provide brief attraction for carp. I don't believe all are associated with food, but some appear to help the production of digestive enzymes within a fish, which in turn triggers off the feeding instinct.

I am by no means scientific by nature, my only background being basic "O" level courses in Biology and Chemistry, but by reading all I could on the subject and borrowing all the latest papers relevant to experiments going on in America and Japan, I have been able to obtain a basic knowledge of what is required. For the most part, scientific papers I've read have only confirmed what friends and myself believed from conclusions drawn in our every day fishing.

A lot of people draw away from the subject of chemical substances, such as amino acids, being of the opinion that they are totally unnatural. Nothing could be further from the truth. All animals give off a certain amount of amino acids, and in the case of water creatures these aminos dissolve freely in the water. Molluscs, crustacea and water snails all excrete aminos and, depending on their size, the concentrations vary between 1/2 to 1 1/2 parts per million. Minute amounts indeed, but enough to be detected very easily by cyprinids.

To show the widespread use of aminos in nature, let me give as examples two birds, the kingfisher and the heron. A kingfisher will perch on a branch above water and excrete its droppings into the water. The excreta contains certain free soluble amino acids, which attract minnows and sticklebacks. The heron has been found to emit amino acids through its feet, again attracting small fish into the area in which it is hunting. All animal excreta contains certain amounts of free amino acids. I read recently that French match anglers add pigeon droppings to their groundbaits, and I have no doubt that the aminos play a big part in attracting the small fish. (For those not familiar with the terminology, a "free" amino is one given off in solution or into air by a substance while other, non-free aminos are only made available during digestion).

I do not intend this chapter to be an essay on biochemistry, because apart from the fact that my scientific knowledge is very limited, I know the subject bores many people. A friend of mine refuses to even talk about the subject. As he said, "If I go to a fishing meeting, I want to hear about fish. If I wanted to hear about chemicals, I'd go to an I.C.I. conference." Yet I believe that if anglers do intend to use chemical substances they should first have a basic knowledge of those chemicals and have sound reasons for using them. So in layman's terms, here is how I see the subject and how I went about using these chemicals.

Proteins, upon which all life is based, are made up of long chains of amino acids. These chains are held together by links known as peptide bonds, which in themselves have no nutritional value. It is the amino acids which the body needs in order to grow and to do this those links have to be broken so that the amino acids can be absorbed. During digestion the links are absorbed (broken) by enzymes produced within the body. In the case of dead animal tissue (e.g. a meat based bait), many amino acids will be released by bacteria breaking down those chains. Not all the released aminos of a meat bait would however go into solution in the water as the same bacteria would absorb most of them. The same occurs with decaying vegetable matter, where bacteria working on them will release small amounts of aminos.

This upper twenty took a Marmite-based bait with added amino acids

Heavy chemistry!

There are twenty or so main amino acids, each of which occurs in two forms like mirror images. These are called the "L-" amino and the "D-" amino. It is the "L-" form on which life is based and so is of concern to the angler. Although the "D-" form in itself has no nutritional value much is excreted or burnt off as energy and the body does at times borrow atoms from the "D-" form to make up an "L-" form, should it be deficient. Bacteria are really the only life form to utilise "D-" aminos, many using them to form the cell walls. One amino acid, Glycine, is different to the others in that its two forms are identical. Although generally termed a "D/L" acid, a truer description would be "L/L" as both forms have nutritional value.

Of the twenty main aminos, ten are termed "essentials" in mammals and fish. Although all twenty are equally essential to growth, many can be made up in the body itself, by borrowing atoms from other aminos when there is more than is needed of these. However, ten cannot be made up and it is those, which can only be derived from food intake, which are termed "essential" amino acids.

The structure of all proteins is very similar, the fundamental difference between different proteins being the position of individual aminos in the chains, and the number of times each one occurs. For example, the aminos Lysine (Lys), Methionine (Met), and Tryptophan (Trp), occur less in vegetable proteins than in animal proteins. Since all are "essentials" and cannot be made up by the body, greater amounts of vegetable protein have to be eaten to provide the body with its requirement of those acids, than would animal protein. This is the very reason why vegetable material is said to be less convertible than animal protein. When a vegetable material is said to be high in protein (e.g. peanut, soya, hemp) it is because those three aminos occur more often in the chains than in other vegetables. However, since the amounts needed are very small, it only takes the addition of a small amount of animal protein to provide those "essentials", in order to provide a nutritious diet.

Away from the protein scene, and on to the reason why I use amino acids. It is because many have been shown to have a stimulatory effect on the feeding of carp. Thinking logically about it, one would expect that the ten "essentials" would show the most marked stimulation. Although some indeed create this reaction, there are some essentials (e.g. Lysine and Arginine) which appear to have very little stimulatory effect on cyprinids.

To find out why this is so, we have to take a close look at an amino acid. The acids are electrically charged and when in contact with alkali (the pH in water), the polarity symbols (i.e. + and −) jump from one end of the chemical chain which makes up the acid to the other rather like the charge in a car battery. They are only stable at one point, this point being named the Iso Electric Valency Point (I.E.V.P.) of an acid. It would appear therefore that to some extent the I.E.V.P. needs to be matched up with the pH level of the water being fished, if full stimulatory effect is to be derived from the acid. This I believe is the reason why some commercial acid baits perform well on one water, and not on another. The pH of some waters is just not matched by the acids used or by the amounts used. (Note: water with a pH of 7 is regarded as neutral; fluids with a pH of less than 7 are termed acid, and with a pH greater than 7, alkaline). To put it very simply, an acid in water of increasing pH would eventually neutralize and cease to be an acid. With each step up in pH value, the chemical nature of an amino acid changes. The crux of the matter is in finding where the acid is at its most effective point and using it in a water where it will remain close to that stimulatory peak.

From early experiments using single acids, I found Glycine to be at its most productive in two waters, both of which had low pH values, being 6.8 and 6.7 respectively. In waters of high pH i.e. 7.4 upwards, it was very unproductive. Since the I.E.V.P. of Glycine is 6.0, it appeared that an acid was at its most productive when the pH value of the water was close to the IEVP of the acid. In order to check this out baits containing Tryptophan, Methionine, and Alanine (all with IEVP's of 6.0 or just below) were tried in the same water, either in compound or individually. The results were very close to those given with Glycine i.e. very productive in waters below pH 7, tapering down as the pH moved up. It also appeared that if the IEVPs were not quite matched, and the IEVP of the acid was just below the pH of the water, then the acid was at its most effective. I must admit I had no idea why this should be so, until only recently receiving papers which show the acids to be at their most soluble when not exactly matched with the pH (ie. not neutral).

To go back to the two examples of "essential" aminos given, ie. Lysine and Arginine, which are not in the same league as far as some of the aminos go for effectiveness. I don't think it's coincidental that their respective valency points are 10.0 and 10.8. There are not many waters around with pH values of 11, where one would expect them to be at their best.

If one accepts that amino acids should have an IEVP just below that of the pH of a water (indeed the pH of the bottom of your swim, since pH values fluctuate around a lake due to decaying materials, and excreta from molluscs and insect life) what more should one look for in order to use them in a bait? When I first saw these baits used, I was not so surprised at their success, but at their very shortlived productive life. Since I knew the base mix being used and later found out the amino acids used with the mixture, I was able to look at the problem in detail. From breakdown sheets of proteins one thing became apparent; the amino acid attractor mix bore no relation to the base mix. I believed that the attractor was good enough to get fish down on the bait the first time, but having eaten the bait, it was nothing like what the fish expected. To put it in a nutshell, it's like lying in bed and having your taste buds aroused by bacon and eggs, so you go rushing down to the kitchen only to find a round of toast. True that first time, you'll eat the toast, because your taste buds have been set in motion. You may even do the same on a second morning out of sheer desperation, but not a third time, having decided that enough is enough.

Amino acids and base mixes

With this in mind, I set about making an attractor mix as representative of the base mix as I could. Using again food breakdown sheets, attractor mixes were made up by adding 1/2 gramme of the dominant acid of each group of the base mix. I might add here that amino acids are split into groups with other acids of similar formulas. Only Proline was left out and Histidine substituted for Lysine, because its IEVP was nearer the water's pH.

That first bait, I must admit, was the most successful yet, on a particular water, and that approach is still one I carry out, trying to make the amino acids represent the base mix as far as I can, without mismatching the water's pH value. A point here of interest is that some of the acids used in themselves show very little stimulatory effect. This is something I'm prepared to put up with as other acids will provide the main attraction, while the non- or slight attractors hopefully help to provide what the fish is expecting to find.

I love eating exotic foreign foods, and my taste buds are aroused by many aromas. Yet when I eat a food for the first time, although I don't know how that food is going to taste, it tastes right. It tastes how my smell senses have led me to believe it would. I have yet to smell something delicious that tasted lousy. Although taste and smell are two completely different senses, I am sure they are closely aligned, working in conjunction with one another. It could be that in fish, this alignment is even greater than our own. Be that as it may, the theory could be wrong, but the approach does work.

Attraction and repulsion

The next point we come to with amino acids which is of paramount importance, is just how much to put into a bait. Experiments have shown that certain amounts stimulate a feeding response, while greater amounts act as a repellent. I believe (or rather have deduced from what I've read) that maximum response is somewhere in the region of 4 to 5 parts per million in water. That all sounds very easy, but how do we achieve a diffusion rate at this level? So many influences abound, that it is nigh on impossible to achieve outside of laboratory conditions. Let me list a few. 1) The density of the bait used; a hard bait will not allow the amino acids to dissolve into water at the same rate a soft bait would; 2) adding eggs to a mix and boiling baits in order to stave off nuisance species, which in fact creates a "net curtain" effect around a bait, creating a semi-permeable layer which allows only those particles or molecules small enough to pass through the holes in the curtain to get out. It is true that amino acids can easily pass through these holes, but passage must be restricted by the sides of the net, slowing down the diffusion rate; 3) the number of active bacteria on a given day. Bacteria will absorb much of the amino acids as they dissolve into solution. The amount of bacteria present will depend on many things such as water temperature, light penetration and possibly ph values and oxygen content; 4) the amount of amino acids being given off by molluscs in the area of the bait. If for example the bait happened to drop bang on a colony of pea or zebra mussels then there could possibly already be amino acids in solution at anything between 1 to 2 parts per million. The addition of a bait dissolving amino acids at a rate of 5 parts per million could easily put the concentration of acids into repellent levels, rendering the area devoid of cyprinids. I say "cyprinids", because I believe eels have a far higher tolerance level. Certainly baits tried in the early days, with greater amounts of amino acids, at times proved real eel catchers.

Another point which will affect how much or how many aminos are used is the fact

ATTRACTORS - & REPELLANT LEVELS '80

At low concentrations, a peak attraction level is reached in the vicinity of the bait.

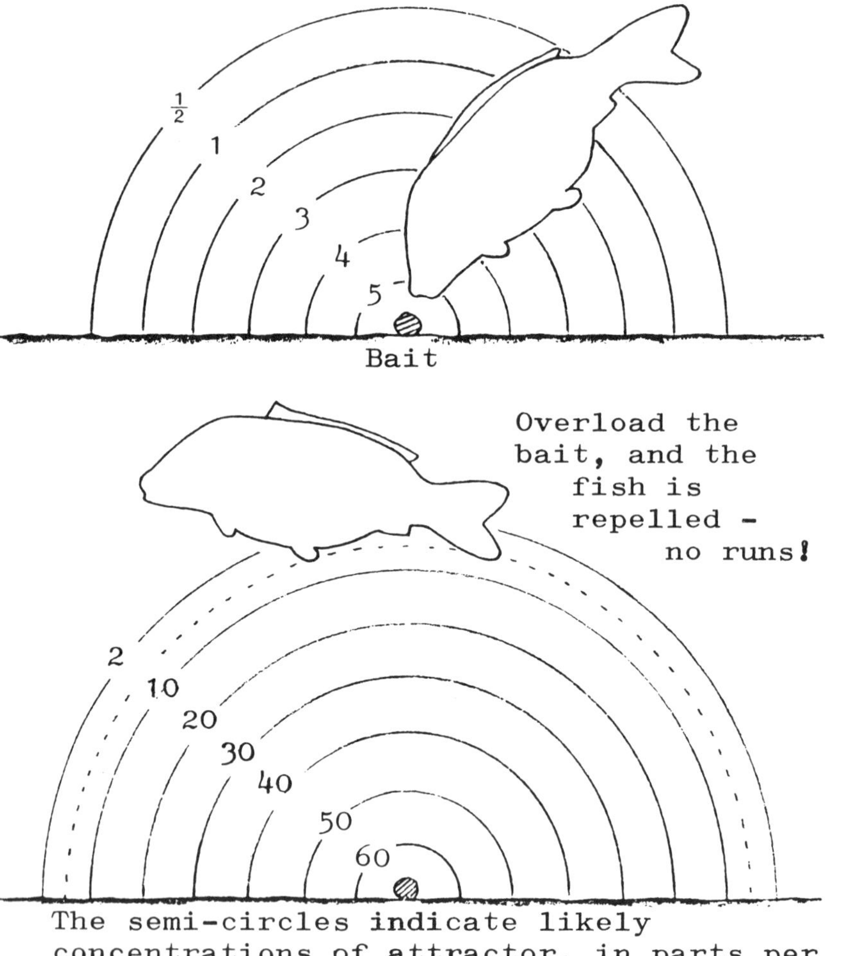

The semi-circles indicate likely concentrations of attractor, in parts per million.

that the receptors of the fish can become saturated and so need greater quantities in order to create any response. Indeed it would seem to me that this is one of the chief reasons why these baits have very short effective lives. Initial response is great because the receptors are highly responsive in the first instance, but the receptors soon become saturated and response tails off to nil. Luckily it seems no damage is done to tissue.

How much to use?

How do we get around all these variables, to produce an instant bait everytime? If I knew the answer to that one, I'd be lecturing at Cambridge instead of chucking scaffold poles around for a living! Obviously a compromise is called for. Rather than try and go to the very edge of the stimulatory peak, risking the production of the ultimate deterrent, I go on the lighter side, trying to stay about half way on the rise to the peak effect. It should be remembered that amino acids can be detected at 1/2 a part per million, so somewhere in the region of two or three parts per million should provide enough of the instant response I'm looking for.

The amounts finally arrived at are the result of fishing with different levels and by watching the response of fish to the baits in certain water. At a pH value of 7.4, the total amount of amino acid used, be it a single acid or eight together (which is the largest combination I have needed to use) is 5 grammes to a 10 ounce base mix. If one attempts to represent the base mix, then I believe one substance (in my case I use vegetable meals) should provide at least 60 per cent of that mix. Theoretically the base should be 100 per cent one substance, but the need to bind a mix or to create a new texture of bait by adding certain other substances, will bring that percentage down.

For every two points the pH value of the water increases, I drop one gramme of acid i.e. 7.6 pH value = 4 grammes acid, 7.8 pH value = 3 grammes acid. Originally the acid was dropped one gramme for even a one point increase of pH, but universal pH indicators such as the liquid and litmus paper types are extremely difficult to interpret to the nearest point, whilst two points is easily enough read.

I think it is possible to get away with adding the same amounts for a two point decrease in pH. I don't myself, but certainly I know of people who have used what I would consider massive amounts of such as 10grammes in a 10oz mix, and yet have had considerable success. The point I believe is this: once a water gets below a pH value of 7, it is what we would generally term a hungry water. Although I would expect these amounts to be of repellent levels, presumably in the final analysis hunger overcomes all things.

Using amino acids is a dicey business – we are really stepping into the unknown. I have spent four years reading all I could on the subject and have obtained all the relevant papers on scientific work going on in that period. I have corresponded with biochemists and have been very lucky in being given the opportunity to go to universities and talk to people who are acknowledged as experts in this field. Yet there are still many unanswered questions because at the moment very little of the scientific work on amino acids has been applied to carp, or in cases where it has not from a carp fisherman's view point.

At the outset of this book I was undecided whether or not to include any information

A high protein bait with added rennet produced this 31.8 beauty

"Amino Acids"

Amino Acids	Group	I.E.V.P.	Essentials*
Glutamic	Acidic	3.2	
Aspartic		2.8	
Asparagine	Amides	–	
Glutamine		–	
Histidine	Basics	7.6	*
Lysine		10.0	*
Arginine		10.8	*Note. Only essential whilst growth still takes place
Cysteine	Sulfur amino	5.1	
Cystine		4.8	
Methionine		5.7	
Phenylalanine	Aromatics	5.5	*
Tyrosine		5.7	
Tyrptophan		5.9	*
Glycine	Aliphatics	6.0	
Alanine		6.0	
Valine		6.0	*
Leucine		6.0	*
Isoleucine		6.0	*
Serine	Hydroxy	5.7	
Threonine		5.6	*
Proline	Imino	6.3	

about amino acids, because I didn't want to see them chucked wholesale willy nilly into waters all over the country. But not to have done so would have been copping out, trying to sweep them under the carpet. It would not have deterred anglers from using them, because the word was out that they caught fish. Although I don't want to lump all anglers in the same boat, many would undoubtedly have used them completely wrongly without first finding out something about them. No doubt some would get into the "more acid = more fish" syndrome.

So to summarize, these are the important issues, if one is thinking of using amino acids: 1) their effective life is the shortest of any bait I know. They should be instant, but it is not unusual for a water to be completely fished out on such baits within a couple of weeks. I believe that the only real reason for using them, and the one which led me to get into the acid scene, is on waters with a very few hard-to-catch fish, where it is very infrequent for a fish to pass over your bait. In such a water, I don't expect prolonged success, but I'm just trying to make sure a fish goes down when in the proximity of the bait; 2) no prebaiting should be carried out. We are working on a stimulus/response and fish don't have to be educated to take the baits. Response is entirely involuntary and prebaiting will do more harm than good. While it is thought that the receptors of the carp can be saturated with the acid general opinion has been that bacteria will absorb any glut in a water. But what if bacteria themselves become saturated and cease to absorb the amino acid? What if for some reason, there is a lack of bacteria present? If this hypothetical situation did arise, prebaited amino acid baits could do untold damage to a water. Certainly in a tank, where saturated conditions can easily be obtained, gill irritations occur in cyprinids. In such controlled conditions the situation can be remedied, but how would one even attempt to do so, even in a small lake of four or five acres? 3) If one is sensible and feels that a water is of the type where an amino acid bait might help catch those one or two big fish, first obtain all the information you can either from your local library, or from the Boston Spa Library. Get in touch with universities and obtain all relevant papers on the subject. Obtain a pH value testing kit and take readings in the swims you intend to fish. Values will vary, some waters more than others, so test regularly. If your water fluctuates to a great degree, make readings on the day, and mix the bait to suit; 4) if one attempts to represent a base mix, first obtain protein break down sheets; 5) always keep amounts on the light side; a little of what you fancy, does you good.

Well, thank God that's over with, you may be thinking. Enough of amino acids! Well, after all amino acids are only chemical substances which go to make up protein, and so foods. How the chains of acids are linked together dictates what type of protein is formed. To build animal protein, other animal protein is far preferable to vegetable protein. It is more convertible pound for pound.

The most popular are casein, calcium caseinate, and sodium caseinate. They are all basically milk but have been refined down so that just the protein is left, the different methods of refinement used being responsible for the different names. All will make a good base for a bait, although I am assured by friends much more into the protein scene than I, that casein and calcium caseinate make the better baits. From this point of view, if

An immaculate mirror from Norfolk

high protein baits are used on a wide scale on a given lake, it would be preferable to stick to these two.

Vegetable proteins, such as soya, peanut, or hemp meal, will also make good bases for baits. But as they are not as convertible as milk proteins, they are not advised where the H.N.V. ("High Nutritional Value") approach is being followed. From my own point of view, I would not advise the use of additional amino acids as attractors when the H.N.V. principle is being applied. Prebaiting ensures that fish will find the baits, and there is no need for the bait to entice a fish down immediately. Whereas H.N.V. baits usually have a very long productive life, baits with amino acids added are often very short lived. The use of one can therefore defeat the point of the other.

Acetates and esters

The word "acetate" is another which has many anglers shying away. It seems to depict some dangerous chemical formula, way above the heads of the average angler. Yet there are few carp anglers who have not used some type of acetate or acetone; they just have not been aware of it. Acetates are simply the product of organic acids (often fruit juices) reacting with alcohols, the general term for the products being "esters". Each different ester has a distinctive smell and flavour. By mixing different esters together, the taste and aroma of an individual fruit can be simulated. Suitable examples are amyl acetate, simulating peardrops, and ethyl butyrate, which simulates pineapple. They are used all the time in the food, sweet and perfumery industries. The vast majority of the flavours sold by the bait firms are made in just this way. It is not beyond the average angler to make his own flavour in this way, failing that, any old fashioned dispensing chemist would be able to make one up. In this way, the angler would not only have a smell and taste not widely used, but would also save himself a fortune.

In the same way that amino acids diffuse into water, so do esters, but only at a slower rate. There is no doubt in my mind that just like amino acids the esters (or fruit flavours) also have stimulatory and repellent levels. I think this is borne out by the number of anglers who suffer fish spitting fruit flavour baits out. In other instances, fish have been seen to go down to a bait, only to shy away, within inches of it. What I think has happened is that the fish has picked up the scent of the bait at a stimulatory level and homed in on the bait. The nearer it has got to the bait, so the concentration of ester increases to repellent proportions.

So it is obvious that levels have to be kept to the minimum. The difficulty here is that a flavour such as pineapple is sold in varying concentrations eg. 1000 to 1 or 300 to 1, while the little bottles often available in supermarkets are I believe graded 50 to 1. As many anglers now obtain their flavours direct from the suppliers, 1000 to 1 concentrates are being used increasingly. At this concentration, it has been found that a 2 millilitre spoonful is all that is required for a 10oz mix of bait. If the baits are boiled not even this amount will end up in the finished product. Amyl acetate, for instance, is highly volatile, and some of it will simply evaporate.

When using these flavours it soon becomes apparent that some work and some do not.

Since all are produced in the same way, I doubt if it is the actual smell of the substance which decides if it attracts or not. I believe the substance works on both smell and taste receptors, and that it is the actual formula that decides if such a smell/taste is a winner. This is similar to the changing effectiveness of different amino acids in waters of different pH values.

A point here about the use of both substances in floaters. Since the esters can be volatile, it is very difficult to know how much will evaporate under the dry heat cooking of a floater. Therefore I believe it may well be beneficial to add the ester after cooking. I would not recommend the use of amino acids in a floating bait. It has been found only very recently that dry heat can alter the structure of amino acids, lysine in particular. This alteration of the structure renders the protein unusable or, to use the scientific term, nutritionally unavailable. It is therefore highly unlikely it will attract carp. This alteration of the structure is a pretty rare occurrence, but since it can and does happen, why risk wasting money?

Back to the esters; flavours can be mixed to good effect, in fact this is basically what is done to produce new commercial flavours. Only by using individual ones first can it be determined if a flavour will be a winner. If, like me, you are of the opinion that carp don't like citric acid, which is found in fruits, don't let that deter you from any of the flavours. Remember those flavours are simulated smells, not the real thing.

Oils and vitamins

Next on the list of substances which diffuse into water giving off flavour and scent (and hopefully attracting carp) are oils. Oils, in the shape of fatty acids, are just as essential to carp as proteins or carbohydrate. True they can be stored in the body of the fish, and so fish are less liable to suffer from fatty acid deficiencies, but the supply must be there, all the same. An American paper, the Loeb report, suggested in its findings that only two oils, namely soya oil and olive oil, show any stimulatory effect on carp. I'm afraid I have to disagree with the learned gentlemen. In my opinion linseed, cloves, corn and peanut oil are all excellent additives to a paste bait, used one at a time of course. I don't expect oils to have the instant effect many esters have, the size of the molecule makes them very slow to diffuse. They have a slow, subtle sort of attraction, which I would have thought ideal for use with H.N.V. baits. The amount of oil used has again been kept to 2 millilitres for a ten ounce base mix. The boiling of baits will naturally slow down the already slow diffusion rate of oils, and in this case I think it may be beneficial to increase levels to 3 millilitres per 10 oz mix.

Not having gone deeply into the H.N.V. bait scene, my knowledge of vitamins is very slight. One group of vitamins, the carotenoids, do appear to have stimulatory qualities however. This is the group used to add pigmentation to the colour of animal flesh. They are added to feeds to turn the flesh of some trout pink, and also to the diet of cage birds, to enhance the colour of their plumage. Quantities used are very small ie. 1/2 a gramme for a ten ounce mix. There are also some ready made fish and bird foods available which already have the vitamins in them. When these additives, or proprietary brands containing them, have not been used before on a lake results can be very good indeed.

Sugars

Probably the broadest group of substances to have success in carp baits are the sugar derivatives. Every one I know of will work to some degree or another. The list is very long, including glucose, sucrose, fructose, cane sugar spirit, mollasses, honey, nectar, dextrose, etc. Even simulated substances like saccharin have been shown to create interest. All of the sugars are of course essential to life, in the form of starch, which is burnt off as energy. Many years ago, I read that sugar, which was in those days being added to match anglers' groundbaits, could lead to a lowering of oxygen content in a water. Whilst I cannot see why this is so, I will accept that it is possible, so prebaiting should be kept to a minimum.

All these new additives mentioned may lead the newcomer to carp fishing to believe it is all beyond him. In fact carp baits have turned full circle. The H.N.V. and particle scenes apart, the most successful baits over the country as a whole during the past two or three seasons have been little more than improved pet food baits. The old sausage, cat and dog food baits were looked at and what was thought to be their active ingredient merely boosted up. Similarly the same baits have been used with the aforementioned attractor substances. Trout pellet and Salmon feeds, which are only after all superior pet food baits with higher protein values than dog and cat food, have also worked superbly when new smells have been added to them. Even without new smells sausage and Kit-e-Kat baits have been given new leases of life, merely by using one of the milk products, such as calcium caseinate, as a binder.

Low protein baits

Low protein bases, using meals made from beans, peas or nuts, have proved just as successful. After all, they work well enough as particles, so it should be no surprise that they work in paste form. While meals made from peanut and soya have a relatively high protein content compared to other vegetables, dari seed, black-eyed beans and maple peas have all been excellent bases. Talking about things going full circle, the flours of these vegetables are little removed from the wheat flour/bread based baits of the fifties and sixties. To give an example, a highly productive bait that consisted of bean meal base, with wheat gluten as a binder, and nectar used as an attractor, is very similar to the old bread paste and honey.

What it all comes down to is that any edible substance will be eaten, if that substance is different enough from baits a carp has previously been caught on. It has been termed curiosity feeding. After the initial feeding on that bait, there may well be no feeling of satisfaction or well-being in which case that food will probably thereafter be left alone. But as pet foods and pellet baits (besides trout and salmon pellets, there are dozens of others, such as pig, pheasant, pigeon, duck and cow pellets) are very nutritious in themselves, the baits are hardly likely to be left alone. I am prepared to accept that the meal baits of low nutritional value may well have the shortest effective life, but even in the curiosity feeding period an awful lot of carp can be caught.

I also think it highly probable that there is a period of time during which carp which are accustomed to accept balls of food as part of their natural diet, and where the majority

A mid-protein, fish meal bait accounted for this superb leather carp

of those balls are of a high protein nature, might actually prefer different baits with high roughage and fibre contents. Again that preference is short lived, but I am sure it has happened in some instances.

"Blowing" of baits

I happen to believe that attractors which act the fastest also blow the fastest. Working on the principle that the greater the stimulus, the more distinctive an attractor is, then the greater the chance it is recognised and caution aroused. This not only applies to fish that have been caught on a bait, but also fish that are in the vicinity of a carp being caught. If the scent or flavour is so strong as to entice a number of fish into a swim, the greater the chance those fish have of tying that scent up with the individual panic of one hooked fish in their shoal. Therefore, I believe strong attractors are best used with low nutrition, cheap bases, as the action will be fast but soon over. For my own part, with so many alternative cheap bases around, I don't mind having to change baits frequently. In fact I welcome it, as it stops me getting bored, and prevents me from putting all my eggs in one basket by relying on one bait. An important issue I think in this age of crowded carp waters, for how are we to know if the expensive preparation we've put all our faith in has not already been used on our lake, and is already etched on the carp's tiny mind to be treated with caution.

That carp do get scared of baits is indisputable, but it only applies where the same carp are being dealt with. Some of the lakes I have fished in the last few years are over forty acres. What with islands and bays, that is an awful lot of perimeter to patrol. While I know some waters where individual fish will patrol every inch of the bottom, in others separate shoals seem to inhabit different areas. That area may be anything from 8 acres to around 20 acres, but the important thing to realize is that when fishing different areas of a large water, we may be dealing with different fish. Therefore a bait which is blown out on one side of a lake, could be a winner on the other side. So first make sure, before abandoning a bait.

As I mentioned earlier there are waters where carp have accepted that their food comes in little balls, so the shape of that food is unlikely to create concern. The main danger will be from recognised smells. I also believe that the texture of a bait is another aspect which can cause carp to display caution. I have noticed that many lakes have periods when a certain type of bait produces and while it is true to say anglers follow trends on a water, I am sure this would not be the case if those trends were non-productive. Many hard-fished waters I know of have acted in this way, first ordinary soft paste baits were the winners, then soft baits that were boiled to give them a rubbery outer skin. Lately on those same waters, very hard boiled baits have produced the goods. I am certain this is because the fish can detect the feel of a bait within its mouth.

Texture

So I believe it pays to try and alter a bait's texture. A soft paste bait mixed with calcium caseinate will after a certain time in water produce a slimy type of texture. There is a

BOLT RIGS FOR BOILED BAITS '80

1" - 3" hook length

1 - 2 oz. bomb

As with shock rigs for particles, the close proximity of lead to hook should be enough to make the carp bolt. However, if this doesn't happen, fix the lead to the line with a leger stop, so it can't move.

SEMI - BUOYANT BAIT

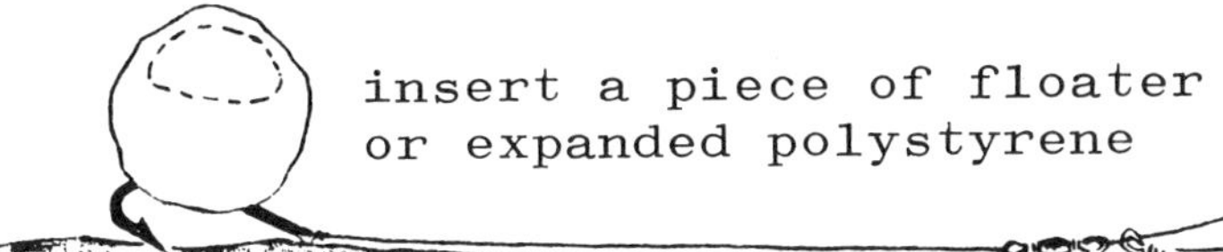

Baits made this way enable the hook to be hidden underneath, and don't sink into silt, weed, etc.

bait on the market producing this slime effect. Adding dry gelatine to calcium caseinate produces a shiny marzipan like textured bait. Again, by the use of emulsifying agents, it is not difficult to present any food you wish in jelly form. If mixed correctly the jellies will stay firm and remain undissolved in water for a minimum of 36 hours. Although I have used this type of bait infrequently, not wanting to use my trump cards till needed, response to the jellies has been very gratifying. Along the same lines, I've been experimenting with free form spawn-like baits. Substances used have included aspen, pectin and gelatin along with a reacting agent. While I have yet to put the baits into use, being more concerned at the moment with getting the texture correct, I can see them being very beneficial in the future.

These extremes of texture apart, even small differences in a bait's feel can be beneficial. While food grinders are now almost in universal use, all mixes come out nice and fine. When the baits are boiled, a smooth-skinned texture is created. I purposely leave my base meals in a rough unground form, about the consistency of breadcrumbs. When these baits are boiled, the outside texture is a mass of tiny lumps.

Crumb and exploding baits

Another area of development of bait form I can see is the wide spread use of "crumb" pastes. In the 60's before eggs and caseins were added to mixes, breadcrumb and sausage rusk were the two well-used bases. After a while in water, these baits would disintegrate. Yet it was not unusual to get runs at dawn, after the baits had been left out over night. The carp had in fact hoovered up little piles of crumb. With the advent of the new baits, this type of disintegrating bait was forgotten, until a joke between Len Burgess and myself, a couple of years ago. Messing around pretending to be ultra cult, we let it be known to some youngsters that we were in on the very latest rage, the "exploding" bait!

Back home, I realised that an exploding bait was a feasible proposition. The theory was this. A well flavoured bait was made up, and instead of using binding agents, combustible foods, such as dry ground rice, barley meal, and a pinch of baking powder, were used. On becoming saturated with water, these dry materials would "explode" the bait, hopefully scattering the flavour over a wide area. This would give the chance to pull in fish from a wide area. The original plan was only to make groundbait samples explode, homing fish onto regular hookbaits of the same flavour. That approach would I am sure work. But looking deeper into the situation, what fish would find on entering the area would be a carpet of flavoured crumb. Therefore I feel it is a better proposition to use a hook bait that would soon break down to crumb, but without any exploding material in it. Anyone doubting the approach will work has only to try laying a carpet of bait crumb in his local lake and watch the result. Crumb is taken without caution, while even going baits are treated with some respect.

It may surprise you when I say that I consider the finest texture of any bait I've seen to be bread. It has a texture all of its own, and is probably the most adaptable bait material there is. I must admit to having tried for years to produce a good flavoured loaf, but as yet have failed dismally. A good piece of bread is like soft coral. I have produced similar

An orange-coloured particle trapped this 27-plus from Kent

looking foods, but without exception they have all floated.

Colour

The final area I come to on paste baits is that of colour. As with particles, I believe yellow, orange and mid-red to be the most visual in water of average depths, while blues show up best in exceptionally deep water. Many people have taken the original particle idea and dyed baits black in an effort to keep off young sight-feeding carp and sort out their older, larger brethren. This is all very well if a bottom happens to be black, but this is in fact quite rare. If one is attempting to apply this principle, the bottom of the swim has to be investigated. Over a sand-covered bottom, a sand coloured bait would be needed. On an algae covered bottom, a shiny transparent green bait. Where a gravel bottom is concerned the bait would have to be of a creamy, mottled appearance. On any of the afore mentioned areas, a black bait would stand out like a sore thumb. Incidentally it is because of these variations of bottom, that I don't try to camouflage line. That I think is an impossibility. At least a green line has a chance of being mistaken as a strand of filamentous weed, while my old favourite, 11 lb Sylcast, has a fair chance of being mistaken for a piece of old barge rope.

Simple Bait examples

1. *High Protein*

3oz casein
1oz sodium or calcium caseinate
1oz lactalbumin
3oz vegetable protein
2oz "Equivite" (vitamin and mineral supplement)
6 eggs

2. *Medium protein*

3oz "5 pints" (dried milk)
3oz texturised soya
4oz trout, salmon, pheasant or duck pellets (ground)
Bind with water or eggs

3. *Low protein*

4oz ground dari seed
4oz Fine Universal bird food
2oz meat extract or "Ovaltine"

4. *The Best Paste for Carp*

Take the flesh of a rabbit, and Bean-flower, sifted very fine; mix these together with Honey and incorporate them in a Mortar, or work them in your Hands into small Balls fit for use; temper it to such a stiff Substance, that it may not wash off your Hook, neither let it be too hard; and if you mix Virgin's wax or clarified Honey with it, it will keep all the Year. If it be too pale, you may make it of a true Flesh-colour by mixing a little Vermillion with it.

This recipe for a carp "special" was first published in a book called "The Gentleman Angler" by one of the early pioneers of carp fishing, George Smith. He revealed his secret formula in 1726!

Chapter 10

Waffling on about carp baits '88

I must admit I was dreading writing this chapter. After all what is there left to say about carp baits that hasn't been said already. The "in search of the ultimate bait" theme has been done, written about so many times, yet has really produced little. When it comes to it what is the ultimate bait anyway? Any bait which catches on the day I reckon. Also how do I write it, so it sounds like a book and not a catalogue? For the fact is producing baits is my living, I can only write about what I use, so that means everything mentioned is a Catchum bait. I can only hope that the reader respects the views as my own, and not as some sort of commercial. In an effort to do this I will try and talk about baits on a broad front and how to get the best from them rather than go into specifics, saying this product is the best, or you have to use so and so to catch regularly. The fact I do work for Catchum and only use their products, does not prevent me from realising that other bait firms produce good products. However as I don't use them, I can hardly write about them. One thing is for sure now, once you accept that there are no wonder rigs about, bait selection is of paramount importance.

Right, having taken my quota of Bob Monkhouse sincerity pills, where do we start? Back on the old chapter I reckon. Right, I said I was struggling on this chapter, so if I waffle on a bit, please make allowances. Are you sitting comfortably? Then I will begin.

On reading that old chapter again I was a bit stunned by the realisation of just how little we have progressed in that direction during the last seven years or so. During the seventies, learning about baits was part and parcel of carp culture, at least as important as any other aspect of carp fishing. It required the gaining of knowledge. The angler wanted to know about the nutritional requirements of the carp, about its digestive system, its vitamin requirements. He wanted to know the amino acid profiles of the proteins he was using, so that his bait could be fully utilised. Which proteins were best suited to the carp's requirements? Was more carbohydrate needed in winter when metabolic rates were slower? Was energy best gained by burning excess protein off, or was carbohydrate or even fat intake better? It was all very complicated with so many avenues to explore, many that ended up in blind alleys admittedly but all the time the angler was learning a little bit more about the carp itself. It was not just a case of trying to come up with the ultimate bait, the ultimate bait was conceived as a food which was nutritionally perfect for the carp. It was a food on which the carp would grow better, suffer less disease, and which was able to promote the healing of damaged tissue. Besides trying to catch them we were also trying to improve their lot.

Very few people today get in that deep, indeed a fair proportion of anglers do not even make their own baits, preferring the convenience of manufactured boilies, about which they know little or nothing, a fact which does not seem to bother them in the slightest. As one such angler said to me "what is the point in my spending hours in the kitchen making boilies which may or may not work? Where there is no guarantee that what I make will be better than a boilie I buy off the shelf. Besides which, the time I used to spend making baits, is now spent fishing. I catch more fish now because I spend more time at the water and what is more every other angler who buys a packet of the same boilies, is actually baiting up for me. In my opinion one boilie is much the same as another, if they are going to feed on them one boilie is not going to be ignored for another. In fact on my water, every young kid comes along with a packet or two of brand name boilies. There must literally be thousands going in every week, no wonder the carp mop them up, they must have become a natural food!"

It is easy to agree with many of those opinions and his reasons for using ready mades, although I cannot go along with the opinion that one boilie is as good as another. A really good bait will be taken first time without any prebaiting at all, and if it is just used by one or two anglers, its productive life may last seasons, as it will not get fished out quickly, which is the case with a bait used by lots of anglers on the same water. The point I am making is that since ready made boilies came on the scene very little progress has been made, simply because few minds are now tuned in that direction.

Even those who are into bait in a big way have found it very difficult to improve on the best bait compositions that were known in 1980. By the nature of my job, I am probably as involved as anyone in trying to improve baits, yet in all honesty I cannot say that HNV baits have been formulated to perform any better than ones used by Fred Wilton in the late sixties. Certainly they are more consistent because of the high quality and availability today of materials such as casein and lactalbumin. Bait companies like my own have also been able to have vitamins specifically formulated to a carp's requirements rather than just use any supplement in the hope it would be beneficial, but this was not genuine progress, just taking advantage of facilities now available, using data and formulas known for well over a decade.

Milk protein baits are good, we have always known that, but they have not proved to be the food which fish would eat in preference to anything else, which was a theory some of the old protein lads believed would happen. It is highly debatable whether a bait of any composition, be it milk proteins, fish meals, meat meals, carbohydrates or spices could ever achieve such a situation, for I can't for the life of me think of such a case in the animal kingdom. If it does not happen naturally, I doubt if we can make it happen. Sure animals, fish included, show preferences, but this does not stop them eating other food. A carp feeding on blood worm, does not spit out a snail or shrimp if it comes across one. Likewise it may be feeding hard on protein boilies. Indeed it is a case that the right combination of flavour enhancers can sometimes get fish going to the extent where it feels it needs just one more to satisfy its appetite. But if that one more it wants happens to be a ball of semolina lying close by, then I am sure it will be taken.

I do believe that by and large protein baits, of either milk or fish meal composition have longer successful lives than simple carrier baits of semolina, rice or biscuit simply because of the benefits that are felt after digestion, but the bait must have a very distinctive label for the fish to cotton on to the fact that by eating that particular food, it will get a feeling of well being. Achieving that distinctive label for the fish to cotton on to the fact that by eating that particular food, it will get a feeling of well being is by no means easy. Achieving it means using a flavour or blend of flavours, that the fish is unlikely to come across in any other baits. This is not as easy as it looks, because the best combinations that really do attract fish down to the bait, are very well know. Any old flavour is not enough. I and field testers used by my company have literally tested hundreds of flavours during the past seven years and only something like ten per cent really do the business when it comes to attracting fish in. Even then a flavour might not react indefinitely in that way in a given water because I am pretty certain in my own mind that on hard fished small waters, at some periods a case of solvent saturation happens. This is when so many baits have been used, all with flavours using the same solvent base that the fish become so saturated with that solvent, that it fails to create a chemical response. That is not to say that a bait so flavoured will fail to catch any fish at all, there will always be the day when a hungry fish picks one up simply because it is food, but the flavour has done nothing in attracting that fish.

I am pretty sure that this solvent saturation problem has been one of the big reasons for the success of flavours based on ethyl alcohol in the last year or so. If I might explain, about four years ago, I and a couple of friends tested out about eight ethyl alcohol flavours alongside flavours we knew to be good. Ethyl strawberry and butter for example, alongside our PG (propylene glycol) based strawberry and butter flavours. At that time the regular PG based ones won hands down. This was particularly noticeable on the lightly fished even sometimes virgin waters in Holland, leading one to presume that in the general course of things, PG was a far more acceptable flavour base to carp. Admittedly we did little experimentation with doseage levels, sticking to the 5ml to a 10oz mix rate we regard as standard with PG flavours. However, the carp's preference was clear.

Then in the last eighteen months or so, I began hearing of many lakes now responding well to ethyl alcohol based flavours, which after the results of our previous tests obviously surprised me somewhat, as I was extremely dubious as to their effectiveness. This despite knowing in theory at least that ethyl alcohol should be the most water soluble of all solvents. It was obvious that we would have to test them out again. This time around, four of the eight caught good numbers of fish, even bettering their PG counterparts! While in the main part this success was on hard fished waters, a very lightly fished lake also responded exceptionally well. I think the main reason was not that the flavours were better than PG based ones, they were simply different enough for them to register a chemical response with the carp as they had not been saturated with that solvent. Also this time around, I gave the field testers full license to experiment with doseage levels. All found that to get the ethyl flavours really going, required a higher level of doseage, 7½ml generally even sometimes as high as 10ml to a 10oz mix. Circumstances and more knowledge about how to use them, have made ethyl flavours now very effective.

This I welcome not just from the fact I make my living out of producing carp baits, but also as an angler. The fact that most waters in the future will see a wider variety of solvents in baits, should I hope stop the saturation of any one. But at the same time I don't think it will make the business of achieving a distinctive label for a HNV bait any easier. For a HNV to really work to its potential, enough of them have to be eaten in the first place for the carp to recognise any benefits, and that will require the best attractors to get the fish down on them, and there are few of these not known to most carp anglers; therefore there is always the likelihood that the same attractor combination will be used by others using baits of little nutritional quality. I think this has happened on lots of waters, to the effect now that HNV baits used there no longer produce more fish than any other boilie. After all a fish cannot recognise the benefits without a label to associate them with and if half

This fish certainly showed a preference . . . I caught it eleven times on the same spice-flavoured bait!

the time that label does not give any well feeling response, as would be the case of say a semolina bait with the same flavour, how can it recognise that label for its benefits?

It is a bit of a vicious circle. Flavours or attractors get fish to feed in the first place. Then heavy feeding is required for a bait to be recognised for its nutritional quality. But at the same time, the flavour must be unique and different for the HNV side-effects to be recognised. Yet if the flavour combination is that good the bait would be eaten anyway regardless of nutritional qualities. All in all despite the fact that we know from less crowded times that baits made on the HNV principle are far superior, I think it very difficult indeed on hard fished waters today to achieve a bait fish actually prefer, on anything other than pure flavour, taste value. On uncrowded private syndicate waters, HNV principles are still well worth pursuing because they are better baits, and better for the fish, but where thousands of boilies go in I don't now see the point. A fish might eat up to fifty boilies in the course of a day. How does it know which ones have left it feeling well? They've all gone in the same hole and out the other end. I mean how long after feeding on the HNVs does the carp feel the benefits? In most animals a change of diet takes several days before any benefits are seen or felt, I doubt if the carp is any different. So really I would think several days would be needed feeding mainly on just the one bait, before the benefits are felt and the bait works because of its composition. I think this could only apply as I said in lightly fished, or really large waters.

The counter argument to the use of HNV baits, is that if you use a bait with little nutritional value, then the carp will need to eat more to be satisfied, and so will be easier to catch. Many people point to the success of particle baits to illustrate this fact. Now where there is a certain amount of logic in this theory you could rightly also say yes, but what if a superior food was also available, surely that would be picked up in preference, because by choice the carp would not eat the inferior food: and so we're back to the HNV principle again, which may be correct but is very difficult to put into practice.

Yes, I know what you're thinking: "What's he waffling on about?" I'm buggered if I know. All this theories stuff's leading nowhere. What do we need from a bait? Simply, something that attracts a fish to it, entices fish to eat one, and is then palatable enough to make it want to eat the lot up. If it does that then it's a good carp bait - right? That simplifies matters a bit. All we are really looking for is something that really attracts, and something that tastes good. Yes, but hang on a second I hear you say, how do you attract a fish, if it's scared of what you are offering it. I have heard this a lot from anglers on really hard fished waters. Some say that they can't get a run on a ball of protein or semolina anymore, but they do get runs on simple bird food bases like nectarblend or sluis.

An alternative to this is bait size preventing runs. Standard 14 to 17ml boilies are said not to produce any more in some places, but donkey choker 25 to 30ml baits do. Obviously in both these cases, the carrier (i.e. the bait) is viewed with suspicion because that shape, size or texture has caught so many fish. The fact that fish can still be caught on something like birdfood, shows the importance of bait texture and that fish do recognise the differences. Think back to when cooked pop-ups were first used. They were absolutely lethal. Sure they stood out, sure they waver about enticingly, but don't forget that the texture of them was entirely different to the standard boilie. Fish meal boilies scored in the same way and I am sure one of the contributory reasons was the difference in texture to milk or semolina baits.

Harking back to the beginning when I said very little progress had been made, I remember back in the late seventies going away on sessions with about a dozen different baits in the car. There would be some lobworms or brandlings, a range of particles, a floater cake or two, always a jelly bait that had been made up with gelatine, a tin of bacon grill, one or two soft pastes in the dry form that only required water adding, plus fish meal, birdfood and protein boilies. I was not the only one, some anglers I knew carried more baits than I! So many different textures and sizes of bait were used, the fish had little chance of getting spooked on any one. What do they get today? The endless round dense ball, all the same shape, usually the same size. Is it any wonder there are days when they cannot handle another boilie? If they are cautious of it in the first place, you are not going to get the best from your attractor however good it is. I am utterly convinced that the angler who makes his bait different in texture and to a lesser extent size, to the standard dense boilie will reap the benefits on hard fished waters.

The dense hard boilie was conceived simply to eliminate nuisance fish problems, but in reality the so called nuisance fish, did not stop us catching carp on soft pastes, jellies, bread, worms or maggots. Particles caught other species too, but this did not stop anglers using them, so why is it practically everything else has been dropped in favour of the boilie? I think basically laziness, not wanting to be bothered with anything else but full blooded runs. But the fact that the other baits were non-selective made you a better angler, because you had to learn about the habits of all fish. You trained yourself to learn the difference between the bubbles of one species to those of another. After all you did not want to waste your time stalking bream when you were after carp. The bait might not have been selective, but the cast was. You put your bait where you knew there was a carp. Even if you got it wrong, you usually had action. I have no time for the anglers who throw other species up the bank; many is the time a blank session has been prevented by the accidental capture of a specimen roach or tench, to which I've been truly thankful. What is more, many attractors worked far better in soft pastes or really loose textured boilies. It was the reaction to amino acids in soft pastes that got everyone so excited in the 70's, but they have never produced the same results in a dense boilie. Actually, with some of the rock hard boilies I've seen used, I think it would be a miracle if any form of flavour or attractor could leak out at all.

The hard boilie has seen everything off just because of its convenience. You can bash it to the horizon without it flying off the hook. Leave it out all night, you'll either catch or get a good night's sleep. It will catapult out a long way, without breaking up. Bait up with it and it will stay in the swim until a carp finds it. You haven't even got to work to find the best feeding areas before you bait up. It will stay in one piece until it's found. If this all sounds like I am very anti-boilie you are wrong. All I am saying is that there is a lot more to carp fishing than just chucking the boilies out. Carp baits don't start and finish with boilies. Sure they are the easiest to use but not necessarily the best. Thinking back to the first year of the Savay Syndicate, one of the most successful anglers that season, my friend Albert Rump didn't, I think, even know about boilies or the hair rig. It didn't matter though because he had picked up watercraft on other waters and the carp he presented his soft trout pellet paste to, never turned their noses up at it, instead they got their heads down on it.

I earlier mentioned how many attractors worked far better, far quicker when used in a paste. Every good paste bait was instant; it didn't need pre-baiting. Even spices such as peppers and paprika as found in the famous Robin Red worked far better in a paste. HNV baits really scored in this form too. It might have had something to do with the protein theory, but more probably I think because the carp could really taste the milk, and they loved it. This has to be because all good attractors work best when they come into contact with water as they do in a paste. Both the dense texture of the standard boilie and the fact that eggs are always used to retain the shape, have to inhibit the effectiveness of any substance in a boilie. When the eggs coagulate on boiling, the goodies inside are literally trapped within an egg cover. I know eggs make mixes easy to roll and bind, but I personally don't believe we will see the true potential of lots of substances be they flavours, spices, amino acids or essential oils, until we get away from using eggs in a bait. It is easy to see that they have to inhibit the effectiveness of the materials within the bait. Amino acids used in paste baits were always in the crystal form. It needed the adding of the water to the paste, to turn them into an acid, then the right combinations really worked. It is hardly surprising that amino acids in this form have not worked well in boilies. They never became enough of a liquid acid to get out of the bait and perform. Any acid that was formed still had to get through the egg cover.

The other point about eggs is that they are the only substance which appears in every boilie. The fact that they provide a coating must mean I think that the egg would always be tasted first. I think on first bite, a great many boilies would have to taste the same. If they all look the same, have the same texture and initially at least the same taste, is it any wonder carp go off them at times? If three components always remain the same, just how different can you make them? It surely makes sense to get away from those three common denominators although I do admit not using eggs does make bait making much more difficult.

Changing shape or size is no problem at all, neither should changing texture be, even if the boilie format is stayed with. Even HNV milk baits can be altered in texture. Although not widely sold by bait companies at this time, many milk products can be obtained in granule or small pellet form. The inclusion of something like Equivite milk pellets for instance to a standard mix gives a bait a bobbley like surface and quite rubbery texture. So if you have every confidence in the HNV type of bait, you can still stick to your principles yet at the same time change the baits appearance and texture.

I see I've come back to the HNV bait theme again and thinking about it, it's not surprising because the vast majority of thinking during the last 20 years has been protein orientated. We have always looked to provide the nutritional meal. Yet all food has its purpose, even if it is just essential roughage. Everything does not have to be protein, to give an example. Look at a history of carp baits for the first sixty years of this century. Everything was based on bread or potato. True not as many fish were caught then but very few people fished for carp. No one put the hours in that today's carp angler does, the tackle was crude and until Dick Walker came along none was designed for carp in mind. Yet the carp angler of that time used bread because he knew carp liked it and he caught fish. This despite bread being about the least selective of all anglers' baits. I think this selectivity idea, from which the boilie grew is taken too far. Maybe some things like particles, paste, bread are prey to any species, but if the angler has done his work and picked a swim with carp in, the carp will have that bait if it wants it and other species will soon be pushed aside. Be that as it may, bread in its many forms is liked by carp and in cheap mixes, I would expect a breadcrumb or rusk base to perform better than the standard cheap bait base semolina. It would certainly be more digestible as it is in part soluble while semolina is insoluble. It would also provide the different texture, I think so important today.

There really are a host of materials that could provide a palatable mouthful for a carp and yet at the same time give a texture different from the run of the mill boilies used today. Let's face it, a milk protein and semolina boilie look and feel practically the same. The success of something like Chum Mixer shows that a bait does not necessarily have to be highly nutritious to work well. Mixers, Munchies, Go-cat etc., are all just basically modified starch, with various meals added. I have had the opportunity several times to visit factories producing these types of dog and cat biscuit, all of which work well either used as a floater or ground up to form the base for a boilie and I've been amazed at how unrefined many of the ingredients were. Soya is often used, but is very basic coarse ground meal containing all the husk. China clay is often added as well to provide colour and calcium, while the bonemeal used is extremely coarse indeed. I also found it extremely interesting that any flavours which needed adding were used in extremely low levels and often included after mixing with lard! Incidentally, propylene glycol the most widely used solvent in flavours used by carp anglers, is used in the biscuit trade as a preservative. So here are a number of products, all extremely coarse with little nutritional value, but all of which make excellent baits. Something used to crunching up mussel and snail will not sneer at a boilie that is not perfectly smooth to the touch. If it's food it will eat it; look at the success of tiger nuts for instance.

I know I've been waffling on again, but what I'm basically saying is that if you fish heavily fished waters and your catch rate has slipped don't think it's just down to finding some new flavour or rig. Start in the first place by changing your bait. Just making it different from the rest could make a hell of a lot of difference. It's time to get experimenting again. Here are just a few materials I know will make a good bait that are not widely used today. Nut meals, ground particle meals, potato flake, isolated potato protein, soya meal, soya grits, meat and bonemeal, beef and hidemeal, sausage rusk, breadcrumbs, milk granules, gravy granules, all forms of dog and cat biscuits, flour, maize-gluten, plus all fish meals which despite having been written about for a number of years are still not widely used and still, in the vast majority of lakes, represent a new texture.

One I have only just started experimenting with myself and one of which I have extremely high hopes as it is not only different but also conforms with HNV principles and may even have a natural attraction is worm meal. At the moment I'm trying to bind it without eggs, so that any natural attraction will not be masked, but only time will tell whether I achieve this and it lives up to my expectations, before my small supply runs out.

Be that as it may, I know every one of those materials mentioned will catch carp, with the addition of a good enough attractor. Carp go down on a bait for a variety of reasons. Sometimes the attractor which may be anything from a combination of flavours to amino acids, to spices or natural oils, is enough to trigger the feeding urge and get fish down on a bait. Often the appearance of that bait may even arouse suspicion in the fish, but it is prepared to take the risk because its senses have been excited. Other times there may not even be any attraction. Think of the times when a fish must eat boilies, when there is no angler present. Boilies which may have laid on the bottom for days, with very little flavour left in them to emit. They will be eaten, simply because the carp knows they represent food and it is hungry.

There is even a line of thinking that baits such as these would make the best hookbaits, as they are regarded by the carp as being safe. After all, who fishes with boiles which have been out in the water for three or four days and which have little or no flavour left in them? Baits which may even have started to sour, but to the carp it is food, food that is safe to eat. I know there have been times when acquaintances have scored using boilies with no flavour in at all and one possibility is that the carp have mistakenly taken the bait as being an old safe one. There is obviously room here to experiment, particularly when the angler spends all of his time on one water, using the same bait. It would be interesting to see the response to baits that have been left in water for three days, before the angler uses them. Not that I am recommending the wholesale withdrawal of flavours from carp baits, in the main the right flavour does attract, but in some instances maybe one without flavour will score on the day. If one thing does not work, try another. It is just a question of responding to a carp's differing behaviour.

I think it impossible to say just what the best attractors are, because ones I previously rated the best in the pre 1980 era have not responded so well in the boilie context, for reasons already outlined, i.e. the dense composition of the standard boilie and the masking effect created by the coagulation of eggs. Some of those things such as peppers and paprika as found in Robin Red can be modified into liquid form giving them a far better potential for working well in a boilie. Amino acids also fall into this category. Having seen just how effective they could be in a paste bait, they could not be ignored. Once again it was found that for them to have any stimulatory effect in a boilie, they had to be in a liquid form. Even then they have to be used at high levels to have much effect in the standard boilie and I would say to all anglers to really get the best from them, a loose textured boilie, consisting of large coarse particle size, is essential. Cut out the eggs somehow and it will work even better.

Several liquid amino acid preparations, including some formulated by myself and others produced by other companies have been tested during the last couple of years. All have worked best when there was an outlet direct to the water, for instance the incorporation of a sponge filled swimfeeder in the tackle, the sponge having first been impregnated with the aminos. In coming seasons I think many will be available, in various concentrations. All I think will work to one degree or another. The amino acid attraction idea is no con, no blind alley, we know that from the terrific results of the paste bait era. What we have to do now is get it right with boilies, because they are here to stay. The point is though, that aminos have to be able to get out of a bait, to attract fish. That is why sometimes in a boilie it is necessary to use as high as 20ml to a mix. Dipping the bait directly into the preparation before casting will also help. It is a far cry from the 3 to 5 grammes used successfully in pastes, but is as I have outlined entirely due to the restrictiveness of the egg bound boilie. Obviously a better carrier is really needed for this kind of attractor and all I can say is that I and I would imagine many others, are working on it.

My thinking today on amino acid combinations differs somewhat from my ideas of 1980. I suppose at that time, I believed that a combination had to be tailor made for each lake to fit in with varying pH levels. One combination to suit this water, one for that. No wonder I dropped the idea. Life is too short to do that each time, there would be no time for fishing.

There was also the realisation that although we knew a few short amino combinations that provided a feeding response, it was not only that combination which was working but also its reaction with the aminos present in the proteins that formed the bait mix. All the best results had been with bait that had sodium caseinate (soluble casein) in them and it was the reaction between the acids and that protein which proved so effective. They were dependant on each other. It seemed to me that a full amino chain was really needed. Some acids might not be attractive but they made others work.

Today I think it better to put every good combination I know within one chain and into one preparation. Those that will attract in the circumstances of a given lake will do so, any that don't react to create attraction will still be of benefit in a nutritional sense. There may be rare times when various factors combine within a given lake (say for instance if pH levels for some reason dropped drastically), that the acids might get no response but they will still be beneficial to the carp if that bait is eaten and so a welcome addition to the bait.

One thing which has surprised me, but as yet I have not drawn any firm conclusions about is the differing responses to synthetic and natural occurring amino acids within paste baits and boilies. If I might explain all the work I and my group of friends did with aminos in the 70's was with synthetic amino acid salts. They were the ones which we found attracted fish when used in the right combinations and at the right levels. However at this moment, liquid preparations of synthetic amino acid compounds, have not had the response of naturally derived ones, which generally come from liver, spleen, or stomach extracts. I should say that this second group have not been entirely natural, as it was felt they needed slight modification to include some acid which either did not occur in the natural extract, or that the acid was in such minimal quantities as to not make any difference. Surprisingly though the synthetic blends have worked well when combined with a small amount of flavour, and also in a protein base which provides additional nitrogen. I think this is very much down to the inter reaction again of aminos, their dependancy on one another: when using synthetic ones this becomes more acute.
I feel here is one of the avenues that can be explored and real progress be made. I feel that the "Sense Appeals" marketed by my own firm have shown that amino acids, small amounts of organic acids and flavours can be combined to really produce very successful boilies. It's just a question of finding what works well with what. Today we have far greater facilities than before, because carp fishing has become big business. A firm like my own for example could have bloodworm, swan mussels, snails or any part of carp's natural diet analysed to find its amino acid construction. We could then have those aminos made up in concentrated form either by synthetically producing them or by modifying an existing natural amino chain, from one of the extracts previously mentioned. The facilities are there, it's if we have the right ideas to benefit from them.

For instance would producing a true snail replica be any better than fishing with a snail? This in itself is not productive because of the old blade of grass in a field routine. One snail is the same as another, why should one stand out? Or would a free release of those acids only persuade the fish to feed on the natural snails? What I mean here is, why should we copy naturals, when it has been shown that we can get fish off naturals and feeding on baits? Would a liquid preparation of milk protein chains be better for instance? Or probably more likely one of fish meals or carp spawn. No-one really knows, all we can do is try something and hope it works. But the costs are such that we must be pretty sure of success before we go ahead with such developments.

Back in 1980, I really thought that the future of baits lay in the direction

The ultimate bait on this day was hemp seed

This beautiful leather was gorging itself on high protein tadpoles!

He popped up on a pop-up!

of getting a bait to produce its own free attractive amino acids by means of breakdown. This meant incorporating enzymes into the bait to break down the protein chains, therefore freeing soluble acids and rendering the bait into a predigested form which could be utilised to the full. I don't think I was wrong in that idea and I'm sure theoretically that it can be done. However I have to admit that I spent getting on for three years pursuing this idea without ever achieving a bait which out performed my standard proteins so I dropped it because I was getting nowhere and from thereon in concentrated on producing better bases and attractors. Tim Paisley and others did I know follow similar lines and it will be interesting to see how they got on, in the chapter I have included written by Tim. Just having the knowledge to achieve such a bait is not enough to say that a bait is better than others. It has to produce better catches to be regarded as superior.

Amino acids of course are not the only things that attract carp. A great number of flavours do that in their own right. I would like to think that flavours in the future will veer more towards natural products purely for environmental reasons but the fact is with very few exceptions, the naturals do not perform with fish as well as synthetic flavours do. For instance fish a whole strawberry or natural cherry alongside a bait containing the same synthetic flavour. I know which one will come out top. Obviously the bait would be far more concentrated, after all they are 1000-1 concentrations. Maybe it is only in concentration that they like that smell and taste. It is not representative of anything. I doubt if a carp knows what a strawberry is. It is simply a chemical combination the carp finds attractive. It could be that the natural contains some volatile esters (over 200 have been isolated in strawberry alone) that a carp finds distasteful or even repellent. A synthetic copy does not carry a true profile, but only picks up on the key notes of a flavour. That is most flavours, expensive nature identical ones are available, but if the natural fruit or origin of any flavour does not entice carp, would a nature identical flavour? Or is it just that flavours are soluble when a natural fruit is only part so?

I know there are a lot of questions so far unanswered, but while it is relatively easy to come up with theoretical solutions, the carp themselves provide so many contradictions in their behaviour to our answers. For instance why should soluble flavours work when in the carp's natural diet there is little or nothing that is soluble?

Or then again does a carp find its food because of soluble excretions or secretions? If so that would go a long way towards explaining why flavours do work, it would also explain to a degree why unnatural baits work. Take a milk protein bait as an example; it is completely unnatural. Milk does not occur in aquatic animals. But its base is insoluble protein i.e. Casein just like a swan mussel for example is composed mainly of insoluble protein. But when a mussel excretes waste into the water, many soluble products including amino

I was on 'sky-high protein' at the time

and organic acids are let out. Is it much different? A flavour drawing fish to insoluble protein, in the same way excretions do in the natural state.

The inconsistency here is that where an amino acid chain can be representative of its base, there is no way many flavours are. They just have to work because of their own abilities. They attract, and a fish wants to find the source of that attraction, whereby it finds the insoluble food. I don't believe any sort of nutritional recognition can be arrived at before digestion of a food, so that food has to be as palatable as you can make it, if all of the baits are going to be eaten. The flavour has acted rather in the same way you might be drawn into a restaurant, because of appetising flavours coming through its windows. That flavour is not representative of one thing but a combination of many. Once in there the standard of the food will depend on whether you visit that place again. This means the food not only tasting good at the time, but also having no adverse reaction to it afterwards. Really it is all the things that make a good bait, i.e. good flavour, good taste and palatability, nutritionally rewarding.

If I was asked just what makes a good flavour I could not give an easy, specific answer, and I mean a truly good flavour. It is said by some, any flavour will catch fish, I don't believe that. Sometimes fish are caught despite the flavour. I am sure this explains some, (admittedly not all) cases when it is said a flavour has blown, when in the first instance the angler just happened to have put his baits amongst hungry fish and they had it. The flavour did not attract those fish, they were just there. So when fish have been less than hungry, or maybe some distance away, the bait has not worked. The flavour has not blown, it never worked. Alternatively even a good flavour might be unattractive, if used at too high a doseage rate, but drop one in amongst hungry fish and they might well be taken. When next time they don't catch, it hasn't blown, it never did attract at that level.

Even the very best flavours have to be experimented with to find their most effective doseage rate, in a given water. Scopex for instance which just has to be one of the most successful flavours anywhere in Europe, has been found to work best at anything between 2½ to 15ml per mix. It all depends on the water it is being used in, and the different levels needed seem to correspond with differing pH values. I should add here that I don't believe this flavour suffers from the solvent saturation problem I spoke of earlier, as the solvent involved, Diacetin, is still rarely used because of its cost. I must admit that I have as yet to come across an unsuccessful flavour using this solvent base, neither have I used the similar Triacetin. Yet the success is not because they have yet to be used to such a degree that fish no longer respond to them. Neither has Ethyl Alcohol yet I and my field testers have had a lot of real bummer flavours on that base. I have to make the assumption that the solvent itself i.e. Diacetin is attractive to fish.

Similar in response to Diacetin are flavours derived from cinnamon: while cinnamon oil is well known, it is not only the oil which produces good flavours. The bark and the leaves are also very effective. In fact I would say that as high as 80% of successful spice flavours are derived from some part of cinnamon. Garlic is nearly as successful. The success of its oil has been well chronicled, but just the addition of powdered or crushed garlic can improve a bait significantly.

Oils can be excellent attractors, but are very much like flavours in that it is a matter of trial and error in sorting out the best ones as some show no attraction qualities whatsoever. Besides the two mentioned i.e. cinnamon and garlic, I can say definitely that most fish oils, particularly herring, sand eel and mackerel do attract as do geranium, eucalyptus and carrot. I think oils work in a different way to regular flavours, even when they have been emulsified. A flavour comes out of a bait, all around it, forming like a halo, slowly becoming more diluted and weaker as it gets further from the bait. An oil behaves differently going directly to the surface in a line from the bait. In this way it is much more likely I believe to attract cruisers or any fish moving in the upper layers of the water. A soluble flavour though I think stands a better chance of attracting fish moving on or around the bottom. I have to say though with oils, that I can find no common denominator in the successful attractive ones, which are not in ones that give negative response.

Oils can also provide another significant role in a bait by providing energy. When incorporated into a bait for an energy function, protein content can be lowered significantly as all the protein can be utilised to make building blocks i.e. growth of tissue etc. In years to come, baits formulated in this way may be essential if we are not to pollute our smaller crowded fisheries, particularly if the water in question has a high pH level, which makes fish sensitive to ammonia.

Let me explain, the protein level of a bait really has no significance. It is the biological value of that protein, the level to which it can be utilised which is what we are really after. If we have a high protein bait that also has a high conversion rate, then there will be excess protein much of which will be burnt off as energy. However some undigested protein will find its way into the faeces, where upon decomposition, ammonia will be produced. Putting it simply, ammonia comes in two forms, one of which is harmless, one of which is toxic. The ratio of the two produced is dependant on pH levels and water temperature. Significantly, more of the toxic form is produced in waters with a high pH, biologists have claimed as much as ten times higher in a pH of 8 as opposed to one of seven. Now while it is highly unlikely that a lethal saturation could happen, I have been told of people baiting 1 acre lakes with 10,000 baits, something I could not believe, so it *is* possible, it could happen. Therefore in this context a bait likely to have excess protein, some of which may be excreted, is not desirable. By all means stick with protein as the bulk of the bait i.e. between 50% to 55% but do not use it for the purpose of energy. Without going into deep scientific studies that might be over the heads of many people, including myself, it has been established that fat is the best source for providing energy in fish; in fact its calculated gross energy is double that of protein and a lot higher still than carbohydrate, which also has the lowest digestibility of all of them. Semolina for instance has been calculated as being only 38% digestible. Is it any wonder I and my generation refer to it simply as a carrier; and yet it catches fish, which only re-inforces my beliefs that flavours, aminos, etc. really do the attracting. If nutritional recognition really happened before digestion, would such a bait really be picked up? Being the least digestible, the lowest form of energy, it does not make sense that it catches so many fish, unless you accept the importance of an attractor.

I should make the point again that I don't really see any dangers in anything but small, hard fished waters but there can be an effect in medium sized waters of say 10 acres (the size here I admit is purely guesswork). Whenever high pH and high water temperatures come together undigested protein as stated will produce a high proportion of toxic ammonia. Now where in a water of such size, the chances of anything dying because of it will be minute, its presence does have a very marked effect on a fish's appetite. I wonder now if I inadvertently discovered this when mixing together my Protein and Boilie mix, simply because I was running out of the former. I feed the fish in my garden pond on this, and within a day their appetite had increased enormously. I think the new diet which roughly gave a 55% Protein, 20% fat, 20% carbohydrate and 5% combined roughage and vitamin content, produced an environment likely to increase appetite, because of low ammonia release. It was pure fluke, but from all I have read over the last few years, considering the conversion of the protein (milks) involved, I would think that about right for small waters.

Fish farmers and feed producers mainly use fish oil as their source of fat: obviously much of this will be down to price but its energy content is also excellent. Now while fish oil in the liquid form may be perfectly acceptable in a fish meal or fish flavoured bait, I can understand many not wanting to taint a lovely flavour such as chocolate malt, or sweet mango. Fortunately fish oil is also available in a solid, granular form in which it has no fishy taste or smell. It has simply been refined to remove the impurities leaving the pure fat. As such it can be recommended for any bait where fat content is felt desirable. I might add that should you have difficulty obtaining it, I am sure full fat soya would do the same job.

I really can give no reason why carbohydrates should work except as a carrier for attractors. But this does not explain the success of bread, potatoes or the vast majority of particles. Take sweetcorn or maize, they may have colour, texture and advantage in their size, but there really has to be more to it than that. Could it be that because its small amount of protein is contained on the outside in the husk that it is recognised, and the carbohydrate plays no part at all, after all it is the least found constituent of a food found in an aquatic environment. If it was really essential surely a carp's natural diet would contain plenty of carbohydrate, the environment would provide it, instead of the diet consisting primarily of protein. As I say I'm mixed up on this one, even the point about protein being in the husk of particles does not really stand up because that protein is mainly in the form of gluten which it is thought cannot be utilised by carp. Bread can probably be explained away by its unique texture but I struggle to explain why the humble spud should have caught so many carp over the years. Maybe it is just like a boilie, just food that is selective in its species.

When I've said in the past that there is no such thing as a carp expert I really meant it. Like myself you can spend a lifetime learning about your subject, its diet, its environment, but there are always those contradictions and inconsistencies that cannot be explained, like the carbohydrates, like appetite stimulators. Now here are food stuffs which really do work, which can turn an average bait into a brilliant one. Yet they are all solids, powders and I've stated my belief that I don't believe anything but the attractor can be recognised before a bait is eaten. The success of these I think has to be down to palatability. They really make a bait taste good, at least the carp see it that way. I think palatability, taste, play a vitally important part in whether a bait is successful or not. Another thing which I think must help their effectiveness is that they are very rich in amino acids which can react with those naturally within a bait or even the eggs. Actually it is most probably the eggs because most anglers blend the stimulators with the eggs, thereby putting them into solution and into their most effective form. Again though, I wonder how much the coagulation of the eggs on boiling affects the potential of them. Without the eggs they might react even better.

As much care should be taken in making a taste as you would making an attractive smell. I wonder sometimes if every single bait is tried once and only those that taste really good get eaten. After all it is a common enough observation to see carp spit out a bait, even when there are no hooks in them. It could well be that when used correctly (a flavour matching up with the appropriate appetite stimulator) that a fish really does find something that tastes how the flavour has led it to believe that food should taste. The flavour being representative of the bait i.e. a fruity smelly bait, tastes fruity, a fishy one tastes fishy, even when say a protein or semolina base is used. The stimulator may completely mask the taste of the bait, and rather in the same way soya can be made to taste like meat or chicken, the stimulator may make milk taste like fish.

While there is no doubting the place of sweeteners in carp baits, I do believe that they are used too much, many times when their inclusion is not warranted. We try to match up flavours with bases, flavours with appetite stimulators, yet why should some anglers put sweeteners in everything? A fish bait or a cheesey or spicy one should not taste sweet. Sweeteners do tend I think to overpower everything, so much so that there must be an awful lot of baits which taste exactly the same. Even if sweet smelling flavours are the going baits on a given lake, I think it would be best if the type of sweetener used was changed regularly, because they all taste different. Most sweeteners on the bait market include saccharin, which has a very distinctive taste, yet there are better ones, admittedly more expensive ones available. There are several now which have been developed for the dietary market which are derived from sweet proteins. These are excellent because apart from sweetness, they have also been found to have flavour enhancing qualities, and experiments I've done with them, show that they will also emulsify many oils; excellent tasting blends can be achieved by combining them with the sharper tasting ones such as eucalyptus. I mention these because of their other qualities yet even the inclusion of a spoonful of brown or icing sugar I think preferable to using the same sweetener every time. If you use anything all the time, you are giving the fish something they can associate with.

One thing I believe very important in a bait is the inclusion of vitamins. In the animal world, their recognition has been more documented than that of proteins and dietary necessities. If they are available animals will find them and I see no reason why carp should differ. Anyone doubting this need only fish a protein bait without vitamins, against one with, for a season to see the difference they make. While I doubt nutritional recognition happening before digestion, I would not be at all surprised if vitamin recognition was possible before, the more so if the environment was deficient of an essential one. While it can be seen that vitamins will help the assimilation of proteins, I see no reason why they should not be used in other bases. A simple carrier can then be the source of something essential, which must improve its capabilities.

I suppose that is the whole crux of this chapter. Try and make a bait nutritionally beneficial because we know in the long run that they work better. You don't have to believe the theories behind that, as long as the indicators are flying. But nutrition is not everything.

Attractors, taste, buoyancy and texture are equally important so ring the changes with those. There are no hard and fast rules, you have to experiment. Remember even text books sometimes have it wrong. Even the so called key to life, the search for DNA was held back years because the books which provided the basis to work upon had miscalculations. Carp fishing and carp diets have yet to become an exact science. Theories are only correct when the results match them. Only your own eyes can confirm or deny that.

I called this chapter "waffling on about bait" because I knew there was no way I could say this is it, this will work, that won't work. The environment with which we are concerned is changing because of angling pressure, and despite what I would like to think i.e. that people take notice of me, the majority don't give a toss. A lot of people reading this are just looking for a new bait. I imagine few will have found one.

What I really want is for anglers to think again, about their baits, about the significance of their captures and about the long term effects on our environment. Just picking up the magazines and looking through articles for the latest wonder rig is not enough, or just the latest flavour. There are no new super rigs. Let's face it there have been a thousand different variations of the hair rig, but none has had such an effect on angling. If it was that bad, why did it catch so many fish? Moved just a quarter of an inch off the bend to become an extension of the shank and it really takes some improving. The only thing that had anywhere near the same impact was when pop-up baits were first used.

Today your bait has to be right. I might be able to give you a fantastic "new" flavour, in fact I could, but it will make little difference if you don't try to make the right carrier for it, or refuse to believe carp in a certain water now will not tolerate tight lines, or indeed if you don't bother to think whether or not that bait is suitable for your lake. I said at the start that boilies and the rig resulted in a stagnation of thought about carp baits. Now is the time to think again, it will mean more work admittedly, but when the rewards come, it will be all the more satisfying. What's more it will have started the thinking process, and you'll be looking at where you go from there. I have found an excitement when things have come together on baits, equally as rewarding as playing a fish. I think if you miss out on that thinking process and only look for convenience, that you are missing out on a vital part of what it is to be a carp man. Sitting at home and not in front of the lake you can't fish, but you can think about how to improve your results. Rod Hutchinson – News at 10, Louth, Lincolnshire.

Chapter 11

Nature's Design

Tim Paisley

Introduction

I asked Tim to write me a piece basically to show someone else's view of carp baits and because Tim pursued an avenue of thought I veered away from. Although there are several points on which we disagree, the main one being on the application of Grecian 2000, I must admit to being surprised at how many thoughts we have in common. Whether we agree or disagree does not matter, as long as we are both thinking about what we are trying to achieve and how best we go about it. My thanks to Tim for his contribution.

Rod Hutchinson.

The main reason for me writing this chapter is that Rod started up in business in 1981, at which time his mind started to diversify (the early stages of disintegration). Up to that time he had a one track mind – carp and carp baits (two track then). All my own thinking on bait originated from the ideas of Rod, and Fred Wilton, and what follows is the outline of the fusion of two lines of thought into a slight extension of a bait principle. Ideas on paper can look a bit frightening; converting them into practice can sometimes seem ridiculously easy. It is the leap from one to the other that is the worrying bit, the self-belief and frustration involved in converting theory into practice. I've done no tank testing so all my baits

changes are tested on the bank: if I make mention of the odd success in the pages that follow it was almost inevitably the outcome of a great many hours of stationary indicators suffered during the refinement of the idea. That is ignoring the hundreds of hours of stationary indicators caused by the lines of thought that were faulty. Stationary indicators are the occupational hazard of carp fishing bait addicts – because confirmed ideas are just not very interesting any more!

I've been carp fishing seventeen years or so but my first venture into southern carp fishing was in 1974. At that time I discovered that however good an angler you are, or think you are, in carp fishing you sink or swim on the basis of the effectiveness of your bait. I became bait-conscious overnight through being out-caught by anglers who didn't seem to have anything special going for them other than a bait the carp wanted more than they wanted mine. But if my attitude changed overnight my success rate didn't, although that was not for want of effort. I caught carp at the start of the season but as soon as the pressure started to tell on the fish and the initial indicator flurry was over, I struggled. I knew I needed help but needing help and getting it were two different animals in the 70s: no one seemed to be writing about baits and no one I knew had any more idea about them than I had. But you meet other carp anglers through travelling and once you really start to try people become more willing to help you. I was told about trout pellets, and luncheon meat, and things improved. The previous season I'd struggled to catch single figure fish; on the new baits I began to catch double figure fish (from the same water – Snowberry).

The progression continued. I heard about PYM (Phillips Yeast Mixture), then about the Wilton baits. (Although PYM was part of the original Wilton bait I still think of Fred's principle and that bait as being slightly separate entities.) PYM was, and still is I would guess, tremendous and gave me my most enjoyable season ever through the glorious summer and autumn of 1975. The significance of PYM was lost on me then. It was just a good bait additive and that would do for me – but there was an unanswerable question forming at the back of my mind. I was just another carp man on just another carp water and while the baits I was using weren't actually being publicised (sic) they did seem to be freely available. We all know all the good bait ingredients now but until someone told you about them it never occurred to you to use them in a bait – or anything like them. So who was coming up with these baits, and what on earth were they using if the stuff I was using wasn't being kept secret any more? The thought intrigued me.

Tim with an immaculate mirror taken on an H.N.V. bait

At that time I wasn't sure what Wilton baits were, but then I had "protein" whispered in one ear and "amino acid baits" whispered in the other within a very short space of time of each other. Hold on a minute! Fifteen months earlier I'd been on crust and flake and my mind couldn't handle the explosion of ideas. I'd travelled too far too quickly and my immediate, and quite unequivocal reaction at the time was "what a load of bait balls". A bait was a bait and to justify its significance by categorising it with a grand-sounding title was the height of pretentious ultra-cultism. My article "Protein, Carbohydrate or Just Food?" which appeared in Coarse Angler in May 1979 was a mellowing version of my original attitude to it all. I didn't really know enough about the subject to write that piece but my ignorance wasn't for want of trying to find out. I hoped that having the piece published might help, and it did. I hadn't known where to look for the reading material I wanted but once others know you are interested in a subject they try to help, even if they can't tell you what it is you want to know.

The 70s bait revolution really was a mind-blower and the arrival of the protein baits raised the emotive question "How do carp know?". Up to that time a bait was a bait and it either helped you catch carp or it didn't. If it was noticeable that each succesive bait had a better food value than the last one that was coincidence; the originality factor was still considered to have the greatest significance.

Fred Wilton suggested that it was the nutritional factor that had the greatest significance and set about proving it by shaping his baits to a theory – rather than the other way round. News travels slowly to the end of the grapevine so by the time I got the full SP on protein/high nutritional value baits their effectiveness had already been established and their track record proven. Of course, like so many others I had to disbelieve it, then doubt it, then set about proving it to myself. I think that in any other field Fred would have got a Nobel Prize for his work; instead he was pilloried for his far-fetched theories.

About the time that I first heard the expression "protein baits" Black Majic hit the headlines. Rod will know far more about the origins of the Black Majic bait than I do: all I know is that it was marketed in Norfolk/Suffolk by Len Bunn and Dick Weale as a result of some information obtained from the Lowestoft Institute about amino acids attracting fish. Black Majic was an "amino acid bait" and some of the results on it were amazing. I don't think the marketed version was as successful as its inventors hoped it would be – which was possibly a reflection of the limitations involved in the use of amino acids.

Every time I heard anything about a bait development I was off to the reference library, or poring over my growing collection of what were then totally incomprehensible science books. Protein baits appear to have been developed entirely independently of amino acid baits but it isn't possible to study a biochemistry book without realising that the significance of one must in some way be connected to the effectiveness of the other; all proteins are made up of complex chains of amino acids. If carp need protein to live, and they recognise amino acids, surely the recognition of the latter must be related to locating and eating the former? That is quite clear to me now but the connection was no more than a frustratingly vague conception at the time. Any natural phenomenon has to be considered in terms of its function in nature. When someone suggests protein baits to you your mind tends to home in on the word "baits", and not the word "protein" – as mine did: you can rather lose sight of the undeniable fact that in nature protein is what carp live on. When we want protein it is stuck on a plate and shoved under our noses in the form of a slab of steak; in nature carp have no such luck. They smell food, stick their heads in the silt or weed, suck and let their systems sort it out from there on. The smell that triggers this observable feeding phenomenon is that of a combination of amino acids and related substances.

The publicity about amino acids was considerable and they were a very attractive proposition as bait additives because of their immediacy; they can be instant. We all love to have a bait we can cast out and watch the bobbin hit the butt without any pre-baiting. I wanted that, but there must have been a period when I doubted the validity of both protein baits and amino acids; I know I wrote to Rod querying them and was surprised to get a letter back full of enthusiam for them. I had some frustrating times in the seventies and I still couldn't get them to work. I'd gone into it all on a very technical level, had identified the water soluble (hydophilic) aminos and was working with them. Then I got a letter from Clive Gibbins who was over the moon because he'd caught a good fish (15 plus – I was as jealous as hell) on an amino bait based on what he thought was the combination used in the Black Majic bait (Leucine, Lysine, Alanine and Glycine I think; or was one of them Methionine?). Back to the drawing board; back to the chemist's suppliers. Relief! Clive's information turned out to be good and I had some tremendous results based on that amino combination fished in a pilchard, caseinate, maize germ meal bait with one or two other bits and pieces in it.

It will sound daft to some of you but for the most part I fish with something until I've assessed its effectiveness then move on to something else. After the success with the amino baits I switched to trying to come to terms with the protein/HNV baits. By this time the Reding bait had been and gone but the Minamino lingered on! I put together a bait made up of Casilan, Bengers and Body Bulk (bait ingredients weren't freely available then) with added eggs and a tablespoon of Minamino. That was 1980 and to say I had no confidence in that bait is an understatement of the highest order: I only started to use it because my first choice bait, which I'd heavily pre-baited, failed to elicit a single twitch. You can imagine my confused delight when the high food bait caught immediately and went on catching all season.

By 1981 the rig and flavour revolution was eclipsing the bait one and the seeds of the present confusion were being sown. I fished low food value baits and flavours for the second half of the 1981 season and the first half of 1982. Initially I caught a lot of fish using Rod's original Cinnamon; everyone caught a lot of fish, let's be right: it wasn't natural and I was far from happy about the bait side of things. My mind is always on tomorrow in carp fishing and the rig-smell thing just felt all wrong. The lesson had taken some learning for many of us, and had promptly been unlearnt by many, but Fred had been right; the fish instinctively select their food sources on the basis of their nutritional value. The carp had to be picking up the low food value baits on the strength of what they thought the smell represented, not for what the baits actually were. By the autumn of 1982 I was beginning to have doubts about the long term use of flavours and was looking for, and experimenting with alternatives. In addition I'd left the crap baits alone and had gone back to the nutritional baits, converting the bait I'd used in 1980 into a recipe that would provide a hard boiled bait within the shortest possible boiling time.

I was convinced of the validity of enzymes in carp baits by this time (Bengers is a trypsin and amylase source) and the base mix of 1980 was strengthened by the addition of an ounce of Davina protein food, which contains bromelain, a couple of ounces of egg albumen and Rennet casein, which now represented 50% of the bait. Enzymes...I can't really skim over them.

I know from correspondence that people try to come to terms with the mechanics of enzymes without acquiring any sort of understanding of digestion and absorption, which are the principal keys to nutrition. The value of a food lies in the nutrients that the consumer's system can make use of from it; this use of nutrients is controlled by the digestive and metabollic systems of the body. Our digestive systems are more elaborate than the carp's, the principal difference being that we have a stomach and the carp doesn't. Our stomach contains hydrochloric acid and pepsin, a very acidic, highly active protein enzyme. Protein digestion is started in the acidic conditions which prevail in the stomach and the partially digested food is forced into the small intestine as a liquified mass. From the stomach onwards our system is very similar to the carp's; the absorption of the nutrients is controlled by the intestinal enzymes. The nutrients are extracted from the food and absorbed through the intestine wall into the system: what the body doesn't make use of is "wasted", to put it politely, and the amount of wastage gives a clear indication of the difference between "food" and "nutrients".

Carp don't have an acidic enzyme which means that apart from any grinding done by the pharyngeal teeth (which are very efficient) their food passes into the intestinal tract untreated. I think their natural proteins are less complex than protein baits, in that they are a live mixture of amino acids and enzymes, which makes them more convertible in nutritional terms than the baits we use. Any help we can give the carp in the breaking down of the bait (in the chemical rather than the physical sense) will make the nutrients more available to the carp and will increase the nutritional value of the bait. The usable enzyme field is very limited and I've concentrated solely on the use of proteins in this connection (although the carbohydrate enzyme amylase is in Bengers).

Trypsin is included in the bait with a view to letting it supplement the carp's natural supply of trypsin in the intestine. I think the presence of the bait trypsin may mobilise the intestine's trypsin, which can be significant. Most baits are on the acid side of neutral signifying that trypsin, which functions best at a pH of 7 + , won't be activated until it is needed – in the carp's intestine: like our systems the pH of the carp's intestine is rigidly buffered against change at a pH of 7.2. I'll make one slight qualification on the triggering of trypsin. Proteins are insoluble and the life of a protein bait in the water depends on the physical properties of the mix. However hard the bait may be it will absorb water and the lake's pH may become an influencing factor in the effectiveness of the bait trypsin in certain circumstances. I have had some very good fish on baits that have been out there a long, long time, when I've been at screaming point wanting to reel in to see if I've even got a bait on. At times, when the going has been really tough, I've had the baits out by early afternoon so they will be at their most effective as natural proteins for the early hours or first light feeding times.

Bromelain is a very active protein splitter and while I stumbled on it independently (it was going to be another in a long line of expensive failures) I have since discovered that its use in carp feeds is not entirely unheard of! Bromelain is from pineapple, and there are a number of versions of the enzyme I think. We include the fruit version, which is very different from, and more efficient than, the stem enzyme and not easy to get hold of. In addition I think I should say that this is not an ingredient to be used irresponsibly; if someone doesn't wish to use our Addit-Digest* I'd suggest that they use Davina in their mix. Don't mess with the neat enzyme because most of you just wouldn't be able to measure to a low enough level. In addition to the bromelain we include the best quality trypsin we can obtain in the Addit, which does push the cost up. Careful bait preparation will ensure consistency with the trypsin but *really* successful use of the bromelain is a bit hit-and-miss. It triggers at a range of pH levels – 4.5, 5 and 6 which gives some latitude for trying to get an initial reaction. We have found freezing to be an essential part of the successful use of enzyme baits. You will have a very reliable bait with these two enzymes, and occasionally you'll get a reaction that will make your season. Work at the preparation and use of these baits and it might help if you make notes of any variations you try. It sometimes takes me up to a month to work out what

* Nutrabaits

happened when I get a silly result! The co-enzymes in vitamin/mineral mixes are an essential part of the digestion/absorption process in that they help the main enzymes function, so don't neglect this aspect of the bait.

I've never used a bait with a protein level of more than about 65%. Biological value is the percentage of a nutrient that the consumer can utilise and it took me a while to come to terms with the contradictory BVs in some of the research papers. Figures for casein vary from 52% to 90%; why? Well the 90% figure represents the use made of casein in an ideally balanced diet. As it is with us the carp's primary requirement is energy, and if you make an inadequate energy provision in the bait expensive protein is used to fulfil the energy requirement. The 90% BV is for a diet with a 20% fat content and a 38% protein content. At the other end of the scale the 52% figure is for a diet with a 92% protein content where no provision is made to fulfil the energy requirement. If you go above 40% protein you are working to a BV of 52%, unless you can provide a better conversion of the bait by using enzymes, and make sure that all the protein is "spared" by including a high vegetable oil content. Quality and convertibility of the protein are more important aspects than percentage.

There are vast sums of money being spent on protein/HNV ingredients and a great deal of this money is being wasted. Too many anglers just can't be bothered to find out what it is they are trying to do. They treat a protein as being just another bait ingredient, stick it in there, march off to the lake with the end result and sit there are the end of the rainbow waiting for fame and fortune to drop on them in large lumps. Protein baits require more thought and care than your own food does because the thought and care has already been applied to your food by the time you get it. Grade, quality, age, storage, preparation, use; in food terms they are all spelt out for you – and you expect them to be. Work at getting it right for the carp because they are almost certainly far more discerning than you are about what they eat.

Before we can get to the ending I've got to go back to the beginning because so far we've taken rather a lot for granted (haven't I?). I went into the text books and scientific papers in 1976 and I've been there ever since, on and off, trying to relate each bait change and development to the scientific principles of attraction, recognition and nutrition. The theory of baits only becomes a science if things happen in accordance with an advance hypothesis, as Fred Wilton did it, or you are able to consistently relate an observable reaction to an acceptable scientific explanation. A great deal of the time you are working blind simply because the precise information you need just isn't available, and the less you know the lower your chances are of arriving at a firm conclusion anyway. Science doesn't operate on guesswork, it is a very precise process – but some areas of icthyology do still represent unproven science: it's worth remembering that everything that is now proven was once only theorised in

A true reward for hard work

An opening day thirty on Seafoodblend

every scientific field. Because carp live in water the full relationship between them and their food sources represents a very precise scientific equation which still isn't fully understood.

Various academics have been working on the science of carp and their food sources for many years now and there is a great deal of literature available on the subject. The Black Majic bait was based on a theory by anglers correlated with information contained in a report by M.G. Pawson of the Lowestoft Institute on the reaction of whiting and cod to a range of aminos. Apart from a broader but less technical report by Professor Loeb of New York the Lowestoft paper was one of the first the knowledge-hungry bait addicts of the 70s had seen, although many of these budding boffins later abandoned their quest for the perfect bait when the bare hook rigs and flavours started to prove so deadly.

But irrespective of what was happening in the carp world the scientific research didn't stop and the findings kept being published. Over the last fifteen years a wealth of material has built up in an area that has to be of great value to carp men. Although all of the papers don't relate directly to tests on carp, as with the Lowestoft paper it is possible to take a "fish" principle and adjust any findings to a specific species by trial and error.

Bait has become a bit unfashionable and a great many carp men have got into the habit of adding 5 mils of whatever on the assumption that it catches – and for some that represents the extent of the thought given to the make up of the bait. If that doesn't work add some enhancer, or change the flavour, or the solvent, but if it's listed in an advert it must work, surely? The carp don't necessarily think so. Initially nearly all flavours worked (some better than others) because their smell went some way towards imitating the carp's natural food scent. They were almost certainly not the same but were near enough to confuse the fish and lead to them being caught on a smell, a hard bait and a bare hook. Some flavours would work over a longer period than others: some would blow out almost immediately, but as there were so many flavours to go at anyway – what the hell? Change the flavour and start again. Mystified anglers are now being forced to change from the less nutritious bases to better quality baits but if an unthinking 5 mils of flavour is still being used the end result may still be a bait with a shortened life.

If a bait is of good enough food value ("good enough" is very vague but will vary from water to water depending on bait pressure and the natural food supply) and catches more or less immediately, then stops catching, the attractor level is right in terms of *smell* (superficial attraction) but over the top in some other way. The first time it occurred to me that this could happen, and was happening, was in September 1982 at Roman Lakes. I went there with an experimental nutritional bait with two new attractors in it. I wasn't over-hopeful I don't think; the mental blockage on flavours takes some dislodging however strong your reservations are. In the event I had a strange sort of day, catching two decent fish in the first half hour of fishing – then absolutely nothing for the rest of the day. This was still early days on the bare hooks and I *should* have caught later in the day. I knew Roman well enough then to understand how the swim ought to fish and the main action should have come in the afternoon with possibly a quick burst at dusk (''Right lads, pack up now'' ''Spherics.''). If the bait had been right there would have been a build up of action, not an explosion, then zero. (To gauge reaction to a bait you have to know the water or you can't be objective.)

That result made me think and I could come up with no other explanation than that the bait had smelt right but that it had tasted wrong, or reacted badly with the carp's system in some other way (there was a fair bit of loose feed out). The longer term implications struck me quite forcibly, and while there are times when you want the carp down on the bait quickly, to have it blown out by dinner-time (lunch-time if you live in Surrey) is a bit limiting – to put it mildly! I didn't want to drop what I was doing with those attractors because they had to be right if I could find the level, but I was a bit nervous of trying them again. Would the abuse of using the higher level put the fish off the right level, or would it smell and taste like something different at the right level? I tried changing the level, but that was when I started tasting the baits: I later started eating them to check for an avoidable adverse after-effect reaction from the fish. (I've got the twitches, too, but if you think I've got problems you ought to see our kid.) In fact the attractor worked at 25% of its original level (which had been one mil), but was nothing like as instant at the lower level. In other words the *carp didn't find it acceptable at the level at which it attracted best.*

It struck me that what had happened could be representative of the growing problem with flavours – and I don't think we can blame the bait dealers for marketing attractors that don't go on working. I've just opened Carp Fisher and checked the first bait advert I came to; there were 75 flavours listed! Now even if you go to the trouble of checking each flavour for instant reaction (as I think Rod does) there is no way you are going to have time to find out just what the effective life of each one is at the optimum attraction level. Understandably the most popular flavours are those that work best when you stick 5 mils of them in the bait and the indicator goes ''bang''. But how long does it keep going ''bang'' for? Not so long or we would all be up for't Drennan Cup every week.

So there was a problem. While the smell apparently represented a natural food smell something about many of the attractors made them unsatisfactory when they were used at the level that attracted best. Some flavours seem to work or be tolerated longer than others, and it is my experience, and that of many of my correspondents, that the flavour problem is exaggerated on waters which are high in the pH range.

But on some waters you want a pretty instant reaction, and a bait that goes on working. The bait will go on working if the food value is high enough, but how was it possible to increase the attractor level to pull the carp down quickly without damaging the long term effectiveness of the bait?

I went back to the old scientific papers, and some new ones that Martin Herbertson kindly supplied me with while he was researching the peanut problem. If carp were reacting to something that represented a smell they recognised what was it they instinctively reacted to? Their natural food scent? But even if it were possible to reproduce the natural food scent would the carp react to it if it was presented to them in hard round balls? Or was the association only valid when it involved them sticking their head in the silt and sucking, or stripping areas of weed for all the edible life it contained?

The research professors have identified the breakdown of many of the food smells that aquatic animals react to and have published their findings. But the individual substances are very hard to quantify when used in baits. Amino acids were used in the 70s but there was a feeling that the baits blew out too quickly (although that wasn't my experience with amino combinations in food baits). Was the quick blow out caused by baits of low food value, or because the amino combinations used were too limited and therefore not representative *enough*? According to the papers aminos and related substances are synergistic, which means that they are inter-dependent on each other for total effectiveness: in addition one or two of the most crucial substances aren't actually amino acids. A breakdown of the stimulatory core of a natural smell usually shows a minimum of seven or eight aminos and other substances in combination. Of the seven or eight some are more critical than others but they all contribute to the full effect.

I'll digress slightly there. When Rod's first book came out I found his chapter on amino acids stunning. I was getting results in practice but I'd got stuck in my theory because it seemed to me that aminos which attracted best were insoluble (hydrophobic) which did not make sense to me. Then Rod's book bore that out, and he had a far greater grasp of their workings than I had; he'd gone to a lot of trouble to find out about them. I started to look at aminos from a fresh angle after Rod's book – and it turned out to be the logical angle. If you forget bait and go back to nature solubility doesn't make much sense, does it? That is not to suggest that there *cannot* be recognition of something soluble, just to suggest that it cannot exist in water as a natural food source. If in doubt relate what you are trying to do to nature's design, which is the purest form of science. When you are dancing in the dark it is easier to look for the biochemical explanation of a relationship between two solids because it means you are on new territory and searching for something far beyond the lay man's vague conception of "smell".

There are a great many lads still doing battle with the science of all this, which is frustrating, but terrific. I think they know they will have to come to terms with water and ionisation to even start to understand it all but while they are beating their brains out perhaps they will look at something else, which might be the key to "recognition" – as opposed to superficial attraction. Hara theorises an amino acid receptor site, but doesn't follow through; I don't think that's enough. Look at the C and N terminals of the aminos, then reverse them at the receptor site, which is valid because enzymes are proteins. You've got a receptor and a transmitter at each site. Does that make under water smell three dimensional via the amino acid terminals and on through the peptide chains? And where does the hydrogen ion messenger originate, at the food source, or at the receptor site? That sounds impossible but then so does radar. Digression over; I hope the heads of the seekers after the truth ache as much as mine did after Rod's first book!

In 1982 I put together an additive based on various recognition factors, nutritional requirements and taste responses and the following year a number of us started to use it. The additive was added to, and the levels of the ingredients were periodically adusted against, the level of the reaction from the carp. The eventual outcome of the rather lengthy trials was the three Addits which Bill Cottam and I have put out and these add up to an additive I'm just not happy fishing without. I had two years on it, and two years off it for comparison purposes. I caught in the off years, but nothing like as consistently, and nothing like the same number of big fish. Apart from the odd freak giants I feel that big fish are big because they have a greater recognition of food sources than other fish and take advantage of it in their feeding. The ingredients we use encourage that recognition. It is my experience that good quality HNV baits result in the capture of bigger fish anyway but a handful of us have had a surprising number of big fish while using the Addits. In my first two years of using them I had more than twenty twenty plus fish from five different waters, with eight of them being over twenty-five pounds and four of them over thirty pounds. I can only put those results down to bait strength because I just ain't that good a carp angler (as Rod will happily tell you).

What we've actually done is go back to natural attractors: by using as many ingredients as possible at low level we've made the bait acceptable to the fish in the longer term while attaining a level of attraction/stimulation which might otherwise be inclined to shorten the life of the bait. The Addits are designed to be used together. They were originally one ingredient but were split into three because of the high cost of the combination. We use the Addits in conjunction with an oil, or a low level flavour, or a combination of both. Whatever you use avoid over-loading the bait.

I think I should perhaps make the point that amino acids are perfectly safe to use. Some time ago I read a statement in a carp book to the effect that amino acids are poisons; I think that must have been a misprint because the statement has no foundation in truth. The ingredients of these additives are listed on the labels, but we don't quantify them. What do you want, blood? (Don't answer that.) All bait ingredients are there for a purpose and you can only achieve consistent results by paying attention to details and grafting at what you are trying to do. There are anglers who are bait-conscious and others who are not, which is inevitable; bait tends to be a personal thing and many prefer the Russian roulette of a new smell or a new "will-it/won't it?" rig every other week, or month, or season.

There is almost certainly an element of chance in catching a particular big fish but consistently catching them is not down to luck or any big secret only the reader hasn't been allowed in on. When you walk on the banks of a big fish water you have one certain piece of knowledge working for you; big carp need good food. The relationship between carp and their food sources is an exact, partially proven science which can only operate at its optimum effectiveness when conditions are *right*. The minimum requirement for fulfilling the equation is that the angler has done everything humanly possible to make the bait right and to get the angling situation right. The effectiveness of the bait, the degree to which it will turn the fish on, will then depend on factors beyond your control. The condition of water varies, both in terms of pH (which is dependent on a number of variables anyway) and temperature. The really exceptional results occur when you get everything right and the conditions conspire to complete the equation for you. If you don't do your part, and keep doing it as a matter of course, those moments may pass you by.

In the seventies we learnt that a bait is a food. A great many anglers have started their carp fishing since the rig-smell revolution occurred and some of them seem to be concerned with everything *but* the content and quality of their base mix and the nutritional effectiveness of their attractors. Nature's design is functional and carp respond to a food source by instinct: nature has designed their system to identify food by smell, taste and after-response. If what they eat reacts wrongly with their system, either through not fulfilling them nutritionally, or because the taste is wrong, or because it disagrees with them in some other way then it will be unacceptable to them – sooner or later.

Earlier I referred to Rod's writings on amino acids in his first book. In the section on aminos he had this to say about food scents that advertise the bait as something it isn't:

"...it's like lying in bed and having your taste buds aroused by (the smell of) bacon and eggs, so you go rushing down to the kitchen only to find a round of toast."

But suppose the toast smells like bacon and eggs, and looks like bacon and eggs, but tastes like toast – soaked in vinegar. Ugh! It just doesn't bear thinking about, does it? I find catching carp difficult. If I'm using a bait the carp don't want I find it impossible. All other factors being equal the more the carp want your bait the better your chances of catching them.

REFERENCES

A typical set of references used to substantiate the findings following further researches

Adron, J.W. and Mackie, A.M., 1978. Studies on the chemical nature of feeding stimulants for rainbow trout, *Salmo gairdneri* Richardson, J. Fish Biol., 12: 303–310

Atema, J., Holland, K. and Ikehara, W., 1980. Chemical search image: olfactory responses of yellowfin tuna (*Thunnus albacares*) to prey odors. J. Chem. Ecol. (In press).

Bardach, J.E. and Case, J., 1965. Sensory capabilities of the modified fins of squirrel hake (*Urophycis chuss*) and sea robins (*Prionotus carolinus*) and *P. evolans*). Copeia, 1965, No. 2: 194–206).

Bardach, J.E. and Villars, T., 1974. The chemical senses of fishes. In: P.T. Grant and A.M. Mackie (Editors), Chemoreception in Marine Organisms. Academic Press, New York, pp. 49–104.

Carr, W.E.S., 1976. Chemoreception and feeding behavior in the pigfish, *Orthopristis chrysopterus*: characterization and identification of stimulatory substances in a shrimp extract. Comp. Biochem. Physiol., 55A: 153–157.

Carr, W.E.S. and Chaney, T.B., 1976. Chemical stimulation of feeding behaviour in the pinfish, *Lagodon rhomboides:* characterization and identification of stimulatry substances extracted from shrimp. Comp. Biochem. Physiol., 54A: 437-441.

Carr, W.E.S., Blumenthal, K.M. and Netherton, J.C. III., 1977. Chemoreception in the pigfish, *Orthopristis chrystopterus*: the contribution of amino acids and betaine to stimulation of feeding behavior in various extracts. Comp. Biochem. Physiol., 58A: 69–73.

Carr, W.E.S., Gondeck, A.R, and Delanoy, R.L., 1976. Chemical stimulation of feeding behavior in the pinfish, *Lagodon rhomboides*: a new approach to an old problem. Comp. Biochem. Physiol., 54A: 161–166.

Dempsey, C.H., 1978. Chemical stimuli as a factor in feeding and intraspecific behavior of herring larvae. J. Mar. Biol. Assoc. U.K., 58: 739–747.

Hara, T.J., 1975. Olfaction in fish. Prog. Neurobiol. (Oxford), 5: 271–335.

Hashimoto, Y., Konosu, S., Fusetani, N. and Nose, T., 1968. Attractants for eels in the extracts of short-necked clam. I. Survey of constituents eliciting feeding behavior by the omission test. Bull. Jpn. Soc. Sci. Fish., 34: 78–83.

Haynes, L.J., Sangster, A.W., Steven, D.M. and Thomas, S., 1967. Chemical factors inducing exploratory feeding behavior in fish. E.F.B.-inducing properties of marine invertebrates. Comp. Biochem. Physiol., 20:755–765.

Hidaka, I., Ohsugi, T. and Kubomatsu, T., 1978. Taste receptor stimulation and feeding behavior in the puffer, *Fugu pardalis*. I. Effect of single chemicals. Chem. Senses & Flavour, 3: 341–354.

Hodgson, E.S. and Mathewson, R.F., 1978. Electrophysiological studies of chemoreception in elasmobranchs. In: E.S. hodgson and R.F. Mathewson (Editors), Sensory Biology of Sharks, Skates, and Rays. Off. Naval. Res./Dept. of Navy, Arlington, Va., pp 227–267.

Holland, K., 1978. Chemosensory orientation to food by a Hawaiian goatfish (*Parupeneus prophyreus*, Mullidae). J. Chem. Ecol., 4: 173–186.

Ina, K. and Higashi, K., 1978. Survey of feeding stimulants for the sea bream (*Chrysophrys major*) (Feeding Stimulants for Fishes, Part I). J. Agric. Chem. Soc. Jpn., 52: 19–23

Kleerekoper, H., 1969. Olfaction in Fishes: Indiana U. Press, Bloomington, Indiana.

Kleerekoper, H. and Mogensen, J., 1963. Role of olfaction in the orientation of *Petromyzon marinus*. I. Response to a single amine in prey's body odor. Physiol. Zool., 36: 347–360.

Konosu, S., Fusetani, N., Nose, T. and Hashimot, Y., 1968. Attractants for eels in the extracts of short-necked clam. II. Survey of constituents eliciting feeding behavior by fractionation of the extracts. Bull. Jpn. Soc. Sci. Fish., 34: 84–87.

Mackie, A.M., 1975. Chemoreception. In: D.C. Malins and J.R. Sargent (Editors), Biochemical and Biophysical Perspectives in Marine Biology. Academic Press, London, pp. 69 – 105.

Mackie, A.M. and Adron, J.W., 1978. Identification of inosine and inosine-5'-monophosphate as the gustatory feeding stimulants for the turbot, *Scophthalmus maximum*. Comp. Biochem. Physiol., 60A: 79–83.

Ohsugi, T., Hidaka, I. and Ikeda, M., 1978. Taste receptor stimulation and feeding behavior in the puffer, *Fugu pardalis*. II. Effects produced by mixtures of constituents of clam extracts. Chem. Senses & Flavour, 3: 355–368.

Pawson, M.G., 1977. Analysis of a natural chemical attractant for whiting *Merlangius merlangus* L. and cod *Gadus morhua* L. using a behavioral bioassay. Comp. Biochem. Physiol., 56A: 129–135.

Sangster, A.W., Thomas, S.E. and Tingling, N.L., 1975. Fish attractants from marine invertebrates. Arcamine from *Arca zebra* and strombine from *Strombus gigas* Tetrahedron, 31: 1135–1137.

Sutterlin, A.M., 1975. Chemical attraction of some marine fish in their natural habitat. J. Fish. Res. Board Can., 32: 729–738.

Tester, A.L., van Weel, P.T. and Naughton, J.J., 1955. Response of tuna to chemical stimuli. Spec. Sci. Rep. No. 130 U.S. Fish Wildl. Serv. 52pp.

Tsushima, J. and Ina, K., 1978. Survey of feeding stimulants for carps, *Cyprinus carpio* (Studies on the feeding stimulants for fishes. Part III.) J. Agric. Chem. Soc. Jpn., 52: 225–229.

T.J. Hara – Chemoreception in Fishes

QUOTES

Whether a fish will eat a particular diet depends upon a number of factors: (1) nutritional status and health of the fish when it last ate, (2) water quality, and (3) nature of the test diet. Factors relating to test diet are texture, consistency, appearance, smell and taste.... The feeding behaviour of a fish under natural conditions influences the choice of bioassay and the ease with which its feeding stimulants can be identified.... In the case of a nocturnal, non-visual feeder, however the situation is rather more complicated, with an attractant as well as a feeding stimulant to be identified.

A.M. Mackie Institute of Marine Biochemistry, Aberdeen.

No chemical has been found to be more olfactorily stimulatory when determined electroyphysiologically than the amino acid.

Toshiaka J. Hara

Chapter 12

Snag Fishing '80

EARLIER, when discussing the location of carp, I mentioned that there are areas where carp will lie up in between feeding periods. These holding areas are often in the middle of snags, or in some place rarely visited by anglers. Although not feeding areas, fish can at times be caught from them, particularly in the period when carp first move in, fresh from feeding in other parts of the lake where food stocks are higher. It would seem that as the carp encounters few baits in these holding areas, any it does come across are likely to be regarded as safe. This being the case, almost any edible item can be used for hookbait. The food that will best behave in the manner you want it to, is the one to choose, regardless of the fact some baits will be "blown out" in the recognised feeding areas elsewhere.

The behaviour of fish in snag-ridden areas appears to be different from lake to lake. In some, once a fish has entered the area it lies up in one spot for hours. In others, particularly amongst fallen submerged trees, the carp slowly cruise back and forwards within the extremities of the snags. In waters containing lilies, it is common to see fish apparently sheltering from the sun under the same leaf for most of the daylight hours. Yet on many of the larger gravel pits, you can see groups of fish all basking in the sun out of the range of normal casting. Although catching fish in any of these circumstances will never be anything like as productive as fishing the feeding areas at feeding times, with the right tactics enough fish do come along to make the efforts worth while.

I would think the easiest of those circumstances in which to catch fish is when they slowly cruise around amongst snags. It is all the better if those snags are close to the bank. You should first get yourself into a position where you can watch the movements of the fish and be able to maintain adequate control of your tackle. As a fish approaches, a bait slowly sinking across its line of sight is always liable to be taken. I can think of no other food that will perform this function better than breadflake. It is best proffered on freeline tackle with the flake lightly squeezed so that it will sink. If the bait is likely to end up amongst the snags if not eaten, then it pays to use a light float, set just below the depth at which the fish are cruising. If a float is used, the choice of baits widens. Any paste can be made semi-buoyant by using sodium or calcium caseinate for a base. There are often convenient submerged boughs over which the carp cruise, and you may prefer to position a bait on such a bough, in order to intercept a moving fish. Cross-currents amongst the snags may be such that the weight of the bait itself is not enough to hold it in position. Obviously any additional item of tackle such as a conventional lead is liable to snag in such an area. The material to use here is plasticine, squeezed onto the line. It has enough weight to hold the bait in place, yet will fall off the line should

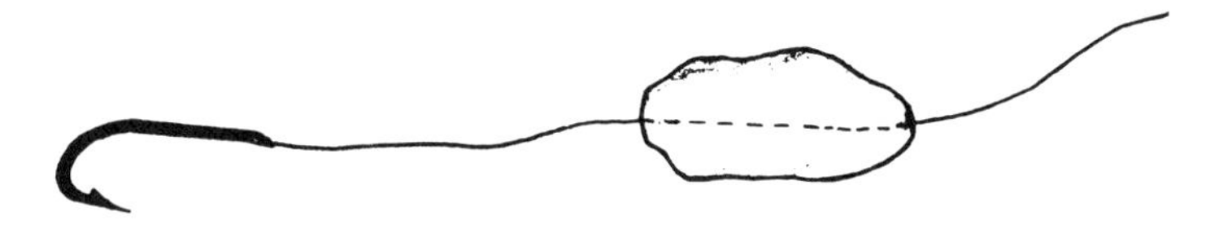

Plasticine squeezed direct on line

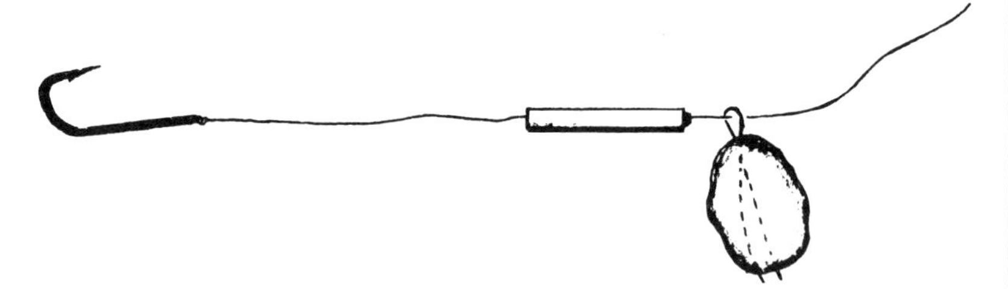

Link leger. Biro tube stop plugged with cocktail stick, plasticine weight squeezed on nylon link.

a fish be hooked. Should you deem it necessary to use a link legered bait, then a simple rig can be made by looping a length of line over the main line, and squeezing plasticine onto the two loose ends. This link leger is stopped at the required length from the hook by a small blob of plasticine.

The tackle combination I prefer to use amongst snags is a soft actioned rod between 1 1/4 to 1 1/2lbs test curve, with 11 or 13 lbs Sylcast line, and a Mustad low water salmon hook. The reel tension nut is screwed down as tight as possible so that not an inch of line is given. The fish can only move within the confines of the length of line cast out, while the soft rod cushions the power of the fish, preventing a break off. The reason why we can get away with the soft rod set up, even with snags in close proximity, is because the fish is not allowed to run. The power of a carp builds up the faster it swims. But in these circumstances the carp is not allowed to swim off. It is held hard and often turned over before it has a chance to build up speed. The fish seems to lose all equilibrium and not know which way to move. They are usually still splashing and turning over as they are being drawn over the net. If you give the fish the chance to get its head down, it will be in the snags before you can say "snapped up" – so don't give it the chance!

The landing net must be positioned before fishing commences, and be of such a size that it can be manoeuvred amongst the snags. It pays to tie up the net so that there is little mesh liable to get caught up, or to use the "pan" type of net, favoured by tench anglers. You should also ensure you have either positive foot or leg holds, as these hit and hold tactics can easily overbalance you.

Fish that lie up in one place for hours are much more difficult to tempt. A bait must be put into the carp's line of vision, and as close as possible, and left there. Occasionally, a fish will move up and suck the bait in. To keep the bait static in front of the fish, make use of any floating material there is, such as branches or lily leaves. It is possible sometimes to get the bait so close to the carp's mouth that, although the fish may have no intention of eating the bait, the action of the water as it breathes in and out can take a light bait into his mouth. You must be alert to this situation and strike accordingly, otherwise as the fish exhales the bait is just as likely to be blown out. I have in the past caught several fish in the shallows of the famous Woldale lake in Lincolnshire by doing just this. None of the fish, I believe, intentionally took the bait. In each case the bait was a single brandling, and when no natural surface material was available, a light float was used to position the bait.

Fish basking out in the open, often a long way from the bank, can sometimes be induced into taking a bait. The method is not far removed from that of inducing a non-feeding pike to snap at a plug, or from a line continually stripped past the nose of a trout. In both cases, it would seem that the fish just get angry at the intrusion of something continually going across their line of sight, eventually snapping at the offender. The method is to float a continuous stream of baits across the fish. When the baits eventually end up in the windward margins of the lake, they can be retrieved, and drifted back over the fish again. Obviously, a natural feeding spell will sometimes occur, and several baits be taken, while

Cold hands support my first Lincolnshire winter twenty

on other occasions I am sure the fish just snap at one bait with no real feeling towards feeding. Both floating particles and small conventional floaters are liable to work here, the tackle rigs being the same as other surface bait methods.

Many years ago, my friend Chris Yates and I experimented with fly fishing methods for carp. Chris had previously taken a few fish by surface-fishing artificial moths. The water in question was not very rich and I understand most surface material was inspected for its edibility. When we came to try the method on a very rich water, we were frustrated by fish inspecting the moths but not taking them. Often a fish would make as if to take the bait, only to come short, refusing it at the very last moment. I wrote to Dick Walker about this problem, and received an answer which had never occurred to Chris or myself. The answer was that the moth, not being an aquatic insect, went round and round in circles when it got caught in the surface film. This made it virtually impossible to present the artificial moth in a natural manner. Rather, an artificial representation of an aquatic insect was called for. It would be nice to say that having sorted out that problem, the method became a winner. Unfortunately activity to the correct flies was very little, conventional surface fishing methods being by comparison far more productive. I did however catch one carp, a fish which was showing no signs of feeding, by continually stripping a small, green nymph across its nose. Again, I feel it was a case of an "induced" take. There have been several instances of carp taking flies in recent years, usually when the angler has supposedly been fishing for trout. However as I have been reliably informed that many fell to "breadflies" and "sweetcorn flies", I would not wish the reader to overestimate the method.

So, when the fish are not feeding in the first place, remember that it could well be that the unconventional approach is the one most likely to succeed.

Chapter 13

Snag Fishing '88

There is very little I can add to this chapter apart from the tackle aspect. I would not now use the soft rods mentioned. Since the use of carbon and aramid fibres, we can now use a much more powerful rod yet still retain the through action which is so vital in 'hit and hold' situations. My choice would be a rod of about 2½ pounds test curve, the length determined by what room we have to play the fish in. With a 2½ pounds test curve rod it is possible to turn even the largest fish over. The 2½lb T.C. Horizon rod sold by Catchum Products, has had a detachable butt section designed to fit the top section. When fitted, it turns a 12 foot rod into an 8 foot rod, ideal where access is limited. The biggest battle is often with yourself. When a fish is fighting like mad to get its head down it is very easy to find yourself giving it line, which would be fatal. The reel clutch must be clamped down as hard as you possibly can. You only wind line in, you can't give any.

Wherever possible I would use dacron instead of monofil though in my opinion most of those sold at the moment for freshwater fishing are not powerful enough for snag fishing. All dacron loses some strength when wet and knotted so because I want a line that will break well over 15lbs, I go for braided lines designed for sea fishing. Sylcast produce a very good one but unfortunately it is white with a blue fleck in it. I'm not sure if it would scare fish off, but just for the confidence factor, I dye it with Dylon cold water dyes.

With a powerful rod and non-stretch line, the hook is going to come under incredible pressure. The strongest now available, a true beast of a hook, is one introduced by Kevin Nash and simply called the Snag Hook. It is extremely thick in the wire and needs careful honing with a file or stone, and although its use is strictly limited to snag fishing, in this situation there is no other hook to compare with it.

At the moment I am experimenting with lengths of braided kevlar. Unfortunately it does not have the limpness associated with other braided lines and I doubt if it could be used as hooklengths as I could see it cutting up a carp's mouth very easily. However it would be ideal used as a leader when fishing amongst lily pads, as it would easily cut through stems. At the moment of writing it is available in lengths of 10 metres in 6kg and 9kg breaking strains, but we will have to see if rod rings can stand up to it.

When fishing into lily pads from any sort of range the standard approach was to try and strike before the bobbin hit the top of the needle. However once the rod was picked up and the strike made, many fish made the lily roots or stems as the rod bent over. I have found that you are more likely to extract carp from lily beds if you leave the rod on the rests, with the clutch jammed hard down on the reel, as long as possible. With the line being pulled straight at the fish, no cushion is given by a bending rod. This brings the fish up to the surface, from where it can be bullied easily through the leaves, rather than the tough stems. Obviously to do this your rod rests must be firmly anchored. Non-twist buzzer bars with a screw at both ends to take a rod rest are your best option.

I must admit to having done little in recent years to induce takes, other than certain ground baiting techniques, but there are times when it is possible to induce a take. This was shown by the fluke capture I had from Savay lake. I was just packing up after a completely fruitless three day session when I saw a pike roll. For no other reason than wanting a bend in the rod, I cast a boilie just beyond where the pike had showed, and then began twitching the bait along the bottom, past its nose, hoping I could induce it to snap at the bait. After about the tenth twelve inch twitch, the rod hooped over. Expecting it to be a pike, hopefully hooked in the scissors, I played it very carefully indeed, and it was some considerable time before I had it roll in front of my outstretched net. Imagine my surprise when the culprit turned out to be a 27lb mirror. I have since tried out the technique quite a few times in the same swim. The only other fish I have taken being perch, and only two of those, although on lots of occasions perch have followed the twitched boilie.

Something which has really surprised me in the recent pressured years is the times carp stay in snags even during the hours of darkness. In previous times I believed carp just entered snags during the day, to keep out of the way, leaving them at night when they felt safe. This is clearly not the case nowadays, pressure is just as likely to drive carp into snags during night-time hours, as it is in the day. Walk around any hard fished water containing bankside snag trees after dark and shine a torch into the water amongst the snags. I think you, like me, will be amazed at the amount of carp you see. However it is a much more difficult operation getting those fish out in the darkness and not one that I would recommend.

A very recent innovation that is a great help in snaggy situations is the PVA tube. When dropping a bait between branches it is preferable if there are no protruding objects on the terminal tackle, be they lead, hair rig or stringer. Using the tube, the complete terminal tackle can be encased, thereby leaving nothing to catch on the branches.

The same method is also ideal for fishing right in the middle of lily beds. In this situation, it also pays to add a number of free baits into the tube along with the tackle. The extra weight just makes sure that the tackle gets down to the bottom before the PVA starts melting. Leads with a hole through the centre, such as the Kevin Nash Cruise, or E.T. Comet leads, are preferable in both cases to a regular swivelled lead, as they are less likely to catch up during the playing of fish.

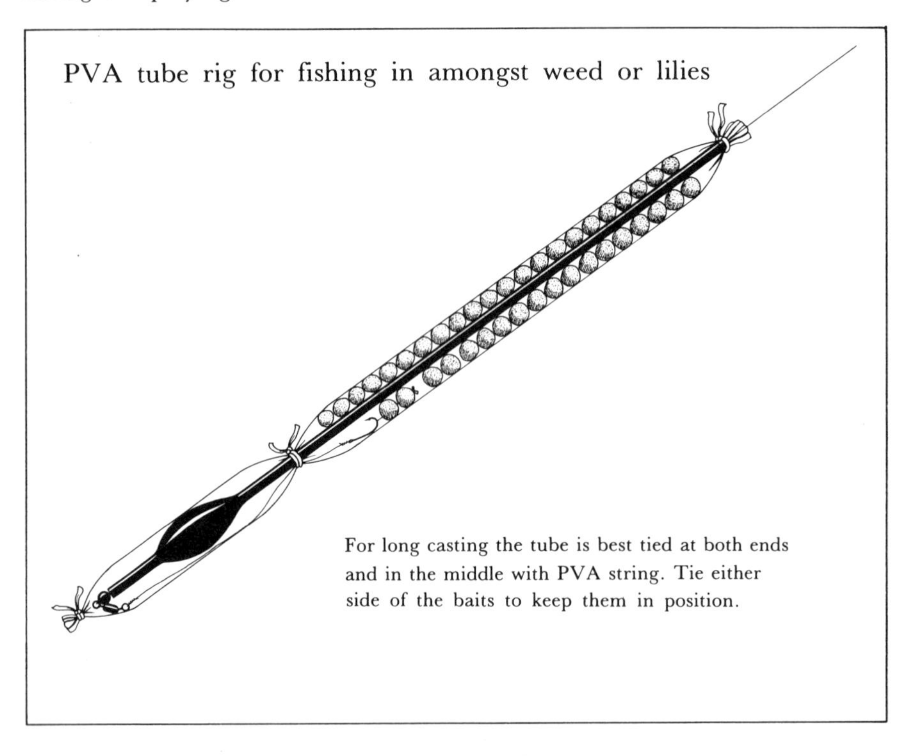

A bait twitched along the bottom induced this fish to take

Chapter 14

The Unexplained '80

HOPEFULLY by this stage of the book you will have picked up points you can apply with a beneficial effect to your own fishing. Logical thinking and the technical application of ideas, however, are no guarantee that the individual will be successful. The angler's complete approach, both physical and mental, will also help to determine this. Dick Walker's famous quote, "Study to be quiet", holds as true today as it ever did. The aim is to become one and part of the landscape. The angler should also try to tune his mind to an underwater wavelength, in an effort to understand just what governs the life cycle in that environment.

Having advocated the above, you may be surprised when I say that once all the thinking, planning, preparation and casting of the baits has been done, your mind should be turned off completely from the job at hand. Everything has been thought out to the best of your ability, so once the baits are out, just let things happen. Watch the water birds, study the trees or lakeside vegetation. There's time to get stuck into that book you always meant to read, or if you're artistic get out the sketch book. Do anything but mentally try to speed up events. Shut fishing from your mind completely. Just let it happen.

It sounds daft, it sounds illogical, it's inexplicable, but it works. Think about the times when you've had a run out of the blue, whilst your mind has been elsewhere. Then think about the times when everything has seemed to go right, when you've been all primed up for action, yet blanked. I think you'll find it works.

Posing with a Redmire 32.8

"Oops"

The Unexplained '88

It's definitely a weird one this. Sometimes you need to shut off, sometimes you need to tune in. I believe there are times when our excitement is overpitched. Overcast, flat calm conditions, thunderstorms, times when you can actually feel the electricity in the air. You see the ripples as a fish approaches your bait. Your body and mind are highly tuned, tense, when suddenly the fish bolts away for no apparent reason. I can't explain it and there is no scientific evidence to back me up, but I believe somehow your mind has tuned in with the carp, some sort of electricity, radio waves, or vibrations have been transmitted by you, and picked up by the carp. It senses danger, panics and swims away fast.

I know at such times, when the air is tense, I have to switch off. Just put your mind away from the carp you hope to catch. Make a cup of tea, or make a meal. Read a book or magazine, it doesn't matter as long as your mind is elsewhere. Then it will happen for you. It may well be that the longer you fish for carp, the more acute these senses become. Many readers may not yet have experienced this phenomenon, but keep at it and you surely will.

In opposite conditions, I don't think it applies, simply because there is not that energy in the air. It's hard enough just to tune in as to where the carp are, let alone get on the same wavelength. During these conditions, I find that the harder I try, the better I do. The carp aren't going to pick up your frequency because the channels are not open. With experience I think you learn what to do in a given situation, so just be alive to it when it happens to you.

Chapter 15

When It All Comes Right '80

THE following incident took place one Friday morning in August at the legendary Redmire pool.

The alarm clock at my side shrieked its morning welcome. It was five a.m. Peering out from over the ground sheet, I could see the lake was shrouded in mist. Cobwebs hung down from the lip of the brolly, glistening dew hanging limp from the frail tapestries. It was a cold dawn. I filled up the kettle, and while it was slowly boiling, climbed a tree to survey the lake. My view was restricted to only a few yards because of the mist, and no moving fish could be seen. I had the feeling there would be little feeding that morning. In one way, I was glad of the mist. It would enable me to bait up my swim whilst preventing any nearby fish being alarmed by my presence. I baited up with approximately four pounds of Chilean hemp, firing it in a direct line out to a distance of thirty yards. At this point, the lake bed dropped off into a central channel. Any carp feeding between myself and the edge of the channel had to come across that line of bait. I had been carrying out this procedure for the two previous days, but up till then only two smallish carp had rewarded my efforts. I was pretty certain that there was a fair amount of that bait still present in the swim.

I re-baited my three rods, casting them at ten yard intervals along the line, and sat back to drink my tea and make breakfast. As I sat beneath the brolly eating my breakfast, dew started dripping quickly from the rim. A lightish breeze had sprung up, chasing the mist across the water. I was thinking how good the bacon tasted when the buzzer sounded to the centre rod and the silver paper indicator glided towards the butt ring. I try to be calm in such situations, yet I always react the same. I leapt to my feet, knocking my tea over in the process. Making a conscious effort to calm myself, I let the line pull really

Sometimes it all comes right

right across the surface before bending the rod into the fish. During the ensuing fight, my mate Chris Yates, fishing on the opposite side of the lake, saw the action and set off around the lake to lend a hand. He arrived just in time to net a common carp of approximately fifteen pounds. Now such a fish would be highly regarded on many a lake. Unfortunately due to the size of fish present in Redmire, such a fish is a disappointment. I returned it without weighing it.

The wind which had blown up had increased, probably now reaching force three or four. It carried with it intermittent broken clouds, which every few minutes masked the sun. The time was now 6.30 a.m. The centre rod was rebaited and cast back to its former position. I put the kettle back on while Chris and I discussed what the day held for us. Chris is a great bloke to have along on a fishing trip, always filled with such optimism that it can't help but rub off on you. I tend to be more of a realist than Chris, usually knocking down logically his optimistic forecasts, but this particular morning his optimism definitely lifted me. For reasons I can't explain, it felt right. I was in the process of handing Chris his cup of tea when once more a buzzer sounded, this time to the nearest, right hand, rod. Once more my pretence of calm deserted me, the tea finishing up down Chris's thigh, accompanied by a high-pitched scream. The line was belting out so fast I feared to put the pick-up in, in case I might be broken up. However all held as the pick-up went in and I gingerly bent the rod. On feeling the hook the fish set off on one tremendous run, not stopping until it reached the dam, which was approximately sixty yards from my pitch, about a third down the length of the pool. The fish made several more equally impressive runs, and I began to worry that my heart would not hold out, before it was safely netted by Chris. This particular fish was one we had often observed, its immense length giving rise to estimates of thirty pounds-plus. However it had little girth to it, but at 27 3/4lb was in no way a disappointment. The fish was a true leather, the intermittent sun brilliantly highlighting its reddish brown hue.

After putting the fish in a sack we just sat back, mentally exhausted from the unpredictability of the fight. I was elated yet felt very tired. Such a fish doesn't come one's way too often. I put the kettle back on while we enthused over aspects of the fight. Chris remarked that is was a pity not to have kept the first double-figure common, and how they'd have made a splendid photograph together. He also insisted that should I catch another fish, and that whatever its size I should keep it to photograph along with the leather. I replied by saying that two fish in a session was more than one could really ask for, and that three was just plain greedy. When you embark upon a session at Redmire, you hope to catch a fish, without really expecting to catch one. When you do get one, and a good one at that, a weight seems to be lifted off your shoulders. It had all left me decidedly light-headed. I felt as if I were tempting providence as once more I handed Chris his cup of tea. I was! This time the buzzer sounded to the far rod, again all calm deserted me, once more the tea landed in Chris's lap. This fish must have heard Chris talking and for some reason felt the need to oblige. It proved to be another double-figure common scaling 15 1/2 pounds. Chris no longer felt the need for a cup of tea and tore round to his swim, hell bent on joining in on this feeding spree.

It would be easy to say that everything that took place that morning was the result of calculated moves. It wasn't, it just happened. I never in a million years expected to take another fish; I didn't even think about one, I was over the moon with what I'd already caught. Yet for some reason I decided to rebait the swim. Out went another four pounds of hemp in a straight line, the rods again being cast out at ten yard intervals along that line. They were cast out and forgotten about. A glance at the clock showed it to be 7.30 a.m. I was tired and very happy as I settled back on the bedchair and drifted off into the land of dreams. Barely had my eyes closed when once more a buzzer erupted. There was no tea to knock over this time, instead I leapt up with such force that the impact of my head on the brolly rim tore it from its anchorage. On feeling the hook, this fish headed directly for me, surfacing practically at my feet. At this distance I was able to identify the fish and without doubt it was the well loved, often caught "38", as we in the syndicate called it. "38" was just a name it had been given, in actual fact the previous two times it had been landed it had tipped the scales around the forty pound mark! However fate didn't have that fish lined up for me. It turned and headed for the centre of the lake and with very little pressure being applied to the fish the line parted. I know it was too much for me to expect to catch that fish on top of what I had already caught, but I was in no state to see reason. I was sick and in a fit of temper threw my rod away into the bushes. I can take it when I've made some mistake on my part, but in this case I'd done everything right.

I was still lying on the bed feeling sorry for myself when I heard a commotion on the opposite side of the lake. Forcing myself to take notice, I peered out through the bankside cover to see Chris net a nice common. Somehow that event brought me together, there I was feeling sorry for myself, when Chris had been watching me all morning getting stuck into fish. When Chris called out the fish weighed 23 pounds, I was not only pleased, I felt relieved that a burden of selfishness had left me. I was back with my feet on the ground. Able to see reason once more, I fished the discarded rod out from the bushes. On checking the ten pound breaking strain line on a balance it proved to be breaking at around five pounds. Somehow the line had deteriorated overnight. Twenty or so yards of line were pulled off and discarded before I was confident that the remaining line broke at its stated breaking strain. The rod was soon fitted up with the appropriate terminal tackle and bait and cast back to its former central position in the line. As I was attaching the silver paper the indicator on the near side rod leapt for the butt ring. This time I was so close to the rods nothing could go wrong. After a short very fast-moving battle another double-figure common lay enfolded in the net.

It was at this point that it occurred to me that there were still more fish to be caught. Bubbles kept bursting periodically all along the line of bait. Somehow I felt that even more bait was needed to keep those feeding fish in the swim. Out went another two pounds of hemp along the ground bait line. For ten minutes or so I knelt alongside the rods, expecting a run at any moment. It didn't happen. Once more I settled back on the bedchair trying to convince myself that I'd caught as much as any man could hope for, that it was sheer greed that made me think there was a chance of more fish. Once more I lit the stove and made the tea. Putting it to my lips completed the formula, and the central rod was again in action. The strike brought entirely the same result as before as the fish ran directly towards me. Again the fish turned and the line parted. The most sickening aspect of it all was that I am convinced it was the same fish as before, the 38. No great fit of temper resulted from this incident. I merely jumped up and down on the rod!

With everything off my chest and all thought of fish off my mind, I climbed into the sleeping bag. A glance at the clock showed it was 8.45. I couldn't sleep as my mind was too full of the events that had happened. Surely an egg sandwich would pull me round? With the fat just getting nice and hot and the egg nice and crispy, a buzzer sounded. I tried to ignore it, but it wouldn't go away! As I approached the rod, I noticed Chris looking out from his pitch opposite. He too had heard the buzzer. In went the pickup and I let the line tighten right to the reel before I pulled the rod round. What happened next I have never seen before or since. The carp leaped from the water like a salmon shaking sea-lice from its back. I swear it came a full three feet clear of the water. It was a magnificent spectacle. Unfortunately the energy expended in performing this feat left the carp very little in reserve to fight with, and after less than five minutes it was in the net. What a gorgeous, beautifully marked fish it proved to be – a mirror carp with scales like gold sovereigns, it pulled the scales down to 26 1/2 pounds. As quick as the fight had been, on seeing the fish hooked, Chris had somehow got round in time to net it for me.

At that moment all the blank hours, all the hundreds of miles I'd travelled to get to the pool, the financial hardship I'd suffered through taking time off work, seemed worthwhile. Such compensation was more than I could have wished for. I didn't feel the need to catch other fish, in fact it didn't even occur to me to rebait the rod and cast it out. I just wanted to relax and bathe in my elation for a while.

The long hours spent sleeping on the bankside living on tinned or fried food eventually take their toll of the human body. An irresistible urge came over me to answer nature's call. About fifteen yards away from my swim, behind a high mass of brambles and nettles, the syndicate members had built a toilet. I was soon installed in it, oblivious to everything but the job in hand. I was aroused from this semi-hypnotic state by a funny sort of repetitive hammering sound. It seemed ages before it occurred to me what it might be. Leaping out of the toilet, I caught sight of the silver paper indicator hammering hell out of the remaining, forgotten, rod which I'd left out. The line was tearing off the spool at such a rate it had jumped over the buzzer-head antenna. With my usual calm and grace I rushed for the rod. Unfortunately, I had forgotten that my trousers were still round my ankles. This deposited me into the pile of bramble and nettles. However that fish meant to have the bait. Despite the time it took to extract myself painfully from the undergrowth and redistribute my attire, the line was still belting out. On feeling the hook, the fish surfaced by the dam wall, sixty yards away up the pool to my right.

That fish gave me the most enthralling fight of all. On the long line, it kited into a bay further up on the right hand side of the lake, and out of my sight. In doing so it also took the line through a bush on the corner of the bay. There was nothing else I could do but wade in to try to remove the line from the bush and get a more direct pull on the fish.

So for the second time that morning, down went my trousers, off went my shoes and socks, and in I marched. Somehow I managed to remove the line from the bush, and with constant pressure forced the fish to move out into the centre of the pool. At this point my feet came across an underwater snag, a long length of trailing tree root. If I had gone back to my position on the bank, that snag could have been a problem, so I decided to play the fish out from where I stood, keeping my foot hard down on the tree root to prevent any mishaps. I conveyed my thoughts to Chris, who threw the landing net out to me. Eventually I netted the fish and it was a very happy man who waded his way back to the bank, his prize in hand. Setting foot back on terra firma, I was shocked to find my legs covered in leeches. I felt like Humphrey Bogart in "The African Queen". The carp turned out to be a mint-conditioned shining common carp, its weight 22 1/4 pounds. If I were a card player, I'd think that I'd a very good hand that morning. Three twenties, one of each, a leather, a mirror and a common, with a trio of doubles to back them up. Sometimes fate looks kindly on us all.

Chapter 16

Carp in Winter '80

THE reader will soon become aware that my views often disagree with previous thinking about winter carp. The reason for this is, I believe, that most angling writers on the subject have been based in the southern counties and their fishing has been done in these areas. Since the furthest south I've fished in winter is Norfolk, with many more hours spent on Lincolnshire waters, the lower air and corresponding water temperatures would seem to explain these differences. From observation of the television weather charts I've noticed that temperatures throughout the winter months in Lincolnshire and in the southern counties average a three degree difference. Bearing these differences in mind, I'll leave the reader to decide which approach best suits his own waters. Any theories or beliefs I hold are all the product of my own experience.

When deciding on a particular lake to fish in winter, I drop my sights slightly. Where my approach in summer is to find a water holding very large carp, irrespective of numbers, in winter I pick a well stocked water with plenty of double figure fish and a chance of something larger. The fact is that carp feed much less in winter, therefore the larger the head of carp the more chance of a fish feeding.

A lot of waters holding large heads of carp have poor natural food supplies. In some cases the lakes themselves are not naturally rich and are therefore unsuitable for the stocking of carp, while in other lakes through careless over-stocking the supplies of food are exceeded by the carp's appetite. Either way, these waters are termed as "hungry", and these are the ones most likely to provide consistent success in winter. We should also be looking for a lake of manageable acreage, as it will soon become evident that it is preferable to have all areas within casting distance of some part of the bank. All the lakes I fish have areas of deep water in excess of fourteen feet, so it is debatable as to whether or not my approach would succeed in predominantly shallow waters in winter. The following is an account of what I believe happens in my own waters in winter, and the methods I have found the most successful.

In the early weeks of October the carp feed heavily, an act I liken to squirrels feeding up for winter. They are at this time probably at their most catchable, due to a slow decrease in natural food stocks. The main feeding areas are the same as the summer ones. The last two weeks of October and the first two weeks of November still find the carp in the same haunts, but feeding gradually slows down. This is because the falling temperatures have a slowing down effect of the carp's metabolism. By the middle of November, reeds and other bank-side vegetation decline into decay. This in turn gives off methane which I presume the carp find obnoxious. This at least would seem the most likely explanation for an exodus from many margin swims. Water temperatures at this time in these swims are generally in the lower forties fahrenheit.

When first presented with the problem of where the fish had gone, I was at a loss. It was only through sustained fishing of different areas that fish were eventually located. In all the waters, each area now inhabited by fish has certain common features. The first thing that becomes evident in mid-winter is that holding areas and feeding areas become one and the same. The carp only feed in very short spells, and they don't appear to want to move far for their food. In each water I have found that the carp have moved into areas deeper than the average depth for the water, but not necessarily the deepest water in the lake. For example in my main Lincolnshire water the average winter depth is ten feet, while the carp hole up in an area having a depth of fifteen feet. In two Norfolk waters the average depth is around fourteen feet whilst the carp prefer a depression twenty feet deep.

While it is fair to say that many waters hold some of these deeper holes, not all hold fish. Fortunately another common feature has arisen in each productive swim. That characteristic is that each swim rarely receives any direct sunlight. The swim remains in a virtual shadow or twilight state. In some cases this arises because of the position of trees around the bank, swims on the west side being protected by trees on the east bank and the low angle of the sun in the morning, while bushes and high cliff-like banks protect them in the afternoon. Another swim has a large buoy anchored in it, again protecting much of it from direct sunlight. The added effects of perpetual twilight and deep water combine to give almost constant temperatures at this time of year. Those temperatures are also for the most part a degree or two up on the shallow areas. The fish have been found to remain in these areas until late February, in some cases well into March. As to why they move out then, there are two possible explanations. The first is the gradual rise in temperatures, the second the slow build up towards spawning. By that, I mean that greater food intake is needed during the gestation period.

Having located the fish, the angler then has to decide how to catch them. To jump the bait issue for a moment, it soon becomes evident that in winter feeding spells are very short. In my waters they are also very predictable. Once the timing of these spells is found out, you can almost set your watch by them. The length of the feeding depends very much on the weather and for the most part the spells seldom exceed thirty minutes, even in perfect conditions. An hour's continuous feeding is exceptional.

In my Norfolk waters, feeding is restricted in normal circumstances to two sessions. These are an evening spell starting between two to two and a half hours after dark, and a morning spell within an hour of dawn. Occasionally in perfect conditions there is also feeding any time between the hours of one and two a.m. Although the timing is different on my main Lincolnshire water, it is just as predictable, being within half an hour either side of dawn and within an hour of midnight. To the angler with the right lake close at hand this predictability is a great boon, because he can fish at the productive times and cut out a lot of blank fishing.

My idea of perfect conditions is totally different to that of other writers on the subject. The general consensus of opinion is that calm, mild, overcast conditions are the most productive. It is my belief that more winter fish are reported in such conditions because more anglers are out on the banks at such times. They are only benefitting from something that is there all the time in winter. If more anglers ventured out in really howling gales in winter, I believe lots more fish would be produced. If there is a really heavy wind on, it doesn't matter if that wind is cold, warm, dry or wet, since I have found the carp will feed well. It's as if they need a kick up the backside to get them moving. Maybe shallow waters don't respond the same. I don't know, again it's up to the individual to decide.

We have to take into account the shortness of the feeding spells when deciding on which type of bait to use. I don't believe the carp feeds to saturation point in winter. Its metabolism is slower, its energy output less and food is taken just in sufficient quantities to tick over. There are exceptions to this, waters where fish are starving and where any food present will be eaten, but I have no interest in such waters as they are unlikely to provide me with the chance of a decent fish. Bearing in mind the need for less food, what bait do we offer? It is my belief that paste baits satisfy a carp's appetite sooner than do particle baits. In winter the consumption of two or three paste baits per session could be enough. The angler here is faced with a dilemma. If any ground baiting is undertaken, a fish may well be satisfied before it comes across the hook bait. If only hook baits are used, then the angler is counting upon them being found before the short feeding spell ends. With that in mind great care must be taken to ensure each hook-bait is as visible as possible, contains ingredients that will help the carp be aware of the bait, and is virtually immune to other species. The bait must also be cast bang on the feeding area. If ground baiting is undertaken, amounts should be kept to an absolute minimum.

Concerning the colour of the bait and with regard to its visibility, I'll come to this later as this is a broad theme covering both pastes and particles. The bait should however be made buoyant enough to prevent sinking into whatever type of bottom is being fished on. To make the carp aware of the bait some kind of attractor or smell is needed. On my lakes I have not found that amino acid mixes work well in winter. I believe the lack of success is because the pH of waters in winter fluctuates due to varying acidic substances given off in the process of decomposition. This in turn renders the amino acids unstable

The product of striking the slightest knock at the rod-top

and often not attractive. Attractors I have found to work well in winter are natural meat and spice extracts. I don't believe the basic mix of the bait makes much difference at this time, as long as it is easily palatable and easily digested. For me a simple base of one third vegetable protein, one third whole meal flour and one third soya husk has been successful. A close friend of mind has also scored heavily with a straightforward sausage meat and rusk mix. I'm inclined to believe that almost any food the carp comes across in midwinter will be eaten. The secret is to make sure the carp finds it.

The same principles apply to particle baits in winter, but they have however one advantage. The sheer mass of a one inch diameter paste bait is the equivalent of fifteen or twenty haricot-sized beans, or half a dozen butter beans. Being able to spread a number of baits around helps the visual aspect, whilst at the same time staying within the realms of the carp's appetite. Bearing this in mind light ground baiting is beneficial. There are no hard and fast rules on the quantities used. Much depends on how many carp the angler expects to have feeding in his swim. I'm inclined to think that an individual carp only feeds every other day or so, but because a number of fish occupy the same swim and feed on different days, this gives the impression of continuous day-to-day feeding. I therefore bait up on the principle that only two or three fish are feeding at any one time. To this end four catapult loads (or the equivalent if a dropper is being used) is enough, whatever particle bait is used, as the total mass will remain the same. Should conditions be such that a longer feeding spell may be thought to be on the cards, then I ground bait again after a fish has been caught, but with half the original amount.

Although particles have the edge on visual appeal, I also do everything possible to enhance their flavour, just to make sure that they're found. To do this, any sauce or soup used in the initial cooking of the bait is made extra concentrated. When the baits are fully cooked all remaining liquid in the pan is retained and frozen. This bait-flavoured soup is then taken on the fishing session, frozen pieces of it being catapulted in amongst the ground bait. As it slowly melts, it gives off the bait's flavour, enhancing the effect.

Just what colours are the most visual in deep water is debatable. Up to two seasons ago, I stayed with the warm colours, mainly yellows and pinks, and I caught fish. Then a television programme made me change my views. It was a Jacques Cousteau feature, during which he explained that deep water and icebergs always appear blue due to their density. Only the short blue rays of the spectrum could penetrate them. This set me thinking that it could be that a blue bait would be the most visual in the deep water swims of winter. Since that time I have had a great deal of success on both particle and paste baits dyed blue. I don't know if the theory holds true, but I do know that the baits work.

I know a lot of anglers set up for small twitch bites in winter. I myself have not found the need; runs have been very confident indeed, only slower than those of summer due to the slower metabolism of the carp. With both paste baits and particles I have found it beneficial to fish with the pickups in the open position. Due to the fact that weed growth is unlikely to present many problems, the angler may decide he can get away with using a finer line than he would in summer. I would not argue with that, whilst at the same time preferring not to do so myself. I use exactly the same line, hooks and terminal rigs as I do in summer and I don't think any decrease in runs has resulted.

Carp fishing in winter, as at all times, is to be enjoyed. The angler cannot do this if he is cold and uncomfortable, so be well prepared. Luckily with the bivouacs, insulated suits, snow boots and so on which are now available, this no longer a problem. So prepared the angler can enjoy uncrowded fishing and thrill to the touch of a cold water carp. There is nothing like being out on a warm humid night in June, but then again there is a beauty to be found in the harsh bleak landscape of winter.

A magic moment with a cold water thirty

These fish came as the lake started to ice up

Chapter 17

Carp in Winter '88

My first reaction on reading through my old thoughts on this subject were "How things have changed". On a second read, "Not a lot has changed". Confused hey? So am I. Well the general behaviour of carp from October onwards, I still go along with. The statement that it is evident that holding areas and feeding areas become one and the same can be true (my experience at that time led me to believe this) in some waters, but is definitely not the case in all waters.

Carp do hold up in relatively small areas, often nose to tail, often forming a circle. This fact can be verified by drifting a boat over any carp water with reasonable clarity. In waters with a small population of carp, it is not unusual to find every fish in one group. In other lakes often quite large ones, the fish are more likely to be confined into more than one group. Four is the most I know of, this being observed in a well stocked thirty acre pit.

Where I have changed my opinion slightly is that I used to believe holding areas were chosen not only because of consistent temperatures in that area, but also because food was at hand. This is definitely not the case in many lakes. In some waters members of a shoal have been seen to break off and travel quite a distance before going down to feed. In a lot of cases this feeding is done in very shallow water. Now while for the main part most of these observations have been made early in the afternoon when the sun has been at its highest, and consequently water temperatures also in the shallows, I have also observed the same, i.e. fish visiting and feeding in very shallow water during the first hour of darkness, a time when the temperature was plummeting in such depths, all of which leads me to assume that carp know very well where the food is, and that they are prepared to move quite a distance for it, when they feel the urge to feed. The holding area is where they spend most of their time and the prime consideration on that choice is, putting it in human terms, being comfortable, which I take as being an area of consistent temperature. But when a carp wants to feed, temperatures don't come into it. They know where the food is and they'll get it whatever the weather. So on this point, to cut a long story short, search out the feeding areas, and once you find one, it is likely to remain one throughout winter. However that spot is just as likely to be a shallow area as it is a deep one. From this we may be able to deduct that if a holding area can be found close to shallows, rather than fishing the holding area itself, fishing the shallows might be more productive. It might be worth also pointing out that in a number of lakes carp have been observed feeding beneath ice i.e. in shallow water! Bear in mind that a shallow area is just as likely to be a gravel bar or plateau as it is a complete area of lake.

Just how much do carp feed in winter? My thoughts on this are outlined in "The Carp Strikes Back", but to reiterate I believe that because in winter not all carp have the feeding urge on the same day, that maybe only two or three might feed at the same time, but as such are easily captureable once the feeding areas have been defined, we tend to get a false picture of winter carp feeding. We may hit the occasional bonanza and land four maybe even five fish, but I would be not at all surprised if that was the total of fish feeding at that time. Most days some fish, maybe only one will feed, but it is open to capture as easy as that. It does not mean all the population of carp are feeding. This in some ways shows how winter hot spots can be so well defined. The carp know where the food is, that is where they'll visit. The angler fishing there hooks or catches whatever amount of fish are feeding there on the day, while anglers around him catch nothing. The few fish with the feeding urge, wanted to be where they wanted to be, and nothing was going to change that.

One of my friends, lucky devil, has a water where he can observe carp all winter long, and where individual fish, because of their size and scaling can be recognized. In his lake the carp hole up in one area, but choose to feed in another shallower spot. He reports known fish visiting the feeding area about three times a week. By the end of January those fish may be seen something like every seven to nine days. The interesting thing from my part was that not all of the fish fed as regularly as this, some would only occasionally be spotted throughout the winter. However the regular feeders on the whole were the larger fish known to inhabit the lake. One smaller double figure fish did muck up the whole picture. It fed practically every day throughout the winter. I might also add that the holding area in this lake is not at all like the first ones I found as mentioned in the last chapter, i.e. perpetual twilight. The area in this water is no more than a clear patch amongst decaying weed, out in the centre of the lake with no cover whatsoever.

I have certainly had to revise my thoughts on the best methods to catch carp in winter due to the success of certain individuals in the Colne Valley area. One group of anglers found a holding area in a certain lake and literally filled it in with bait, using anything from five hundred to two thousand boilies each session, in the middle of winter! The fact that they were very successful indicates that they had come up with a winning method. However there must be hundreds of anglers who have filled in a swim in winter and had no success. The difference here being that these fish being in a natural holding area did not have to move for their food. By regularly fishing and baiting in the one spot, they turned a holding area into a feeding area. I am pretty sure this was the case because those fish had been known to inhabit their particular area for several seasons, but conventional winter carp fishing using very little bait had failed to produce. I think it is debateable though as to whether this approach would work on every carp water.

Most of the successful winter carp anglers I know use very few, sometimes no free offerings, apart from those attached by a stringer to the hookbait. This being in line with the general thinking that a feeding spell in winter is very short with little food consumed. There are always exceptions, particularly where hungry waters are concerned. Two friends of mine have had tremendous captures of doubles by heavy baiting with peanuts and tiger nuts, neither of which are recognised as good winter baits.

My personal approach nowadays is to use much smaller baits than I would do in summer. By using several small stringers off the hook, threaded with little 10 mm particle boilies, I can use the same amount of food weight wise, that I would using large boilies, and at the same time create a much more visual image to the fish. The point being that during a short feeding spell we don't want the carp to miss our bait (see diagram).

There is no doubt in my mind whatsoever as to the time we are most likely to catch a really big fish. That time being during the months of December and January. It would appear that in most cases the peak winter weight mirrors the weight of a fish at spawning. Why fish are at their peak weight in the middle of winter is probably down to several factors. The first being that they have had time to get back in condition after the rigours of spawning in the summer. It could be that good food (mussels, snails, shrimps etc) is easier to find, due to the absence of weed beds. Oxygen content is also likely to be higher which could well lead to better utilisation of the food intake. Add to this the heavy squirrel like feeding of October and early November and it is easy to see them being at their peak in December.

The really interesting thing is that the larger fish in a given lake are very likely to be caught at this time. Maybe the reason why they are large fish in the first place is because they feed over a longer period than their brethren.

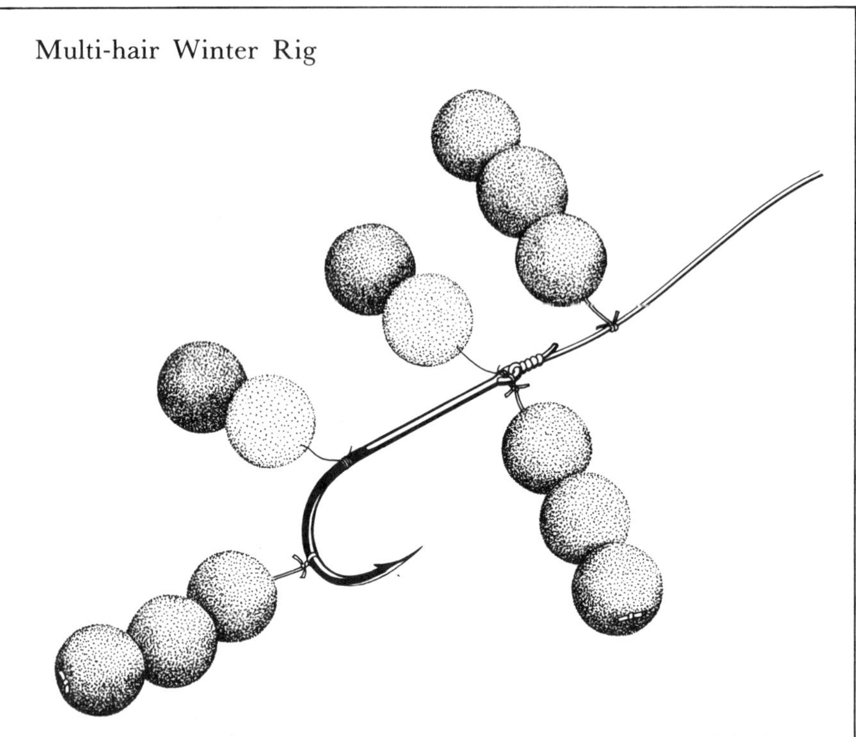

The hairs with 3 mini boilies are made from microthread PVA. The true hairs have a buoyant boilie nearest the hook and a regular boilie on the oustside

In years gone by I used to think that young growing fish required the most food intake. I now think the opposite. Big fish have to feed more to sustain their weight. Some of the largest carp to come from Lake Cassein for instance, are also the ones which have been caught the most. One specimen currently weighing in the middle sixties, has since its first capture at fifty four pounds in May 1985, been on the bank at least twenty times, and I would suspect there were many more times its capture had not been reported. Having stated my belief that big fish feed the most, for the life of me, I cannot explain why some big carp rarely get caught in the summer months. The only possible explanation is that they are feeding entirely on natural food stocks throughout this time.

Regards the subject of whether one type of bait is better than another in winter, I admit to being slightly confused myself. Theoretically a carp has decided it wants some food intake, and it knows where it will find it. As such anything palatable should suffice. Flavours, attractors, colours etc, are only there to make sure that the carp finds the bait. All very simple, but is it really?

Maybe, things we regard as being palatable in summer, are not viewed the same in winter. Looking back on the paste baits of the pre-boilie age, all of the best ones had some fat content. This was particularly so in the case of sausage meat which to my mind was one of the best all time winter baits. Significantly trout winter feeds also contain much more fat than in their summer feed. I have tried to analyse why for instance Ritchie MacDonald had a great deal of winter success using oil based flavours. Now, the particular salmon flavour he used I knew thickened up so much in winter (my company bottles it, and we have to heat it up to go through the machine), that I could not see it having any attraction effect. My belief is now that the oil gave the bait a fat content which made it palatable, maybe even more digestible. He didn't really need an attractor because he baited what he knew to be a holding area. Be that as it may, in winter I now use a very simple high fat base mix in which I have every confidence. That is 5 oz Rennet Casein, 5 oz semolina and 4 oz of full fat soya. Colour wise, blue baits do work in deep water, but as I now often fish shallower water, white, yellow and orange are the colours I use the most.

My preference in flavours as an attractor is still with the spices. Ultraspice, Megaspice and cinnamon I find as good as any. If the bait tastes particularly bitter, blending with a small amount of malt type flavour, i.e. maltrex, chocolate malt, will remove the bitter edge. I suspect the effectiveness of these flavours is due to their easy solubility in cold water.

As explained in the bait chapter, amino acids used in the seventies were in crystal form, and the fact was for whatever reason, that they did not attract in winter. However since that time, close friends have used compounds of amino acids in liquid form throughout winter, and have caught many good fish. They did not catch any more than I did though, when I fished the same swims with baits without aminos, therefore, all we can truthfully say is that they have no detrimental effect. They may indeed have been of benefit, as I regarded my flavour much more suitable for winter use than the one they were using. Given that the compound they used has since been refined, and has been much more successful than the original in summer, I think the coming winters will see a lot of experimenting with liquid amino acid compounds.

Right up until four years ago, I believed carp to be a lot less tackle conscious during the winter months. If they were going to have it, they were going to have it, was my view. Then during a long three day session out of sheer boredom through lack of action, I started striking at any movement of the rod top. Imagine my surprise when on the first strike, I hooked into a mint conditioned leather of 25 lb. Rod tips were immediately pushed up high and the rest of the winter was spent fishing as if I was after chub or roach. If a good knock came on the rod tip, I'd strike. If a tiny tap, or a knock I wasn't ready for occurred, I'd take the rod off the rest, take the line from the clip, and feel for any movement, striking if there was any. I ended up having my most successful winter, taking a number of fish over 30 lbs. I am convinced now that many potential winter catches do not arise, simply because the angler does not recognise that bite indication. Simply sitting behind the rods waiting for a full blooded take is not enough.

Last winter my friend Mark Lawson was able to observe carp on his hookbaits. Instead of bolting away when they pricked themselves on the hook, carp were actually spinning around on the spot in an effort to eject the hook. One thing he noticed was if the hook length was over six inches long, which I would hazard a guess that 95% of carp anglers use, then most times the carp was able to eject the hook. Can you imagine what sort of indication you would get if a carp was performing in that way with your bait? The answer is surely just an occasional tap on the rod tip. Not knowing about this form of behaviour would leave you dismissing such indications. Having said that, when the temperature really drops hard prior to an ice up, I don't think carp behave in this manner. They know its their last chance of a feed up for a while, and on such occasions I think caution is thrown to the wind. Besides which it is a very difficult business hitting knocks on the rod top in darkness with a harsh frost falling around you.

One thing which really surprises me and which is something for which I can give no adequate explanation is the speed at which carp return to some of their summer haunts once a thaw occurs after an ice up. This is particularly noticeable in areas that hold lily beds in summer. Generally these are in shallow water, which must be a great deal colder than deeper parts of the lake, yet you can practically guarantee carp arriving in those areas. I would imagine that once more the key is food, yet I have never regarded lily beds as being prolific food holding areas. Be that as it may, look to the remains of lily beds to find carp once the ice melts.

I find winter carp fishing very much an attitude of mind. The chances are that the lake may appear completely lifeless. The bankside will be bleak, often thick with mud and it is all too easy to be affected by this, and convince yourself that you are not going to catch anything. It is absolutely essential to keep warm and your spirits high. I think you have to work harder to be successful in winter, but this is a good thing because it keeps up your interest. Tell yourself that somewhere out in the lake a carp is feeding. Be of the attitude that you only have to find it to catch it. Check with other anglers on all signs of activity. Find out precise spots from where carp have been taken, rather than just the general swim. Chances are that the spot will produce again.

Keep warm, work hard, tell yourself that you are going to catch carp and you will.

Chapter 18

Ambition Achieved '80

AT the very outset of this book I expressed an opinion that all values the angler holds must be his own completely and not those of other anglers. A lot of anglers consider a "winter carp", to be one caught after November the first. Some even consider late October fish as such. To me a "winter carp" is one caught in winter conditions. The hardest part in winter is facing the elements; the style of fishing doesn't change, whilst carp feed much more in winter than the "summer only" angler believes, I cannot accept as a winter fish one that is caught in practically shirt sleeve weather, in water temperatures still near summer levels. The early weeks of November can often produce these conditions – back in 1973 I caught a 22 1/4 lb carp in such weather, but I could not in my heart of hearts accept that fish as a winter one. Surely conditions had to be winter-like. With this in mind I set myself a water temperature limit, below which I considered conditions as winter. That temperature was 50 degrees fahrenheit – the date of such temperatures was immaterial.

Although I had dabbled at winter carp fishing since reading articles on the subject back in 1968, it was not until 1975, when bivouacs and good insulated clothing came on the scene, that I persevered, fishing right through the season. My ambition throughout the long, dark winter months that came and went was to put a twenty pound-plus fish on the bank. During the following four winters, I was very successful, catching far more fish than I ever expected when first undertaking these winter campaigns. Norfolk proved to be a very lucky area for me, only one winter session failing to produce at least one double figure fish. (That particular session didn't really count as my lines had only been in the water half an hour when the lake froze over completely.)

Despite this success a twenty pound fish refused to pick up my bait. Far from getting despondent, this fact bullied me into fishing even harder, getting out at every possible opportunity. Early in January 1979 a cold spell hit the whole country, the lakes I was concentrating on being particularly hard hit. They were iced up bank to bank and remained in this state until the first week of March. At this time I was ringing all over the country every night trying to find some water open. On hearing that the lakes had cleared, I made plans to get off at the earliest possible opportunity, and I was able to get away on the Thursday evening prior to the last week of the season. The long three and a half hour car journey was hazardous to say the least. Falling sleet made the roads atrocious. On the journey I decided just where I was going to fish. The previous season I had watched an angler take two twenty pound fish on the last day of the season, from a swim which is under ice and so unfishable for long periods in winter. I arrived around 1.00 a.m. in the morning. The sleet had turned to torrential rain and a near gale force wind was blowing. Due to the dark and rain it was impossible to see the surface of the swim, so I switched on my car headlights to check that it was free of ice. Finding that it was, I decided to get my baits in as quick as possible, as in the conditions prevalent at the time there was a fair chance of a feeding spell some time between one and two a.m. I quickly catapulted six free offerings of paste bait into the swim, followed by one with a hook in it. The bait was presented on a fixed pasternoster rig, as I intended to hit any taking fish as quickly as possible due to snags at the far side of the swim.

Before I could fix up my second rod, the indicator slowly rose to the butt ring and I struck into a plump 10 3/4 lb mirror. I immediately recognised the fish as one I had caught on the last day of the previous season – because of a tail disorder it had been christened "Stumpy". I quickly rebaited the rod and soon had all my rods cast out and in their rests. By this time, I was completely soaked due to the unremitting rain. I always try to keep as dry as possible in winter otherwise a long session becomes impossible to bear, but in this case I was more concerned with taking the greatest advantage of the short feeding period left to me. Within five minutes one of the indicators rose again to the butt ring. The resulting strike met a heavy thumping resistance. The fish moved off slowly, almost irresistibly along the opposite bank and I knew I was stuck into a big fish. For maybe five minutes the fish moved up and down on the same length of line alongside the opposite bank. I was having great difficulty in determining just precisely where it was. The spot being fished was 80 yards from my position, and so entailed the use of a fast taper rod. I don't like using fast tapers because not as much of the rod points down the line as when using a compound or slow taper rod. However, the distance involved and the need to strike through a hardish bait dictated its use, but as I've said the lack of bend in the rod made it hard to know the fish's exact position. I became aware of a grating on the line; I realised that the fish had moved behind an island far out to my right. I ran quickly along the bank to my left, winding down on the fish, giving it all the pressure I dared in an effort to bring it back out into open water. Just when I thought the measure was taking effect the rod sprang back straight. The only word to describe my feelings at that moment was sick, pig sick. It had taken me four hard winters, fishing through at times atrocious weather conditions, to get stuck into a big fish, only for the hook to pull out. Inspection of the hook showed it to have broken at the barb.

It's funny but when I'm feeling on top of things I don't notice the elements, however the disappointment had left me very cold, and I was shivering uncontrollably. I got into my car, and turned on the engine, setting the heater full on. Slowly the feeling began returning to my body and the heat brought on tiredness. Settling my head on the car seat in order to catch forty winks, I noticed the isotope indicator on the remaining rod slowly rising. Rushing from the car I arrived at the rod before all had pulled tight. A long, sideways sweep of the rod and another fish bumped at the end of the line. Luckily the rain stopped, and the moon shone brightly through a gap in the clouds. By closely watching the rod top against the moon I was able to keep check of the fish's position. Although I knew it was a good one, I also knew it would be nowhere approaching the weight of the largest fish I had previously caught, as this lake just did not produce fish of that size. However the long wait for a "winter twenty" had me wanting to land that fish more than any carp before. When I shone the torch into the net I knew I had done it; the pounds and ounces were irrelevant, for it was a "twenty". The scales confirmed my belief, 21 3/4lbs of mirror carp. I fixed up the bivvy and the bed, sleeping through till way past dawn, a very happy man.

If you can't beat 'em, join 'em!

Chapter 19

A Never-to-be-Forgotten Evening '80

ON a Wednesday afternoon in the last week of September 1973, I was witness to an incident that will remain with me for the rest of my life.

I had arrived at Redmire Pool the previous morning and unaccountably had taken a twenty pound-plus fish on my first cast. No swim preparation had been undertaken and no groundbaiting, yet within minutes of a bait hitting bottom a good fish had taken it. From the moment I landed it not a single fish moved. There was no bubbling, no colouring of the water, and the whole lake appeared dead. For twenty-eight hours I periodically patrolled the lake, yet not a single movement did I observe within those mysterious depths. I am by nature an optimist, yet at the same time try to be a realist. In that short space of time, I had come to the opinion that the rest of that week would be a waste of time. I was at the time still trying vainly to hold down a regular job and so after only a day and a half at the lake, I decided that in the circumstances it was best I return home, while I still had a job to go to.

As I was packing away my gear the sky clouded over and a slight drizzle began falling. The mountain of gear required three journeys to see it all back at the car. As I began the last trip back to the car the sky really blackened and the drizzle turned to heavy rain. Slogging my way through the mud, I stopped for a breather at the famous "Willow" pitch, scene of the capture of the record carp over twenty years before. I sat down, lit a cigarette, and gazed across that famous water. As if in a dream, a huge back slowly emerged from the water. The back was dark, almost black, and carried the uniform scaling of a common carp. Slowly more and more of the fish appeared, until its whole length from tail to mouth could be seen. It's a stupid thing to say, but I was under the impression the fish was enjoying a shower, as the rain cascaded across its broad back. I must have been watching the fish for many minutes before it dawned on me that its length was immense. I bit my lip and slapped my face, to make sure I was not dreaming. Surely this couldn't be true – I was witness to a fish at least four feet long!

But I wasn't dreaming; I turned my head and then looked back and it was still there not twenty feet from me. I was bewitched, held in a trance, my eyes not moving from that enormous back. I could count the scales, the rays on the fins, the image was so alive. Without my noticing, the rain stopped falling. As it did, the giant sank away into the cloudy depths.

Many weeks later, I was to discuss this event with that legendary angler Jack Hilton, who had been the first to report a sighting of a four foot long fish. Jack asked me just how long I thought the fish was and I replied "Nearer five feet than four". Jack's opinion was the same. I asked why, if that was the case, he had always stuck to his four feet long story. Jack's reply was that people didn't believe him when he said four feet, and if he'd said five, they'd have thought him plain crazy!

With this event still fresh in my mind there was no way I could go home. Tackle was quickly reclaimed from the motor, and camp set up in the "Willow" pitch. That night no runs were forthcoming, and dawn broke amidst a violent thunder storm. Such conditions had in the past been very favourable and with this in mind I was alert, perched on the front of the bedchair, eagerly awaiting a run. My anticipation was rewarded as the buzzer sounded, and the silver paper bounced in the butt ring. I hoped it was the big fish, but that was not to be. The fish turned out to be a twenty-plus mirror carp, whose capture I had witnessed the previous season. It was identified by a growth on the lower jaw, and by cataract-like films over the eyes.

That afternoon, the peace of the lake was broken by the chugging of an old motor cycle. My mate Chris Yates had arrived for a long weekend stint. During a chat over tea, I recounted the tale of the huge common. Chris was suitably inspired, choosing to erect his pitch opposite me. In the evening we visited friends in a nearby village. During this visit, we were invited for a meal the following evening. Conditions hardly seemed favourable for fishing with a full moon due, so we gratefully accepted the invitation. Conditions the following dawn and on into the day did not lend themselves to the feeding of large fish, and although we were both aiming to catch big fish, we knew when were "flogging a dead horse". Luckily in Redmire at that time there were always a few small carp, up to about fifteen pounds, which fed in all conditions. They were relatively easy to catch on light float tackle, so we whiled away the hours enjoying the sport of the small fish.

At 6.15 p.m. I called across to Chris, reminding him of our dinner date at 7.00 p.m. Chris called back, saying that he'd just give it another ten minutes. I wound in my tackle, and set to the task of smartening myself up. Considering I was thick with mud, and the only footwear I had with me was a pair of waders and a pair of slippers, it was a case of making the best of a bad job. Hair wetted and slicked back with lake water (alive I might add with shrimp and daphnia) I climbed out from my swim to present my immaculate presence to the Yates. As I climbed the stile, I was able to check the time on my watch because of the full moon. It was 6.30 p.m. As I did so the ratchet screamed out on Chris's beloved centre pin reel – he was stuck into a fish. When you have fished a lake for a certain time you become familiar with how fish of certain sizes behave. Small fish shoot off fast, full of the joys of youth. Big old fish move off slowly, ticking the ratchet like an old grandfather clock. The fish to which Chris was attached was tearing into battle with all the vigour of an Irish Kamikaze pilot. It was fairly steaming off, and it had to be a little fella. I shouted out to Chris that he was not to mess about, to get the little fella in because we had a dinner date. I was soon at his side, marvelling at the speed the old centre pin reel was spinning. Chris remarked that he knew it was only a small fish but that it was fighting so hard he couldn't get it in. He was positioned on the dam wall and from here the fish had the whole length of the pool in which to run unhindered. Ten minutes later, it was still no nearer to being netted; in fact it was now a full sixty yards away down the pool. We had come to the conclusion that it was a small fish, foul-hooked. But surely even a foul-hooked fish would soon be exhausted?

The battle was now a slow affair, Chris managing to retrieve a yard or two of line before the fish would make a short surge, taking all that line back. By 7.00 p.m. the fish was only 20 yards from the dam, not because of any pressure Chris had put upon it, but because it had for some reason decided to run towards us. Half and hour later the fish had been coaxed in close to the dam. It didn't run, but seemed content to lie on the bottom in fourteen feet of water directly under the rod top. It didn't matter what pressure Chris applied, the fish just refused to shift from the bottom. Christ was only using 6 lb B.S. line, and this was barely adequate to lift a dead weight of perhaps twice that amount.

This was ridiculous – the fish had been on over an hour. We were both frozen, since that particular evening had fallen to the first frost of the season. Our breath floated away in huge clouds over the moonlit landscape. Away in the village no doubt our absence was being discussed and not in the most favourable terms. A piping hot meal that had taken hours to prepare was slowly drying into an unrecognisable crust. Drastic measures were called for. Away to our right the water shallowed up, creating an area tight in the corner of the dam under three feet deep. We decided to create a disturbance to the left of us which would hopefully drive the fish up onto the shallow area. We threw stones and practically whipped the water to foam with landing net handles before the fish grudgingly moved off in the direction we wanted. However it refused to go right up into the shallowest water, once again stopping and lying doggo where the bottom shelved off. The depth at this point was about four feet. Once more the fish was immovable. There was only one thing to do – I'd have to go in after it.

In normal circumstances I don't think twice about having to enter the water to net a fish, but this time it was so cold that to say I was apprehensive would be an understatement. Still it had to be done, so it was off with everything right down to my birthday suit, and in I plunged. The shock of the cold water on my body was immense; I had to get the netting over as soon as possible. I got the net down in the vague direction of the fish and called to Chris to switch on his torch. As the light penetrated the water, a huge white scale-like foam drifted into the spotlight. It hit us like an electric shock. "You jammy bugger Chris, you've got the big fella'', I yelled out.

Where before I had been calm, although in a hurry, now panic took over. What if I messed the netting up, and lost Chris a record fish? I'd never be able to face him again. I must have accidentally knocked the fish with the landing net arm, for quite suddenly it bolted out into open water. A terrible grating sound vibrated through the air, and somehow the line had got caught around the landing net arm. I felt the pressure on the net and had to let it go, otherwise the line would be broken for sure. The net ended up hanging from the line, some ten yards away to my left, the fish once again lying on the bottom about 20 yards out from the dam. Somehow I had to free the net, so I marched out slowly towards it, the water rising to chin level. When I was only a yard or so away the bottom disappeared, and I sank from view. Coming up to the surface I grabbed hold of the nearest object, which happened to be the landing net handle. Once again I sank from view, but miraculously the net fell free of the line. By this time, I was pretty close to hypothermia. My only thought was to get out and get warmed up. The next three-quarters of an hour were spent drying out over a gas stove and drinking hot soup. Eventually feeling was restored to my shaking body.

When I returned to the dam wall, Chris was still there, rod in hand and the fish still wasn't beaten. It had now been on for two hours, and by that time we were quite convinced it would be a new record carp. It was once more lying doggo, just off the dam

The sweetcorn kid arrests another

wall, but now had less energy left. It was possible to lift the fish off the bottom a few feet but fear for the tackle made it impossible to lift it right to the net. In the condition it was now in, we were pretty certain that if we could again coax it into the shallow water, netting would be easy. So again it was a question of chucking stones and thrashing the water. The fish moved in the right direction, but stopped in precisely the same spot as before.

Was it worth the risk of exposure once more to enter the icy waters? It had to be, this was a record fish! This time everything went right, Chris managed to lift the fish off the bottom for a moment, and I slipped the net under it. On grasping the net I was filled with disappointment. I knew it wasn't the big fella, it just wasn't heavy enough. After the antics of the past two and a quarter hours, my disappointment was hard to hide. "Sod it Chris, it's only a little-un." Size is relative – after speculating on the weight of the big fella anything less would appear little by comparison. As it was, the fish turned out to be an immaculately conditioned common weighing just over 24 lbs.

When we were to discuss it later, the disappointment was put into perspective. Sure, it was no record carp, but the thrills, the excitement, the doubt of landing the fish, the whole box of tricks was something which could not be bought or manufactured. We had taken part in an event that would forever be etched in our memories, a fight which would be re-fought many times in years to come. That huge white scale shape we saw in the torch-light? That turned out to be the landing net, floating up to the surface.

Note: You may have read Chris Yates' account of this epic capture elsewhere – we really thought we'd cracked the record at last! You seldom get the chance to read and compare accounts from different viewpoints of the same capture, and especially not one as dramatic as this. While Chris is an incurable romantic, I'm more down to earth, and maybe it shows in this tale. Of course, it might have something to do with the fact that I was the poor beggar who had to jump into five feet of ice-cold water – twice!

Chapter 20

The Day it Happened '80

Thursday
June 19th 1980.

I drove home from the lake, taking the tiny country-side roads. Pheasants jerked their awkward way into the hedgerows, rabbits hopped into the long grass. High above, a kestrel hovered, waiting for some unknowing fieldmouse to make its move. Driving slowly with the windows open, I tried to take it all in. It had been a disappointing start to the season; I wanted to clear my head, cast away any preconceived ideas I'd had before the season had started.

But one thought kept coming back to me, "If the fish aren't feeding, you can't catch them". The start had been cold and heavy rain had dropped water temperatures which even before had only just crept into the sixties Fahrenheit. On the Monday afternoon my mate Brian and I were already anticipating hard going. We had fished the large Southern counties gravel pits for a few seasons and knew how they needed plenty of sun on them, before they would warm up and get the fish moving. I remarked to Brian how small lakes were so much different: "This is real Redmire weather. If there is anyone on the rota this week with his wits about him, he'll be in for a real killing".

Passing through Hitchin, I popped into Alan Brown's tackle shop, to return a rod I'd borrowed. Alan greeted me with the words, "Hello Rod, have you heard the carp record has gone?". My first thoughts were of anger, I immediately presumed some tame, farm bred fish had been dropped in a water and been caught for promotional purposes at a pit which I knew was soon to be opened on a day ticket basis. All the years of travelling I had done, all the time spent perfecting baits and methods had counted for nothing. For if the truth is know, I had been chasing a record carp, even if I didn't admit it, even to myself. It had been a race against time, for myself and friends knew it was only a question of when a farm bred fish would be "set up" for a record. Once that happened the mystique, the aura of the carp record would be lost, as one fishery would vie against another for bigger fish. All enchantment would be gone as the carp record would take on the same ridiculous ever-changing situation as the trout record.

"Yes, it went opening day at Redmire. Fifty one pounds, six ounces, Chris Yates caught it. It was Jack's forty," said Alan, interrupting my thoughts.

From anger, my mood turned to elation. A true wild bred fish, and at fifty one pounds plus, surely a record that would stand for quite a while. I had been fishing two pits, which each held individual fish which just might have inched their way past the old forty four pound barrier. But fifty one pounds – boy, it was a whole new ball game. I felt as though a huge weight had been lifted from my shoulders, no more record obsessions, I could just get out and enjoy what came my way.

Above all, I was overjoyed because Chris had caught it. Apart from being one of my closest friends, he above all people deserved the new record. Eight years earlier, he had been cheated by ounces when a huge common he had caught emitted enough spawn for him to just miss out. On that occasion he had every right to feel disappointed, but instead he was overjoyed at catching such a large fish. So the record has gone to a true gentleman – who said "Nice guys never win?"

Congratulations Mate!

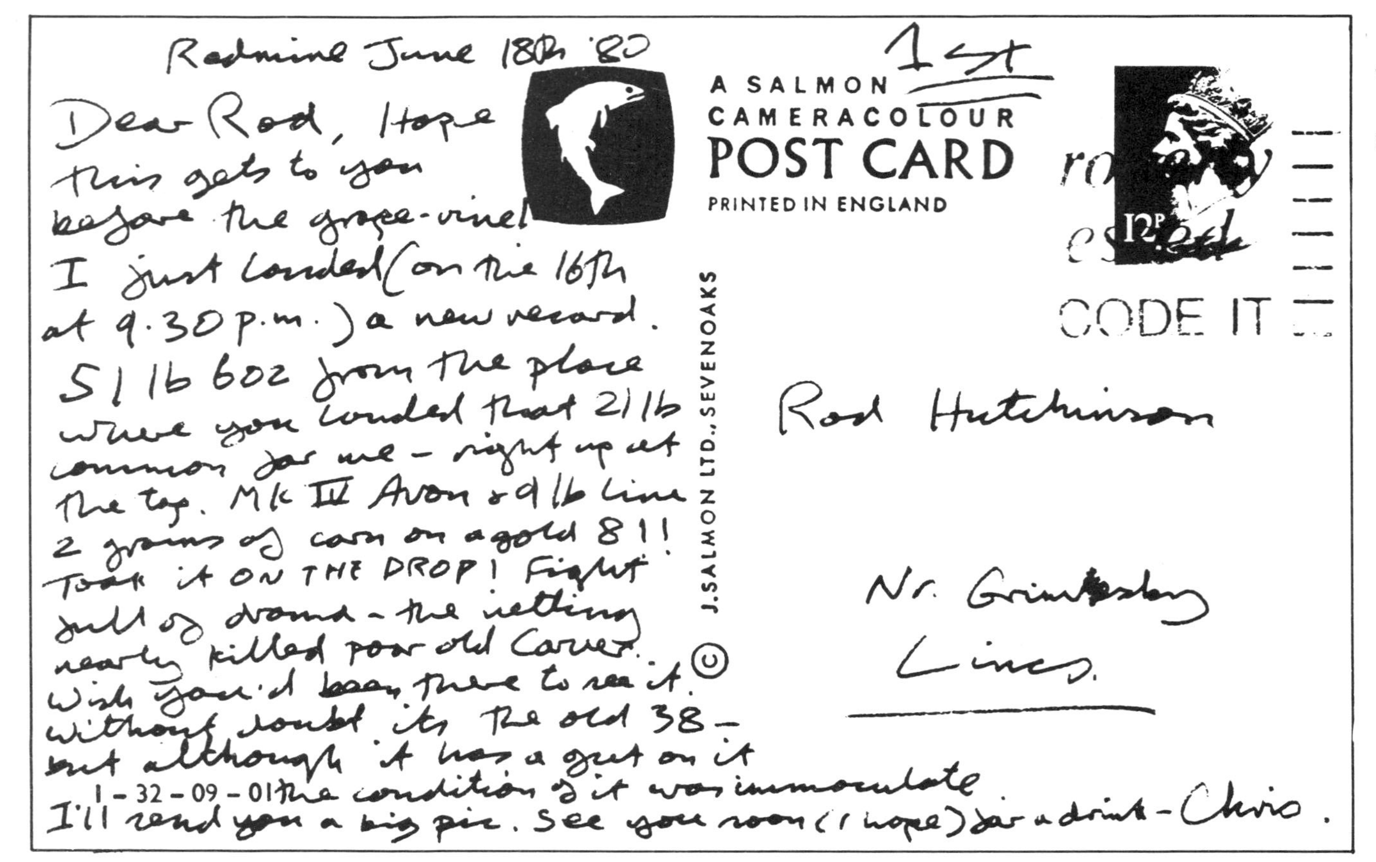
Redmire June 18th '80

Dear Rod, Hope
this gets to you
before the grape-vine!
I just landed (on the 16th
at 9.30 p.m.) a new record.
51 lb 6 oz from the place
where you landed that 21 lb
common for me – right up at
the top. Mk IV Avon & 9 lb line
2 grains of corn on a gold 8!!
Took it ON THE DROP! Fight
full of drama – the netting
nearly killed poor old Carver.
Wish you'd been there to see it.
without doubt its the old 38 –
but although it has a gut on it
the condition of it was immaculate
I'll send you a big pic. See you soon (I hope) for a drink – Chris.

1 – 32 – 09 – 01

1st

A SALMON
CAMERACOLOUR
POST CARD
PRINTED IN ENGLAND

J. SALMON LTD., SEVENOAKS ©

12P

CODE IT

Rod Hutchinson

Nr. Grimsby
Lincs.

A memento of fishing history

Chapter 21

Dear Rod,

from Chris Yates
Redmire
June'80

REMEMBER our first session at Redmire? You were sitting on the dam when I arrived on that grey Sunday afternoon. I wanted to say: 'Mr. Hutchinson, I presume,' (it being our first meeting) but if I remember right neither of us said anything at all for a few minutes. We just gazed, awe-struck, at that small stretch of water. So this is it, I thought, this is the place we've read about and known about since childhood.

'Boosh!' A huge, gold common carp turned on the surface and you made some ridiculous exclamation. We were like a couple of kids who'd got into Oxford without taking any exams. We were going to have to learn it all in our first term, or be discovered and 'sent down.' Well, that's how it felt to me. I know we'd caught some good fish in our time, but Redmire! Would my test-curve be able to stand the strain? You'd fiddled about with small baits in the years previous, you'd hooked and lost a big carp using hemp-seed, I'd used sweetcorn the previous season but lost confidence in it after half an hour (thank God!). We understood the problems that faced us, but could we solve them? It was going to have to be small baits, but what bait? And what about presentation? Hooks, rigs, rods and lines we'd decided upon, but maybe we'd have to rethink even those fundamentals.

We were three weeks into the new season and only two carp had been caught. One for Jack, one for Bill, everyone else had blanked. What chance did we have when I'd been told (by one of the others) that Redmire carp were almost uncatchable. Just the reputation of the place alone, its history, its unique tradition; that was a challenge in itself without the brick-wall of ultra-crafty fish!

Remember all those mad ideas? Floating maggots, 'long-trotting' with crust down the length of the pool, fly-fishing with artificial moths, bamboo-shoots and water-snail cocktails.

"Eat up all your corn and one day you might weigh fifty pounds"

And then you got one on an ordinary worm! I remember your shout, from the top of a willow in the shallows, as you held onto a branch with one hand and a bent rod with the other. A Redmire carp! So what if it only weighed six pounds, we laid it in the bankside grass as if it was something mystical. Then, after solemnly photographing it, we let it go, thinking perhaps that it was the only fish we were going to see out of the water. But then you hooked a bigger one, off the island, also on a worm, and things began to seem less monumental! Pity you lost that one, you berk.

My moment came when I lost my appetite for sweetcorn and only ate half a tin for my supper. The other half went into the lake, plus one baited hook. The sun had been an hour gone and I was just beginning to lose sight of the rods (each one with a different bait!) when the silver-paper on the old Mk IV Avon began to rise up and then jump in the butt-ring. Oh joy! A Redmire run! Oh krattz! I'm bound to mess it up. Swish of rod, squeal of reel, splash of frenzied angler as he leaps into weed-bed to keep hugely powerful carp out of submerged willow! Eleven pound common, but it looked bigger in the half-dark. I carried it down to you in the net and you seemed impressed. 'It took that stupid corn!' I said, still wondering if I'd really got it right and that the fish hadn't taken a worm or a snail instead.

Was it a fluke? Had that carp just breathed in at an unfortunate moment? We fished on and we both started getting carp with corn-baits. On our final evening of that first week you nearly drowned yourself landing a 16 pounder for me. It was the biggest common I'd seen. 'I never thought I'd say it to a Southerner,' you muttered, 'but well done!'

We found a good pub that night (Jack the Road-Man still remembers you).

We'd begun our new term like a couple of kids, but we'd grown up a bit by the end of it. You went on from corn to ideas about preoccupation and then to your wild projects with maples, chick-peas, beans of all sorts, hemp, grapes, black-eyes, pickled mangos, boiled adders poops. You left me miles behind, you hare-brain, you son of a wholesale seed-merchant, you great barn of grain.

Perhaps it was an excuse for a lack of imagination that I came up with the theory that if you continued with just one, successful bait, eventually you'd catch the biggest fish in the lake. Of course, we know now that idea is as full of holes as your socks! The common mind of a carp population soon realises the mistakes of its individual members. Maybe it was just that I was so confident in the stuff that I kept on coming back to corn after brief successes with other baits. After a few years we went our separate ways. You'd caught twice the number of twenties, yet, somehow I'd managed to bump into the biggest fish (I always was a bit jammy). You went on catching big carp from all over the country, I went back to my beloved wildie-waters and didn't have much time for the big-fish-circuit (though remember that night I met you and Brian on that island 'somewhere in Kent' and we might've had some good fish only you got struck by lightning!)

Then, years later, I had another opportunity to go back to Redmire and I took it. And the carp still took corn, though very cannily. All the elms had gone, like the teeth knocked out of a familiar smile, but the atmosphere remained. Redmire still had its quiet magic. I think it's haunted by the friendly ghosts of departed carp-anglers. Anyway, as you know, I had one or two unspectacular seasons, losing a lot of good fish, landing very few big ones. And now, as you've heard through 'the grapevine', using my favourite bait, my favourite technique (light-tackle-stalking) and under my favourite conditions at my favourite part of the pool, I hooked and landed (that's a lie, I didn't land it, John did) 'old 38,' now a new (as bright as a new pin) fifty-one pounder. FIFTY-ONE POUNDS! After all those years the record fell to me! I was the last one I expected to crack it even though I knew there was always a chance; I'd never really thought in terms of fish that size. Sure, I knew they were there, but I'm still too dazzled by the sight of a big twenty to look beyond that to something bigger, even though I've caught them. Does that sound sense to you? Probably not. And you'll think I'm even dafter (that same old loopy Southerner) when I tell you that, back in January, I had an odd premonition that I was going to get the record. '44 + ' I wrote in my fishing-diary. So, in a way, though I was still overwhelmed when it happened, I was half prepared when it did. I'd had Fate smile on me, for some curious reason, yet I'd sniffed out the fact, some time previously, that she was going to smile. But enough of all this idle meandering! There's a muggy wind blowing and I know it'll be driving the carp into the corner of a little pool, not far from my cottage. I might get a 'double' before tea.

I'll see you soon, and show you a portrait of the '51'. My only regret, after I'd released it, was that you hadn't been there to see it.

Splintering Rods, Best Wishes and Full Sacks,

Chris.

This time he was cheated by ounces

This time he cracked it!

Chapter 22

Cassien '85

"The Sting"

The huge increase in the popularity of carp fishing during the 80's created its own problems, namely pressure and anglers literally fighting for the best swims. Just being a good angler was not enough any more, that angler also needed plenty of time. The old adage of being in the right place at the right time was true to a degree, but what if you knew the right place, but had not the time to wait around until you could get in it?

As the start of the 1985 English season came up, I was getting more and more despondent. Running my own company had brought about responsibilities I was not used to. To get in the swims I wanted to be in on my favourite waters would entail camping out at least two days prior to the start of the season, and that was time I simply could not afford. Yet if I arrived any later, I knew it would just be a case of wishing and hoping about what swims were left. It is nice just to be out on the bank, it's nice to be part of the cameraderie amongst anglers, but as nice as those things are, they don't compare with the feelings you get when you're catching fish. Even if the fish don't respond straight away, if you know you are in the right place it is up to you to ring the changes to ensure you catch those fish. If they are not there, you haven't a cat in hells chance of catching them. I don't know if other anglers have changed with age the same way I have, but patience is no longer a virtue in my book. While I can marvel at the dedication shown by true big fish hunters such as Ritchie MacDonald and Phil Smith, who can sit on a water

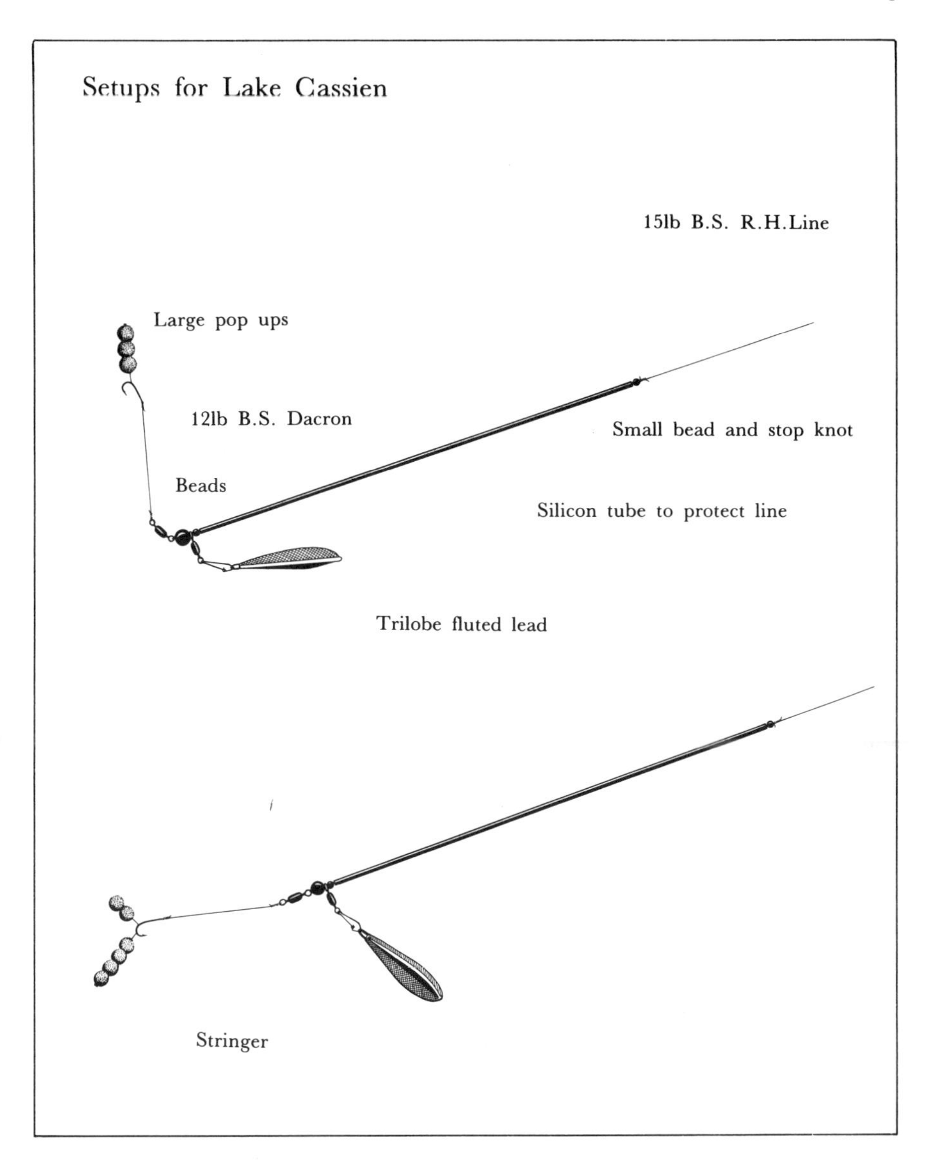
Setups for Lake Cassien
15lb B.S. R.H.Line
Large pop ups
12lb B.S. Dacron
Small bead and stop knot
Beads
Silicon tube to protect line
Trilobe fluted lead
Stringer

for whatever time it takes until they catch the fish they are after, I know I get bored if I don't get at least one run a day. Any big fish I had designs on would be forgotten about, should there be a chance of catching a double to two. I simply like catching fish too much to ever consider myself a true specimen hunter, while being on a water knowing I'm in the wrong place seems a waste of time, when I could be catching fish elsewhere.

I had that craving to go fishing, to catch fish, yet did not know where I could go and practically guarantee myself a choice of swims. Two days before the off, the idea came to me, the "big sting", why not Lake Cassien? Surely any English anglers who had it in their plans would not miss the start of the season on their local lakes. Most people prefer to start the season on a water they are familiar with. Me, I just wanted to get away from the crowds and be able to do my own thing. Just the angler against the fish with no outside intrusions. So, it was a big water, so I knew little or nothing about it, it was all so much the better. I could go in with a clear mind not cluttered by preconceived ideas.

I thought hard about it, apart from the occasional local angler and a few sorties by English anglers in the previous couple of months, the place was virtually unfished for carp. They could not know what pressure was, what lines, hooks, leads and rigs were. Food was just food whatever it was. They had not seen enough to gain any preferences. What was liked by carp in English waters would be liked by the French carp. It was so simple, just take the tried and tested baits. Sweetcorn would work everywhere, peanuts were practically as good, plus they were larger and would present a more visual presence and they were also very easy to prepare. On the boilie front I didn't think there was a better all round bait than Seafood Blend. It seemed a better choice than a milk protein bait, considering that the carp were practically virgin fish, living for the most part on a diet of shellfish. Even if they didn't recognise the round boilie shape, they would know it as food from the natural aromas of the fish meals and prawn extracts. Having not been bombarded with boilies before, there would be no pre-occupation with a certain size, all that was wanted was a big, bright bait to try and catch their eye, whilst being smelly enough to draw the fish in should the bait not be seen. Big 20-to-the-pint baits, boosted up with Crayfish or Scopex flavours would be the order of the day.

On the afternoon of the 15th June, I was on my way stopping off at Harlow to pick up fellow Savay member Jim Hepper who had agreed at short notice to accompany me. Jim a lorry driver by trade knew the route well and also had good knowledge of mechanics whilst mine was nil. Now, although breakdowns had become a fact of life to me, I didn't fancy one a thousand miles from home, in a country where I couldn't talk or understand the lingo. Should anything go wrong it was a decided advantage to have someone along who knew what he was doing. It also gave a certain feeling of reassurance to have a 6feet 4inch bruiser along, at a time when there was much ill feeling abroad towards the English in the aftermath of the mindless behaviour of morons masquerading as football fans at the Heysel stadium.

Due to ferry cancellations and our old van only having a top speed of 50mph it was 4.00 p.m. the following afternoon before we had our first glimpse of Lac de St. Cassien. It was Sunday afternoon and we could barely see any clear water, such was the concentration of wind surfers, canoeists, swimmers and pedalos! Now I was used to the crowded beaches of Majorca but I'd never seen such a concentration of people in my life; Magaluf or Blackpool on a hot Bank Holiday is the best way that I can describe it. I felt so disappointed and Jim's face could not disguise the fact that he felt the same. After buying permits from Chez Pierre's cafe, we lay back in the van and fell to sleep. Disappointed, shattered from the twenty four hour journey, it was off into oblivion.

As tired as we were, the intense heat made it impossible to sleep for long. I woke up after about three hours, not knowing where I was. I got out of the van, shook my head and wiped my eyes. The boats, the people, the cars had all disappeared! After waking Jim, we quickly set up our plumbing rods and made our way down the cliff like path to the waterside. Before dark could fall, just one meaningful feature had been found. A point that jutted out on the entrance to a small deep bay, shelved beautifully at about 45°, giving a depth of fifteen feet only a rod length out. It was a natural food trap, which could be efficiently baited by hand. With darkness falling, we baited the swim heavily with a mixture of corn, peanuts and boilies. Jim was to fish the swim in the morning, while I not having found any other swim in which I had any confidence decided to wait till dawn, in the hope of spotting feeding fish, before I made my choice.

We could barely sleep that night, such was our eagerness to get fishing. Every half hour or so, throughout the darkness one of us would prod the other "did you hear that?" as huge fish rolled out in the lake. With dawn coming up Jim made his way down the path to his swim while I headed back south along the road that overlooks the lake, window down, eyes peering through the slowly lifting gloom for rolling fish. This proved practically impossible in that light but all my senses were tuned, my ears would have put Mr. Spock to shame. On the first splash I heard, the van was pulled up and out came the tackle, After fighting my way down the hill and ripping everything on the gorse and thorny bushes, I found myself on a small beach, flanked either side by small deep looking bays. The swim was the exact opposite of Jim's, a cast of thirty yards or so was needed before ten feet of water could be found. Leaving the float out as a marker I swam out with the large bait bucket tied around my neck and treading water, scattered corn and peanuts around the float.

The rods, special beefed up Spirolites with an extra spiral whip of carbon to give them extra backbone had been made up the night before. The tackle consisted of large Shimano 4000 Carbomatic reels, loaded with over 200 yards of 15lb line that bears my name. The terminal tackle was a fixed lead set up, using a 2½oz Trilobe fluted lead. These leads rise quickly to the surface on retrieve and so minimise tackle losses in snaggy swims, while the fact that it was fixed, ensured that should a fish pick up the bait, the lead would be lifted from the bottom, again minimising its chances of getting snagged. Because the lake bottom was strewn with short tree trunks, bushes and boulders the hook lengths were kept short, ranging from three to six inches. Twelve pound dacron was used on two rods, 11lb monofil on the other. Hooks used were size 2 Mustad O'Shaughnessy, a good sharp black carbon hook that's really tough. One rod was cast out with two large cooked boilies, so that they would rise directly from the bottom, six inches from the lead. The second rod consisted of two large 1½'' boilies, used in conjunction with a six bait stringer, while the third rod used, the "cheating rig", which has already been described but for those who have forgotten already, is a boilie some sweetcorn and peanuts, all on one hair. If the fish are showing a preference for any one of the baits, well, you're still in with a chance. After casting out and tight lining up to the leads, the rod tips were pushed high into the air, again in an effort to eliminate many of the snags.

Maybe thirty minutes after casting out, in time honoured fashion, that is at the exact moment that I was pouring out a cup of scalding tea, a fish rolled on the marker. It was bloody massive! The hot tea went all over me, and I didn't even feel it. I was frozen to the spot, the image still clear in my mind. It was weird, I felt almost frightened. A beast like that could knock the living daylights out of you. I hoped that because of my misdemeanours of the past towards their English cousins, they didn't have it in for me. Suddenly the crude, cod fishing type tackle I had with me felt very inadequate. I'd played a clapped out Renault 4 on eleven pound line before, but there I was doubting whether 15lb line would subdue such a monster. I felt a level of excitement I'd only known once before in my life and that had been during the playing of my first ever carp. This was something else; I was a boy again, chasing a monster. "I'm gonna have you baby, you better believe it".

Focusing my eyes back on the marker, I channelled all my thoughts towards the fish I'd seen, here was the romance of all boys adventure stories. I'd played Roy of the Rovers many times, now it was time for Tarzan Lord of the Jungle. This was get your act together sunshine time. Do it right, leave nothing to chance. It's a hard thing to explain but all my life, although I'd thought a lot about my fishing I never had to really try. I didn't know what it was to have to work for my fish, I just seemed to do my little bit and the fish just seemed to come to me, but now I'd seen just what the lake could offer, I was determined to work my balls off till I caught such a monster.

''Now then you rod tops, let's get it on. Start a twitchin' and a whippin''.

Suddenly behind me was a noise. It was Jim, panting and sweating. He'd run all the way from his swim, practically half a mile away. He fell down on his knees, putting his head between his legs, in an effort to regain his breath. ''How many'', asked Jim between gulped breaths. ''Not had a thing mate, but I'm confident'', ''No, how many have you seen'', Jim gasped. ''One definite and a couple of small swirls that could have been carp'', I replied. ''Look, I've see at least a hundred and one, not fifteen yards from the bank. Bloody massive fish, I had a thirty first cast, and I've lost two others in the snags, now get your arse round near me. There's a stack of fish just lining up to be caught''! Now, I may be slow on the uptake; despite that it took me precisely one thousandth of a second to make my mind up and the other 999 to pack my gear up.

Running down the hill towards Jim's swim I could hear the crashes as huge fish threw themselves from the water. ''Hear that'', cried Jim, ''save your breath mate, I've heard nothing else since we jumped out of the motor''.

We were only yards from Jim's rods when one of them leapt in the rest and was away. Jim was on it in a flash, the clutch screaming for all it was worth. Boy did the fish go, in one straight run, it took over a hundred yards of line off his reel! Slowly though the pressure told and fifteen or so minutes later, a beautiful unmarked leather of 28 pounds graced the net. If a twenty eight pound fish took over fifteen minutes to land, how long would it take to subdue a forty or even fifty pounder? I trembled at the prospect.

There were still fish around, though not in the numbers Jim had spoken of earlier. I set up to his right, fishing onto the shallow side of the point from which Jim was fishing. As the sun got higher though, it was evident that the carp were moving into deeper water. Jim had one more chance that morning but unfortunately the fish snagged him on some unseen obstacle. Taking the boat out over the fish made no impression on it at all, indeed the harder Jim wound down on the fish the more the back end of the boat would rise from the water! After being on the point of capsizing half a dozen times, Jim had to give up and pull for a break. By 10.00 a.m. with the sun high and the air very hot indeed, all signs of feeding fish had stopped.

My idea to beat the crowds by fishing first week of the English season had really come up trumps, Jim and I being the only carp anglers on the lake. We spent the afternoon drifting up and down the lake in a hired dinghy, checking out depths on a borrowed echo sounder. Not knowing anything about the depths, we came to the conclusion that the old echo sounder was on the blink, so many times did the depths appear to go right off the screen! It was not until we put a handline down that we actually realised that the depth in places did go beyond 100 feet! It was purely academic, we didn't for a moment expect fish to feed in those depths, the food surely had to be in the shallower water, which for the most part meant close to the margins. From the success Jim had already had, between ten and twenty feet appeared the best bet.

We moved back into Jim's swim for the evening, but apart from one or two fish showing at very long range, little appeared to be moving. As darkness fell we packed up our tackle after first baiting the swim heavily, with approximately ten pounds of corn and peanuts, plus around two hundred boilies.

The second morning produced an almost repeat of the first day. Jim catching three more fish, a thirty one, a twenty four and a double, while another apparently larger fish once again got him snagged up. Meanwhile, yours truly on the shallower side of the point, didn't get so much as a sniff. We had moved into our swims about half an hour before dawn to find fish already rolling in the baited areas. Yet it had been a full two hours before any runs occurred. It was not until the sun actually rose above the mountains behind us, that there appeared to be any interest in the baits. Our conclusion was that our highly flavoured baits had drawn in masses of crayfish, which in turn had drawn in the carp. While the sun was still behind the mountains, the crayfish felt relatively safe in the half light on the shallow, but once the sun shone directly down, they immediately hid beneath the rocks or moved into deeper water. It appeared that the carp preferred to feed on the crayfish, but once they disappeared, the carp were then quite prepared to feed on the baits. Certainly in the time before the runs occurred a tremendous amount of little pulls and tremors came on the rod tips, and it was not until these crayfish pulls stopped that we could (or should I say Jim could) expect any runs. Jim said simply, that the carp liked the sun on their backs before they fed, but I'm sure it was the disappearance of the crayfish which led to the runs.

By 10.00, the carp had moved off and as there seemed little point in staying in the swim I'd been fishing, I took a rod and float and spent another couple of hours plumbing for another likely looking area. On the opposite side of the bay which Jim was fishing, I found a large plateau like gravel bar, heavily weeded on the top, with a depth of about twelve feet of water covering it. Surrounded as it was by depths of twenty five feet or more, it positively screamed out carp. I was confident I'd found the spot where I'd catch my first fish.

Just how good the spot was, I didn't find out, for come the following morning I'd not been in the swim half an hour when Jim yelled at me from across the bay to give him a hand. The greedy bugger had two on at once. By this point I was more than a little pee-ed off. Jim was on his eighth or ninth run, while I had still to really settle into a swim. Still even if I was not catching fish, it was still nice to see them on the bank, so it was off in the boat, to the aid of Jim!

The fish on his left hand rod was despatched quickly. Jim then leapt into the boat to do battle with his other fish, while I was left to do the unhooking and weighing of the first. It was a peculiar looking specimen with a twisted tail, though fit and healthy just the same, and weighing just over twenty three pounds. After sacking the fish, I could only watch as Jim was towed up and down, some hundred or so yards out. A couple of times it looked as though he would land it, when the fish thrashed on the surface, however the carp just refused to be beaten and after thirty or so minutes, Jim's rod sprang back straight, the line having cut on some snag. Jim reported afterwards that the fish looked to be a mid-thirty. His morning didn't end there either. In the next hour he hooked two more. The snags claimed one again, while another superb conditioned leather of twenty seven pounds was landed.

"Ere Jim, how many is that you've had now?" "Seven", came the reply, two thirties, four twenties and a double and another four lost. "I was wondering Jim, any chance of letting me have a morning in the swim, just to get a fish under my belt?" I asked apologetically. "Yes, I don't see why not", said Jim. "As a matter of fact I was thinking about moving. After all we've come a hell of a long way and I can catch twenties and thirties at home." It was funny really I thought, there was Jim craving for a monster and all I wanted was a fish, any fish, a double would do, a twenty would be heaven!

So the dawn of day four saw me creeping excitedly into Jim's swim. Jim, meanwhile was still trying to get his boots on. The night had been extremely warm, with Jim electing to sleep outside the van in the open air. Unfortunately for him he'd been attacked by a battalion of mosquitos wearing size twelve boots! His ankles were up like balloons, while his face looked like a cross between a punctured football and one of those potato men you play with as kids.

Two hours later and nothing had happened! It was just my luck to move into the swim, just as it had gone dead! Jim hobbled down the bank towards me. "How many have you had", he asked. "Nothing, not a twitch, nothing, absolutely zilcho, I've not even seen one", I replied dejectedly. "You will now". said Jim, "the sun's just come out over the mountain, that always gets them going". One hour later, nothing. Two hours later, with me by then starting to shrivel up in the hot sun, still nothing. "Oh, I give up, it's obvious that they are not going to have it, this morning". With that the left hand rod top, donked a couple of times, pulled right over, "whack", the indicator smacked the rod and she was away like a good 'un.

Boy, was I terrified about losing that fish. I generally play carp pretty much on the light side, yet I'd seen Jim lose four fish in snags, and he is a bit of an animal with them. I didn't want my one and only run getting snagged, so there was only one thing for it, hold on for dear life and not give it an inch. If it was going to go anywhere, then it was straight through the rod rings! Cramming on the pressure for all I was worth, I turned the fish on its first run, forcing it to kite into the bay to our left. Once in there I felt pretty safe, as every one Jim had lost had been out in the main lake; the bay itself appeared to be pretty much snag free. Even so I kept the pressure crammed on, never once letting the fish get its head down. I suppose it was ten minutes or so before Jim lifted the net around the fish. Never had I been so relieved in my life before. "It's a good 'un", said Jim carrying the fish from the water "Do you reckon it's a thirty", I asked. "Dunno," said Jim, "I think so". I let Jim do the weighing; after catching my first fish, the weight seemed almost irrelevant. "Congratulations," said Jim, "you've got a new personal best, forty three and a quarter". I was dumbstruck, even if I didn't catch another fish, the trip had been worthwhile. I had a few drinks that lunchtime like you do and continued the celebrations at a nearby restaurant, going through the complete menu.

Back at the lake we decided to try our luck in a new area close to Chez Pierre's Cafe. Jim chose to fish from a small island in the bay to the left of the cafe, while I chose a shallow well weeded area to the south of the same bay. Each swim really looked the part, only time would tell whether they would live up to their appearance.

I was in position well before dawn. Conditions were close to perfect with a moderate south westerly wind blowing into the shallows that I was fishing and likewise into the side of the island which Jim was fishing from. However, despite the conditions I didn't hear or see a single fish. One thing we had learnt in our short time at the lake was that if fish were present, they generally showed themselves, it therefore came as a complete surprise when shortly after dawn one of my rods roared off. Twice the fish became weeded up, but each time strong pressure had it on the move again. It came to the net with a mass of weed around it. So much weed in fact that as I lifted the net, I had the impression that I'd caught a massive fish. It turned out not to be the monster I thought; however, it was indeed a super specimen of fat bellied mirror, pushing the scales to 35lb 12oz, I was well pleased.

Jim meanwhile had a most frustrating morning. Being extremely tired, he fell to sleep on his rods. The buggeration factor came into play, like it always does in such a situation. One of his Optonics decided to pack up and it was of course the rod on that Optonic on which he had a run. He awoke just in time to grab his rod butt as it slowly disappeared into the depths. He could make little impression on the fish as it had by this time tied his line around every tree stump and boulder in the south arm! Eventually his line broke, whereupon Jim threw himself back on the bedchair and back into the land of dreams. An hour or so later his sleep was disturbed by the sound of his two remaining working buzzers. Once again, he had two runs at once! It was several minutes before the sleep cleared from his head, and he sickeningly realised that he was playing anglers either side of him, both of whom had decided that Jim's swim looked the ideal spot into which to cast their spinners.

Big Jim gives it the wellie!

The first Cassien fish we saw on the bank, a thirty

A personal best, forty six pounds eight ounces taken in just three feet of water

A 34.08 mirror from 'The Island Bay' in the South Arm

Suitably posed . . . back goes a 24lb mirror

My first forty goes back to fight another day

Not a fish showed, yet this cracker roared off with my bait

"Back you go sunshine"

Returning a 29lb leather to the South Arm

This nicely scaled fish came after casting to the deep water

The stuff of dreams, my first fifty pounder

Jim's fabulous last minute trio

Jim was not a happy man. From over a hundred yards away, I could see the steam coming out of his ears!

Over lunch we discussed our tactics for our next assault. Jim was going to stay put on his island. Though having to admit that he had not seen a single fish, he just had the feeling that it was a big fish area and felt very much that the one he had lost came into that category. I was happy to stay in the same swim for despite not seeing any either, I had put a beauty on the bank and felt sure that given the same conditions again, numbers of fish would have to be in the area. I might point out at this stage that our fishing by this time was only of about four hours duration per day. The weather was much too hot for fair skinned types like Jim and myself, with the temperature topping over 100 degrees farenheit each day. We did try to fish from beneath the shade of our brollies one day but within an hour, my wavelock umbrella started to melt! Evening fishing had been a dead loss for us, so we stuck to the routine of baiting up heavily as darkness fell, moving into our swims as soon as we legally could, an hour before dawn.

I broke this rule for the first time the following morning. Sometime around 3.00 a.m. a real hooligan of a gale sprang up, shaking the van from side to side, making it impossible to sleep. Getting out of the van to stretch my legs, the sheer warmth of the wind, stunned my face. If there were such a thing as perfect conditions, for the swim I had baited, then these just had to be them. I walked down the cliff path in darkness to the swim, simply to experience the conditions. Carp were crashing out everywhere, the swim was absolutely alive. Back at the van, it was impossible to sleep, knowing that down below the carp were going crazy. After deliberating for an hour or so, I could contain myself no longer. It was out with the rods and on the with back pack.

Down at the swim, I decided to bait up again, my actions being based on the fact that I knew good numbers of carp had been feeding hard for well over an hour, and I didn't want a situation where they had finished all the bait and began moving off. The wind was so strong it made baiting by catapult or throwing stick impossible, the corn and peanuts being blown behind me, and into my face. All I could do in the situation was to bait up the margin in front of me by hand. I was more than a little disappointed not being able to get my baits where I wanted them, but in the end it did not matter. Within half an hour one of my hookbaits with three large boilies on the hair was picked up in just three feet of water. The fish with no depth beneath it, didn't seem to know what to do, except thrash the surface directly beneath the rod top. Within a couple of minutes I had it beached, whereupon I dived on it, scooped my hands beneath it and carried it to the safety of the bank. Straight away I knew that it was big, a true monster of a carp. Subsequent weighing showed that I'd beaten my personal best once again with a truly gorgeous mirror of 46lbs 8oz. As dawn came up, I was in again. This time with a smaller but equally good looking specimen of 29lbs.

When I went round to tell Jim, his appearance led one to believe he'd been to hell and back. He had had but one run, that coming from one of the truly big fellows he had been after. He had fought it for well over an hour, without ever getting the upper hand. It had eventually like many before, snagged him and nothing he could do could get the fish out. In the end, prolonged pressure only succeeded in straightening the hook. Not surprisingly he was very despondent, and had come to the conclusion that although the small island swim was indeed a big fish area, such was the predominance of snags, that it would be virtually impossible to land such a fish from that position. We had but three days of our holiday left, and he desperately wanted to beat his personal best.

I suggested moving across the lake to the opposite bank where I'd seen good numbers of fish showing for the past two mornings. Jim was in agreement for despite his urge to catch a truly big one, I think also he felt the need just to catch a carp once more.

Our move opposite certainly paid dividends. By 10.00 a.m. the following morning we had landed another five carp, all over twenty pounds. Four had fallen to my rods, fished out into a reedy bay housing two islands, the best of which was a 34lb 8oz mirror, while Jim fishing out into the main lake had a mirror of 24lbs. During our sport, a great many more fish had been seen crashing out around the two islands opposite my swim and not surprisingly Jim took the boat out later that morning to investigate the area. Arriving back some couple of hours later, he could not move swims fast enough. He had found a gravel bar running out from one of these islands and in the weed at the foot of the gravel bar had found a group of nine carp, three of which were extremely large, together with a gigantic tench, which he said would have broken the English record by a good ten pounds or so! He did have some misgivings about the new swim. It was once again alive with short tree stumps and even bushes. These appeared to be all to the left of the swim however and Jim felt that if he could force any fish to the right, that he would then land them.

That evening the weather changed for the first time during our visit, with the air turning cool and huge black banks of cloud moving in. It was not to our liking or to the liking of the carp or so it seemed, as they were conspicuous by their absence. By 10.00 a.m. the following morning we had not seen any fish or had any runs. Around 11.00 the sun started slowly filtering through the clouds and as it did so the odd fish started to show way out in the deeper water. Being for ever the optimist, I cast out a bait consisting of two large orange pop up boilies at one of the fish that showed, though in truth hardly expecting anything to happen as I knew the depth where I had cast to be in the region of forty feet, not a depth at which I expected (at that time) fish to feed in.

Maybe ten minutes had passed when the rod tip hooped over and the indicator started its agitated dance. On putting in the pick-up the rod was practically torn from my grasp and this to a fish sixty yards away! I just knew that it was another big one. Tightening up the screaming clutch, I leant into the rod for all I was worth. Even at that distance, I feared for a break, so much was the rod creaking and the line singing out as if tortured. Some seventy yards or so out, an enormous back broke the surface, (Jim said later that even at that distance, when he saw that back he said fifty to himself). "Bloody hell", I said to myself, "this is it. This is granddaddy himself". Having seen it there was no way I was going to let it get away. Everytime it tried to get its head down, I hauled it back up. There was this terrific feeling of being at one with my tackle, of having the ultimate confidence knowing it would not let me down. I had in my opinion the best rod, line, hook and reel available to man. It wouldn't let me down, the only thing that mattered was that I did nothing silly – I didn't. I had the fish on the surface thirty yards out and just kept it there, coaxing it all the way straight into the net. Once on the bank, I must admit to over-estimating the carp. It was indeed colossal, far larger than anything I had seen before in my life and I was thinking in terms of over 60lbs. I was not however in the least disappointed with a weight of 51lb 8oz. In fact when it was pointed out to me that the weight was the same as the English record carp, it really spelled out just what an achievement Chris Yates' record fish was. To think such a monster had been caught back home, really showed how difficult a record it was to beat, or even come close to. To think that I had, on a whim decided to fish France just to escape the crowds, yet had caught a fish as big, gave me a tremendous feeling of satisfaction. Maybe for just a fleeting moment, I had felt as Chris had done on his historical morning. Finally, I had done it all right. Huge fish were not just there to be dreamed of, they were there to be caught. Any carp in any part of the world was now fair game.

Later that morning, I caught a smaller specimen of twenty three pounds, again by casting long into the deeper water. Jim's swim however failed to produce, no doubt due to the change in weather conditions. When we had seen lots of fish close to his island, southerly winds had predominated. That morning however the dark clouds were moving in from the Alps to the north.

Sometime during the night, the skies cleared and dawn brought the promise of another hot day, the last of our holiday. Shortly after dawn, the gods smiled down on us and gave us the warm southerly wind we'd been praying for. My swim suddenly became alive with carp. At times two or three fish would roll at the same time! The great angler in the sky though decided that I had had my share of good fortune for the week. He teased me a bit by letting me hook three carp, but then decided that they were not going to grace my net on that occasion. Each fish finding a snag from which they were impossible to move.

How funny that the previous six fish I had caught from that spot, did not know about the same snag? Then again it may have been some submerged tree trunk that got buffeted back and forth by the wind. Maybe the snag had not been there the previous two days.

We had planned to pack up at 10.00 but by half past Jim had still not made a move. I could see him across the bay huddled behind the rods, willing the indicators to move. Slowly, I started packing away my gear in a very animated fashion, hoping Jim would notice and take the hint. With my back toward him I heard him suddenly yell, "Rod, quick give us a hand, I've got two on at once" I turned to see Jim with a bent rod in either hand! Now I was well and truly stuck. Jim had the boat. What was I supposed to do, swim out the hundred and fifty yards or so? Running around the bay, trying to find a shallow spot in which to wade across, I heard Jim yell again, "Rod for Christ's sake, get yourself over here. I've got three on at once, three buggers did you hear me?"

Before I could get across, Jim had sorted it all out for himself. Somehow he managed to net two fish at once, while the other rod he just dropped, leaving the pick up off. But lo and behold, fate smiled on him that morning. The fish on the third rod decided it didn't much fancy a fight and just laid on the bottom, waiting to be wound in, while only feet away were lots of snags into which it could have dived had it so wished. Jim's largest fish looked every inch a forty pounder, but was empty due to the fact that it had recently spawned. His next largest was only slightly smaller, both however broke Jim's previous personal best by good margins. Both were mirrors weighing 37lb 12oz and 35lb 8oz respectively. The third fish, the sleeper, weighed in at 24lbs. It was a quite remarkable achievement to hook and land three fish of such quality, all at the same time.

We drove home in high spirits. The "sting" had come off for us. Nine fish over 30lbs had been landed, including a fifty and two forties. Jim had broken his personal best twice, while I managed it three times. It truly was the stuff of which dreams were made.

Jim plays and lands the last of his fabulous trio

Chapter 23

Dear Rod from Chris Yates '85

The Watery Mead
Someday

Dear Rod,
I've just heard the news.
Join the club! No, not this disreputable Golden Scale Club. I mean the 51½ pound Club. Congratulations!
Very best fishes,
Chris.

P.S. I've checked the International membership lists and it would appear that we are the only two qualified members of the 51½ lb Club. Now I know you take great pleasure in debunking the tellers of ghost stories, the mystics, the seers, the visionaries, the superstitious and the ordinary non-materialists like me, who think there are more than five senses, more than three dimensions and more to this planet than meets the eye. However, you've got to admit that this latest coincidence is interesting & unique & weird.

Had I told you when we first met, in 1972, that within a few years we would both catch a 51½ carp, from different waters, you would have swallowed your pipe laughing.

But what is the significance? What is the cosmos telling us? I asked me Mam & she said; 'Make another cup of tea, there's a good lad.'
C.

Chapter 24

When It All Goes Wrong: Opening night 1980

BY the time I reached the lake on the evening of the fifteenth, all the recognised hot swims had been taken. It was 10 p.m. before I decided on one, a gap in thick reeds, with trees overhanging into it, and a moderate South Westerly wind blowing straight into my face. Plumbing revealed a depth of four feet, dropping off to ten feet at a distance of ten yards out. In the conditions it looked the ideal margin swim. When 10.30 p.m. came around I was all set up, and the swim baited with two pounds of particle. Not being the type to enjoy sitting around twiddling my thumbs, I shot off to the pub for a last couple of pints. Leaving the loo at the pub, I walked straight into a brass door stop, which had been hung from the ceiling, obviously by some dwarf from Bertram Mills circus. The blood running down the back of my neck did little to ease the excitement and by 11.15 p.m. the adrenalin was flowing.

Back at the lake car park, it was now very dark. The lake looked very different. It was the first time I had fished this area and it took at least twenty abortive attempts before I found the path through the trees to my chosen swim. When I did eventually make base camp, I discovered that I had chosen the venue picked by the International League of Dive Bombing Mosquitos for their annual dance, and all of their fifty eight billion members had turned out. Usually, puffing the old pipe sorts them out, but this lot were obviously all females and flocked to that mild, slow burning, St. Bruno haze. In no time at all I felt like a burning pin cushion. My face looked like one of those knobbly potatoes. Still these things are meant to try us, so it was on the with the show.

With no torch available and the overhanging trees making things as black as the Oval on test match day, just getting the baits out was in no way a simple operation. The first hook was baited easily enough, but the second hook remained bare, although somehow I contrived to impale two pieces of particle on the index finger of my left hand. After what seemed hours, all was sorted out and baits cast into their positions, although with one bait in a bush and the other wrapped tantalisingly around the head of a bullrush, they were not in the ideal place. Much pulling and tugging followed after which came the inevitable tangles. More sweat, more mosquito bites and more cursing before the satisfying plop of bait hitting water was heard. While adjusting the buzzers, the wires from one of the heads somehow snapped in my hand. Luckily I had a spare in my rucksack, one lent to my by a friend the previous season. It had not been until I had suffered three bleep ridden, sleepless sessions that I had noticed the fine print engraved on its case: "Not to be used out of doors". Still it would have to do, until dawn came.

Half an hour after casting, a very confident, impossible to miss, run developed on my left hand rod. I missed it! Another half an hour went by before a real belter of a run came to the right hand rod. I waited until the line was really tight before striking, and immediately felt the satisfying bump of a big fish on the end of the line – and also the sickening realization that my rod top was stuck fast in the branches of an overhanging tree. Needless to say, I lost the fish.

Around 2 a.m. the moderate wind turned to gale force, bringing with it driving rain. As I was bang in the face of it, it was no time at all before the brolly was uprooted and the ground sheet blown off me, both ending up in the bushes behind my swim. I was soon as wet as a bank holiday in Skegness, but the situation did have its brighter side, as the weather kept the mosquitoes off.

Just before dawn a suicidal little mirror contrived to hook itself. At fourteen pounds not what I was after, but I was pleased just to get a fish on opening night, and above all it had given me a tremendous scrap which, let's face it, is what it's all about.

By 10 a.m. I was doing the rounds looking for signs of feeding fish. In the back bay were three carp, two of which were of considerable proportions. They were moving around with their dorsals just breaking surface, looking suckers for a surface bait. I hurriedly changed the rig on my rod, baiting up with a piece of magical, unrefusable floater. Casting just ahead of the fish, imagine my dismay when my floater sank like a bag of nails, as did all subsequent free offerings. Oh, well, back to the drawing board. I fed the rest of the concoction to the coots.

Later in the morning I found two fish bubbling profusely, heads down in eight feet of water. Not wanting to put particles directly over them I baited up with cubes of meat-based bait. It should have sunk very slowly, not disturbing the carp it was meant for. However, it floated, and to give the bait its due, the coots loved it.

Knowing that it just wasn't going to be my day, I upped swims, moving to the tip of a peninsula on the far side of the lake. By then it was after midday, and I wasn't expecting any more chances. However about fifty yards out one or two fish could be seen moving so I catapulted out about twenty balls of "instant" paste bait, and cast my hook bait in amongst them. The sound of food hitting the water was a signal to every coot

It's not always the big ones that give the most fun

on the lake that it was dinner time. On this lake, the coots take anything and everything – in fact I heard they ran off with a bloke's "brolly camp" one night!

Unperturbed, I left the bait where it was – after all if I couldn't catch a carp, I might as well get a coot. It's all action after all. To my surprise the buzzer erupted, and the indicator literally flew. There was no possible chance of me missing this run, and I didn't. Pick up in, pull tight, strike over the shoulder. The rod snapped in my hands! The top joint flew down the line like a polaris missile and I was left on the bank trying to play the fish on two feet of rod. There was a huge crash out in the lake and a very big carp surfaced. Would you believe it, it laughed at me? A couple of seconds later, it threw the hook.

Shortly afterwards, an angler came up to me, asking if I'd had any luck. I'm in court on Friday!

Chapter 25

Cassien Revisited '85

We're bombing on through the night; lights flashing by on the wrong side of the road; roundabouts hitting us at weird angles. Little towns with strange sounding names are buzzing with Saturday night activity.

I've got my foot down and Roger shows no interest, head buried deep into his French translation book.

"What do you think Rog? What do you expect?"

"I want a good time", said Rog, lifting his head from the book: "I'd like to catch some fish, but I've really come for a holiday. It's a new adventure for me; I've never been abroad before so I'm just going to enjoy myself."

"You'll do for me Rog." I replied.

The hours flash by with only short breaks to pay the toll fees. On through Paris – Paris by night, the world's most romantic city: you'd never know it, nose to tail with a juggernaut. Auxerre services loom and it's time for a break and a couple of hours' kip. Beds out in the car park. A clear sky, full of stars; a warm wind with an air of expectancy.

All too soon the alarm goes. Half dead we crawl into the self-service cafeteria. Roger's been warned; no bacon and egg here, just croissants and coffee.

"I know what croissants are" says Rog, "they're those whirly things like buns. Alf Engers makes them."

"I don't think he's made these Rog, but you never know with Alf!". Visions of Alf, legs pumping the pedals, veins bulging, tearing down the autoroute with a bread-basket strapped to the back of his bike come to mind.

Back in the carpmobile, two feet on the pedal, only another 500 miles to go. At my side Roger is practising his French.

"Eeya, how do you pronounce this?"

Deux bieres s'il vous plait. I do my best to show him but after 24 years without using the language my touch has gone. However, Roger seems suitably impressed. "Dare bear sieve oo play (two beers if you please)" emits with monotonous regularity as the miles flash by. On through Lyon and time for "dare bear." On by Avignon.

"We're making good time Rog. Reckon we've got time for just one dare bear".

The traffic's less crowded now, half of it bearing off right to Espana on the N.8. The sun beats down, not a cloud in the sky; only a hundred miles or so to go. Roger's "dare bears" now betray a trace of excitement. Porsches, XJSs flash by filled with sun seekers heading for St. Tropez, Cannes and Monte Carlo. One Corniche convertible driven by an evil looking Arab – all draped in gold goes by us.

"Flash bastard" says I.

"Bet he can't catch carp" says Rog.

"Bet he don't want to" said I.

As we get closer to our destination the hills become bare and black, legacy of the recent forest fires which had swept through the area. With their climate the whole area is just one huge tinder box. Off the autoroute.

"Well Rog, here we go; only a couple of miles mate".

"It's only five o'clock" Rog replies, "we should have time for a couple of dare bears before sorting out our swims, shouldn't we?"

God, the place is jam-packed. Everyman, his cat, his dog and his budgie are here: wind-surfers tearing around like dorsals in a stock pond. The French are on holiday, every single one of them it seems. I try to point out bays and bars, but it's impossible; you can't see them for people. Into Chez Pierre's cafe and I let Roger off the lease. Up to the bar he bounds.

"Dare bears sieve oo play".

Two Kronnenbergs are uncapped and handed to him. He walks across smiling from ear to ear.

"Ooh, I like it 'ere, ain't it lovely" said Roger, "Ay, and don't they speak good French?"

"They should do Rog, they live here".

Pierre walks through and recognises me, coming over to greet us. Pierre's English is on a par with Roger's French but with sign language and a little translation by his wife he gets by and we find out what has been happening. Pascal, who spoke English, has moved on from the cafe for a while. The opposite bank, which previously could be reached by negotiating murderous mountain tracks has been closed due to the forest fires. Even as we spoke smoke loomed up from behind a hill a couple of miles away. There were quite a few anglers about it seemed, some English, some Dutch and some German. The

French anglers apparently left the lake alone during the holiday period. The "dare bears" flowed and it seemed a shame to leave, but we wanted to find some swims and bait them for the following day so we made our farewells.

We started out in swims I had fished with Jim Hepper on my previous trip, but even as we crept into our swims at dawn I knew that all was not as it should be. No fish were rolling anywhere. On our last visit some mornings we had seen up to a hundred fish. While we'd been away the huge Mistral wind had obviously moved a lot of fish but where do you start looking in such a vast lake? Be that as it may we were stuck with the swims for that morning and about an hour after casting out I had a couple of plucks on the rod top. The crayfish had moved in on our baits. Half an hour later the top whipped over and line poured from the spool.

"I've got one, and it's a big 'un".

Ten minutes later I felt a bit of a fool as Roger lifted the net around a 16½lb mirror.

"She may only be little but it's a French carp," said Rog, "That's the important thing; we might not see another."

By nine o'clock in the morning fishing had become impossible. We had swimmers, snorkel divers and wind surfers on our baits.

"Looks like the attractor works Rog", said I "wonder if the fish will like it?"

Time for a swim, a few "dare bears" and Roger's introduction to French cuisine. Pastis with the starter, wine with the main meal and fromage, then creme caramel with cognac; what more could a man want? Just a few dare bears in a quiet bar while the sun lost its ferocity. Thinking about where to fish that evening Roger announced:

"Let us go where no man has gone before."

And so we did, hiding away in a quiet bay away from the crowds. That evening we both lost huge fish. Roger's came adrift when his line cut on a rock close in while my fish had swirled at my feet twice before getting into a snag only a few feet out from the bank. As dawn came up I knew I'd be lucky; two magpies flew overhead. Sure enough in the next four hours I landed four fish all of which fought like crazy. 21 pounds, 24¼, 30¾ and a fabulous 41lb mirror. My fourth forty in two trips; incredible. We were in for an even bigger surprise. On taking the photos we found that we had doubled up twice on fish caught the previous session. The 24¼ was one Jim Hepper had caught at the same weight, while the 30¾ mirror was Jim's first fish from the lake. They were identified not only by scale patterns but by the fact that both had terribly deformed tails. My captures had come nearly two miles from where Jim had caught them! It made us wonder just how many fish there were in the lake. Even before we'd left, it had been established that a 46.8 I had caught on the previous trip was a fish caught at 55lb by another English angler back in April.

It was a day for celebration as Roger kept reminding me as each "dare bear", pastis, cognac etc flowed down the neck.

The day had been a good one and after putting our rods out again that evening we thought we might just as well have a bottle of wine to finish the day off. A couple of glasses had flowed when my buzzer sounded and the rod jumped in the rest. Such was the ferocity of the run, even on open pick-up, that the rod was pulled from the rests, the bale arm snapped shut and the 15lb line broken like cotton on a straight pull – all before I'd even managed to put my glass down. Better luck came my way half an hour after casting out at dawn. After the usual ferocious Cassien battle a gorgeous 30.8 linear mirror graced the net. Shortly after Roger also banged into one and he put his first Cassien fish on the bank, a 33.8 mirror.

Life was lovely, with the sun beating down. We went for our customary swim and drank a few more lagers to celebrate our captures. That evening we planned to move out across the lake to the swims where Jim Hepper and I caught a lot of our fish from and with three days left we were confident we would put quite a few more fish on the bank. However, on driving back to the cafe a lone magpie crossed our path. What devilish scheme did he have in store for us? Surely now we had both caught and the prospect of even better swims in front of us, a silly magpie could not ruin things. "No point worrying lets have another lager" said Rog.

The peaceful calm was soon shattered as the sound of wailing police sirens pierced the valley. Heads turned to look to see that the police were escorting a massive wide-load trailer, at least 50 feet in length. Oh no, it was the Middlesex Mafia! The whole job lot, Reggie and Ronnie, Crazy Alf and the Semolina Kid. The trailer was full of boilies!

"Looks like they mean business." said Rog.

Minutes later the trailer pulled to a halt; bait and tackle were unloaded in minutes flat, boats were loaded up and the whole cortege proceeded out to the swims Roger and I had planned to move into.

"Looks like they've done their homework" said Roger.

"Faeces" said I, or words to that effect.

"It doesn't matter" said Rog, "they're here to catch fish; we're here to have a good time."

"Can't we do both?" said I.

"What I think" said Roger, "is that we should have just two more 'dare bears' and then the world will look a lot better. Then we shall try where no man has gone before."

We certainly did that; we were so pissed even we don't know where we fished that evening. Roger, though, obviously fell upon the right spot; I just fell in! We were some distance apart, out of view of each other, and as far as I was concerned my baits were out of view of all carp. That evening and the following morning I had a class one, hundred percent blanko. No twitches, no pulls, nothing. I went for a swim and such was the clarity of the water that I could see every single bait still lying there on the bottom.

"How you done?" said a voice from behind me. It was Roger, looking very happy.

"Nothing whatsoever; I haven't even seen a carp. How about you?"

"I've had a great big mirror carp. It nearly pulled me in. Cor, it wasn't half powerful."

"How big Rog?"

"I don't know, but it's a whacking great whacker."

"How big do you think it is?" I asked.

"I don't know. I've never seen one this size before."

Minutes later the pointer swung round on the dial of the Happy Hookers; thirty, forty, fifty — the pointer dropped back.

"Sorry Rog, you've just missed it."

"What do you mean? How big is it?"

"Forty nine pounds eight ounces." I told him.

"I'm not sorry; it's a whacker. I think we should celebrate." said Rog. "Oh no" said my head.

What a fabulous fish it was, a huge golden leather.

"Eeya, " said Roger, "Look at his belly. He likes his boilies, don't he? Ain't it nice here?"

For some reason we went for a drive up in the Alps that afternoon, looking for another lake reputed to hold huge carp, but lost our way in the mountains, ending up only 7 miles from the Italian border. Sitting on the top of the world drinking "dare bears" and bathing in the glory of his big fish Roger was in a philosophical mood.

"Do you know what the best job in the world must be?" he asked.

"Taster in a lager factory?" I enquired.

"No."

"OK. I give up." I said, fearing the topic would get into depths too depraved.

"The best job in the world must be the weather man's in the south of France. All he has to do is wake up each morning and say 'today will be bright and sunny with temperatures in the 80's, winds light and variable' and he'll never be wrong: no chance of the sack or nothing."

"Oh, how great minds work." I thought to myself.

We drove back late afternoon through bustling villages crowded with gents in panamas and shorts playing boules upon the village squares. Roger kept pointing out all the groups of people sitting outside the cafes, drinking and laughing.

"Look at them, they're all having 'dare bears'."

Having got lost we tried a short cut over the mountains. It was scary, just tiny ridges cut into sheer granite. All down the mountain side were burnt out wrecks of cars that had gone over. "I've not been so scared since I drove a Lada." said Rog.

We got back to the lake in the early evening. It was like a mill-pond; conditions hardly looked promising. Just to cap it all the lone poxy magpie flew overhead, laughing. Needless to say that evening and the following morning session we both blanked.

However, life was good. We lay in the sun, and swam in the crystal clear water. Eating bread and pâté flushed down with a bottle of local wine for breakfast it didn't seem to matter much that the fish had departed from our area. In fact we were both more upset by the fact that the following morning we'd have to head back for the cold of England.

There was only one thing for it, we'd have to make the most of the last day, and so we did: "dare bears" in Pierre's, a fabulous four course meal in the restaurant; pastis, wine, cognac etc then off to the mountain bar for a few more "dare bears".

"This is the best holiday I've ever had." said Rog.

"I know" said I, "but wouldn't it be nice to catch just one more 'carps'."

We got back to the lake about six. I have to admit I had had it. My mind was blown, my liver was shot, my legs had turned to rubber. It's been a long time since I had a session at Savay and nowadays I just can't keep up with the likes of Roger, or Jonesy, or the Tooth. Yet Roger was his usual self, in fact on top form. In true Fisheries fashion he was sitting on the back of the motor, can of lager in his hand, swaying from side to side saying "this is what carp fishing's all about". I don't think my liver agreed.

Somehow I made it back to the swim. Pushing the rod rest in with all my might I hit an unexpected piece of soft ground. "Oh no!" I felt myself going but was unable to prevent it. "Sploosh", head first into the swim. Back to the motor for a change of clothes and back to try again. Half an hour after casting out — I couldn't believe it: the buzzer screamed and the indicator flew. I was so surprised that I just sat there for several seconds watching the line whip off the spool. Eventually I shook myself from my daze and struck into it. Miracles happened: it didn't snag, didn't break me, and the hook didn't pull out. As I drew it grudgingly to the net I was saying silently "Please don't come off, please". Well it didn't; straight into the net first time. As I grabbed the net the lone magpie shrieked over head. I put two fingers up to it: "Up yours" I cried. By Cassien standards the fish wasn't a monster, but it was a cracker all the same; a long, beautifully scaled mirror of 24lb 8oz. Ain't life beautiful.

Now I know this might sound out of order to many people, kids and dads, but like Bob Jones once said to a rather disappointed lady, "I'm only a man".

What a way to start the day!

This thirty had been caught on our previous trip by Jim Hepper

Almost fifty. So was the fish. Roger's superb leather.

The 'one last carp' I asked for

Built for speed, this fish 'went like a train'

Probably the prettiest carp I've ever caught, a thirty pound linear

When dreams become reality, my 58.04 leather

Happiness is watching it swim safely away

I was so chuffed I just had to celebrate. One more fish was all I wanted and I'd caught it. I fell to the temptation of cracking open the last bottle of wine. Laid back on the bed, mind floating on a sea of rosé, body glowing with the evening sun; the perfect end to the holiday. We'd both had forties and thirties, and had a terrific time

"Whack." An indicator hit one of the remaining rods. "Bloody hell, another run!" I can't say I leapt to the rod, because it's impossible to leap and sway at the same time, but I got there. In with the pick-up — and the bloody thing pulled me in! In my haze I'd forgotten to slacken off the clutch! All I could do was run into the water following the fish while I frantically tried to release the clutch pressure. I was up to my neck before I achieved it, but somehow it was done.

I knew instantly it was big and, shit or bust, this one wasn't going to get its head down into any snags. I flipped the lever over to backwind and screwed the clutch up tight: it wasn't going to get an inch. The rod was bent double, line singing out vibrantly in the evening air. The water erupted about forty yards out before the fish put on a terrific burst of speed, pulling me off my feet and onto my knees in the margins. It gained a few inches of line but no more; I simply wouldn't let it.

How long it took before it was circling round in the margins I don't know. The light was dimming and my arms and back ached terribly. First shot at the landing net I couldn't get it in; it lay across the arms and just wouldn't fold in. I was cursing and swearing under my breath. "I bet I lose it after that," kept flashing through my mind again and again. Ten minutes later I had it back again, this time heading straight for the spreader block. "Here we go baby" I said aloud as the lips touched the spreader block. I couldn't lift the mesh! The damn mesh was snagged on a root. Out she swam again. "You bastard," I cursed to myself, "I know I'm going to lose you". Fumbling around trying to release the net with one hand while a monster carp surged away on a tight line I'd just about given up all hope of landing it. Eventually I tore the net away from the root, put both hands on the rod and said to myself "Here we go, in for the bigun". Rod bent to the limit I heaved. In she came, straight into the net. I lifted; she was in, she was mine. The water erupted as the fish lashed the margin to foam. "Crack", the landing net shattered! It didn't matter; I'd dropped the rod and had hold of the mesh. I could barely lift it from the water it felt so heavy.

Kicking open my holdall I spread it on the ground before lowering the net onto it. In the half light the fish looked massive. The hook was embedded in the bottom lip so firmly I had to bite the line and bring the hook out from the front. Hell! I was shaking like a leaf from head to toe. I felt shattered and cold and every bone ached; my head was throbbing, but boy, was I happy! Wrapping the net around the fish I turned to my tackle bag to find my scales and torch. "Flap, flap, flap"; I looked behind me, The beast had leapt from the net and was back in the water! Furiously shaking its body, although grounded, it was slowly but surely making headway towards the depths. "Geronimo. Oh no you don't you —." Not caring I dived over the rocks, smack on top of it. With a combination of stangle-hold and half-Nelson I collared it and hung on for dear life. Inching my legs round in a half circle I managed to get my body between the fish and the deep water. "You ain't going nowhere sunshine but in the sack." I heaved her ashore onto the holdall and kicked a sack into the water to wet it. That done and the sack wrung out, in she went. Onto the scales; the moment of truth. Round the pointer sailed to half way. Exactly 60lb; magic! Into another wet sack and weigh the first. One and three quarter pounds, making the fish 58lb and a few ounces.

I've been fishing for so many years now that I know big is not necessarily beautiful, and that big fish aren't particularly hard to catch; but the moment those scales whacked round was the most magic moment of my fishing life. People will catch larger fish, but no one will ever feel as I felt then. The sheer triumph over adversity was what made the capture so worthwhile, so rewarding.

I didn't sleep a wink that night; instead I just sat on the bank watching the sack. Even after all that happened I was still terrified the fish might somehow escape from the sack. Can you imagine it? If you told someone you'd caught a fifteen pounder but it got out of the sack they'd say "Well it happens". Tell them you'd caught a fifty eight pounder but it got out of the sack and you'd get "yer, yer, tell us another one."

When dawn came up and I could see the full sack lying there I was so relieved it was untrue. I went for a swim, lay in the sun and nodded off. It had all seemed to happen in a haze; hell it *was* in a haze. Even when Roger was taking the photos my mind was somewhere else. I was totally intoxicated by the fabulous fish I'd caught.

Days will come and days will go: fish will come and fish will grow. Larger fish will be caught, and I hope I get my share, but they won't match that moment, that magic: I was there.

Chapter 26

Large Carp Waters '80

AT the time of writing the record carp, a fish of 44 lbs, still stands to Richard Walker. This record has stood for twenty-eight years, coming from Redmire pool, a small three acre lake on the Welsh border. The closest a fish came to breaking that record was a 43lb 12oz common carp, taken by my friend Chris Yates from the same water in 1972. That year two other anglers captured forty pound fish, although in both cases the fish caught was the same. In the seven seasons which have passed since those captures, only two other fish over forty pounds have been taken. One of those two came from a lake used for holding large imported carp, and as such cannot rank with the other large fish caught, which have lived the majority of their lives and grown to their immense proportions in the lakes from which they were captured. The other forty pound fish came from a gravel pit in the Southern counties in 1979.*

That very short list of forty pound fish could lead one to assume that there is little chance of the record being broken by a truly wild bred fish in the near future. However contrary to the above facts, I believe that the record can go and probably will within the next two or three seasons. If we experience drought conditions in the next few years, similar to those of the seasons '75 and '76, I believe the record almost certainly will go. The reason for this statement is that in '75 and '76 the loss of much water confined carp in closed areas. Within those areas there was much competition for food, which in turn made those fish so much easier to catch. I know of three waters which hold fish approaching or bettering record size. Each one is extremely large, and each lake contains long continuous gravel bars which are in some cases only inches below surface level. If drought conditions came, I could see these large pits developing into a number of much smaller lakes as the

* *May 1980*

In my pitch with a brace of twenties from a large gravel pit

water levels fell. In such conditions this could well put every fish within casting range and therefore catchable. At the present time, on the large waters i.e. anything from 50 acres upwards (in one case 600 acres) I am sure some fish never come within casting range of the angler.

In order to catch such fish, or indeed any large carp (a large carp to me being over 25 lbs) we must look to what governs the growth of a fish, and what makes a water capable of providing those qualities.

Carp have long been a valuable food source on the continent and in the Far East. It was with the housewife in mind that cross-breeding of carp strains was first undertaken. The aim of this breeding was to produce in the shortest possible time a carp heavy enough to make a decent meal and also to produce a fish with few or no scales, so saving the housewife the messy job of cleaning the fish. (It should be remembered here that all carp strains derive from the wild fully-scaled carp). Early cross-breeding produced fish which indeed grew far faster than their wild-bred ancestors yet kept many of their characteristics, one of which was a long life span. Subsequent knowledge has proved that in the correct environment that lifespan can be between forty to fifty years. Another characteristic of early cross-bred fish was their ability to grow in length and bone structure for up to fifteen years.

It was the progeny of these early cross-bred fish that was used for stocking waters such as Redmire Pool, and Billing in Northamptonshire, in the early 1930s. Both these lakes were relatively new at the time, Redmire pool being a flooded valley originally intended for trout fishing and irrigation purposes, whilst Billing was a disused gravel pit. Not surprisingly the carp grew well, as trout have since done in similar new rich environments. In both cases during their growing life there was little competition from other species for the available food. These original stock fish and their early offspring grew on to reach their full weight potential, both waters producing forty pound fish at their upper limits, whilst other fish made weights in the upper twenty and thirty pound ranges.

Over the course of the years, both environments changed. Although still rich in food stocks, I doubt if the quality is now the same as the original freshly flooded environments. They settled down, in much the way the trout reservoirs have done. In later years the carp were also to have competition for their food. In Billing this came from the increase in other species, whilst in Redmire that competition came from subsequent offspring, year after year. When I last fished the pool in '74, there was no doubt in my mind that it was at that time overstocked. I also believe that each new generation was slowly reverting back to the wild carp ancestry. Many small fish which were caught had that long lean look of the wild carp about them. It also relevant that the wild carp is very slow growing compared to king carp strains. This does go some way to explaining why generations of carp produced since the capture of the record fish have not attained a weight of anything like their predecessors. Since all fish now in the pool can be traced back to only a few parents, breeding between those fish now present will produce offspring closer and closer to the wild carp.

I also believe this to be the case in Billing. Although the survival of the offspring is nothing like that of Redmire, and it cannot by any stretch of the imagination be said to be overstocked with carp, the many small fish present again bear all the marks of wild carp. I know of no official stockings of king carp strains since the original one, whilst I do know that many wild carp have found their way into Billing, coming from a nearby marina and also from the River Nene. Breeding between these wild carp and offspring of the king carp strain will again slowly produce a reversion to the wild carp strain.

This does not however mean that neither water is capable of turning up a record fish. Although a carp only grows in length and body structure for a number of years, the end of that time need not see its maximum weight. That time merely produces the full frame of the carp. Upon this frame, due to fluctuating food stocks, and also the general health of the fish, the weight carried will differ. I know of one fish which finished growing many years ago, yet has a weight fluctuation range of six pounds. One famous, much recorded fish at Redmire pool, which generally weighs somewhere between 38 to 40 pounds, I could see bettering the record 44 pound figure if circumstances were such that it saw *a couple of seasons rich feeding.* I doubt if either water now contains a record sized fish that has remained uncaught over the years, yet there is always the chance of an old original or early generation fish adding the extra weight in the right conditions.*

Apart from the two waters mentioned, what are we to look for in other lakes when searching for big carp? The first thing I look at is the carp themselves. It's easy enough, if the fish present show themselves often enough to get an accurate estimate of their sizes, but when fish hardly show or they do at such ranges as to make estimates complete guess work, then we must look into the history of the carp in that lake. As cross-breeding of carp strains developed on the continent, fish were bred which grew much faster than the early strains. These new fish held less of the wild carp characteristics. It should be remembered they were bred for the table, not for the angler, so one of these characteristics was a long life span. Another was the length of time in which fish kept growing lengthwise. Scale readings taken from carp, from waters all over the country, have shown one significant point. It is now rare to find carp which grow on into the fourteenth year. Growth even into the twelfth and thirteenth years is not common. Normally lengthwise growth stops at eleven or twelve years. It is not rare to find carp which only grow into their tenth year.

From this, we can conclude that carp which grow for the longest length of time offer the best chance of attaining large weights. I might add that those fish growing for the greatest length of time were fish stocked in the 1940's and early fifties. The shorter growth period fish were stocked in the late fifties and early sixties. It would seem that this long growing characteristic is slowly being bred out of fish by the fish farmers. I might also add that as the life expectancy of present day carp is now shorter, the chance of a fish being around long enough to increase its body weight after its lengthwise growth is over, also diminishes.

As regards the lake itself, I would be looking for a water which at the time of the stocking was very much in the Redmire or Billing vein, that is, a newly-flooded valley or new gravel pit working. If those fish were allowed to grow on through the years with little angling pressure and little or no competition for food, then so much the better. There are some pits which although flooded many years ago were kept on as working pits. They were stocked, but fishing was not allowed for many years because they were still being worked. Other pits were so large they were not looked on as feasible fishing propositions until stocks bred and multiplied. There are hundreds of such pits around the home counties and large cities, which sprang up after the war due to the need for large quantities of materials for rebuilding. It is to these that I look for big carp. It is rare for these waters to be overstocked, or to have a glut of small fish species. In fact it is common to find small heads of every species growing to specimen size.

There are I believe two main reasons why this is so. The first is that many of the pits were stocked by the large gravel companies. As fishing was only a small offshoot of minor concern to them, only small scale stocking was undertaken. I was witness to one such stocking of a newly finished pit back in the early sixties. If my memory serves me

*The accuracy of Rod's prediction was demonstrated when on June 16th 1980, Chris Yates caught this particular fish at 51 1/2lbs, a record weight for a British carp (length 35'').

correctly, the stocking consisted of just twenty small carp, one hundred small tench, two hundred bream between one to three pounds, and around two thousand assorted small roach and rudd. A mere drop in the ocean as far as the size of the pit was concerned. I was also assured that these numbers were about average as far as that firm's stocking policy was concerned. The idea was that these fish would grow on and breed, eventually multiplying into a good head of fish.

The other reason is that I believe the majority of food available in gravel pits is more suited to the feeding habits of large fish. In order for a large percentage of fry of any species to survive, there must be an abundance of the right food needed for fish to grow on at that stage of their lives. Daphnia explosions, common in clay pits and old gravel pits, where the bottom has built up a thick layer of silt, are rare and even non-existent on many of the newer waters. Although daphnia plays a very important part in the infant fish diet, I believe it plays little part in that of the adult fish even when in profusion. Given a diet of higher order creatures (shrimp, caddis etc.) daphnia is not needed, nor ingestion geared to that food form. Lack of silt pockets in new gravel pits also means that there is only a small bloodworm population. Again, I believe this much publicised food source is much more essential to the diet of infant fish than to adults. Once the larva has progressed to a larger size it becomes more important to the adult fish. This I believe is why such pockets are hotspots for adult carp. Over the years constant flow over gravel and sand, and the wind battering the banks, which slowly erode, eventually creates greater areas of silt, thus making them more suitable for infant fish. I'm sure it is no coincidence that it is the very old established pits which often have a stunted, overpopulated fish problem. Fish will only survive in numbers where the feeding is suitable for fry.

Chapter 27

The Potential of Carp Waters '88

As I write Chris Yates' record 51.8 still stands and for how much longer I can only hazard a guess. Rumour was in the summer of 1987, that it had been broken but not claimed. This is a possibility as the largest known fish in the British Isles at this time had been caught in previous years up to 45 lbs or so, yet it had never graced the angling journals, as the water has a strict publicity ban. That fish was growing all the time, and it is not beyond the realms of possibility that caught in spawn, that fish could have equalled or passed Chris Yates' record. If the rumour was true, I could understand the captor not claiming the record. He'd know he'd caught it, so would others in his area, yet at the same time he would have preserved his fishing. Be that as it may, I have to admit surprise at the lack of growth of known big fish in England. Going back five years, I expected the record to go within eighteen months, but all of the fast growing fish I knew of, levelled off once in the forty pound range. The massive fish Ritchie MacDonald caught from Yateley, which at the time was the most likely candidate, has in subsequent captures lost weight. It seems very much as though forty five pounds or just over is about the ceiling English fish can attain, anything larger being almost freakish.

Climatically there is no reason why English fish should not grow to the same size as fish in Belgium, Germany and Northern France, all of which have produced carp in the mid fifty pound range. I believe that the main reason for this is angling pressure. The fish caught in the other countries were in all probability caught for the first time at over fifty pounds, while any carp in England by the time it makes forty pounds will have been caught several times.

Once a fish is a known forty, the pressure will be even greater, as there will be anglers pretty much around the clock after it. It is very difficult indeed to catch such a fish without giving any damage be it a split fin, or just a tear in the mouth. That damage has to heal before growth can continue. Add to that the sheer trauma of being caught may put a fish off feeding for several days, even weeks. I think it essential for fish to grow unhindered, if they are to make the weights of their continental counterparts and much as I wish this were possible, I cannot believe there is a lake in England holding really big carp that are not fished for, or have been left alone for a number of years. The only possibility of such fish being caught I believe, is if the ban on the importation of fish is lifted. I cannot see more than a couple of natural English grown fish making 50 pounds, as much as I'd like them to.

World wide, I don't think we yet know just how large a carp can grow in perfect conditions. Reliable sources reported fish of ninety five, and one hundred and six pounds from South Africa in 1987, although the means of capture have not yet been ascertained. Both fish came from a huge dammed lake, many parts of which have yet to be fished, so it is doubtful that these would have been the largest fish in the lake. It is also doubtful as to whether we will ever know the potential of the lake as terrorist killings are common in the area, I'm told.

I know little about the natural diet of those huge carp but I would guess that it consists of substantial sized food items. Taking St. Cassein as the rule, the size and abundance of the crayfish population is obviously to my mind the key to their growth. I have fished several larger lakes in France, but none has had such abundant rich food, and none has produced fish of the Cassein stamp either. Lakes on a par with Cassein no doubt exist; food will be the key to sorting them out. Crayfish, freshwater crabs and swan mussels, all in abundance are the things to look for. Add to that climatic conditions that encourage year round feeding and low stock intensity and you truly have a big fish water.

It would not surprise me if a truly huge fish was caught from one of the large navigation canals, either in Holland, Belgium, Germany or Northern France. The few I have fished have really surprised me in the quality and abundance of food such as swan mussels. Fish in these waters can escape pressure and still be on rich feeding. All the year round feeding can be expected due to warm water influxes, plus any ice which may form in winter is soon broken up by boat traffic. I also like the fact that most have fluctuating water levels. Although concrete banked in many places, some also have areas of natural bank. When in flood, land animals such as worms, grasshoppers, slugs etc, provide rich and abundant feeding.

Although I have friends on the continent who disagree, claiming that the water is too cold, I can also see massive carp inhabiting the huge lakes of

Northern Italy and Switzerland. I was amazed at the amount of food in Lake Geneva for instance, with vast shoals of small fish everywhere I looked, yet this lake must have the heaviest boat traffic of all lakes, and must suffer some pollution as a result. This water like most of the ones I've visited in the Alps, is remarkable for its clarity. Water clarity being a vital part of photosynthesis in plants helps along the necessary food chain required to breed big fish. Now while there is no getting away from the cold water argument, I see no reason why this situation should last much longer than it does at Lake Cassein. Besides which it never freezes to depths of 60 feet anywhere and captures from Lake Cassein have proved food in some source or another occurs at these depths. To reiterate, if there is food a-plenty, no pressure and a reasonably mild climate for 8 months of the year, carp can be expected to reach weights in excess of fifty pounds.

While this may not be the case in the British Isles, excellent fishing and good sizes can be achieved with a little management and forethought, and I should add a slice of luck. I would like to give as an example a lake I managed to acquire back in 1981. Because I believe one of the main reasons for slow growth in carp is because most lakes have too many bottom feeding species, I deliberately chose a water with very few fish at all. It had formerly been a trout water, and apart from a handful of tench which had been stocked, plus the odd pike and perch which had arrived via nature's mysterious ways, only sticklebacks and a few surviving trout inhabited the water. As such it could be stocked to the intensity I required. Various figures and ratios were advised to me by fishery management people, and two kept cropping up. They were 500 lbs of fish per acre for good growth, 300 lbs per acres for maximum growth. I decided to go all the way with a policy of 250 lbs total fish per acre.

The water itself was dug out as recently as 1978 for its sand. Within three years much of that sand had a 3 to 6 inch covering of black silt, which was alive with bloodworms. Canadian pond weed had established itself, the weed being alive with shrimp. The fact that the lake was fed by a chalk stream meant the water had an extremely high pH level of 8.3 making it suitable for larger shelled animals. Some swan mussels were already present (their stocks have since multiplied), while the water snail population was and still is to this day, the largest I have ever come across in any water. Spring also saw large areas absolutely black with tadpoles, another abundant and nutritious food source. It was reasonable to assume therefore that any carp introduced would make good weights, even allowing for the cold North Lincolnshire winters, which may see the lakes completely frozen for as long as eight weeks.

However, having chosen the water, and having raised the necessary money for lease and stocking by forming a syndicate, I found myself in a dilemma. Every source I had for decent sized carp in the 18 to 25 pound range let me down for one reason or another. It seemed every fishery's owner in the country was after large carp and any which did become available were mostly at completely unrealistic prices. By March, with our first season coming up on the water, I had but four carp present for the syndicate members to fish for! I should add here that it was my intention not to fish the water for at least three years, simply because I like surprises. At that time any fish I caught would hopefully be new to me. However under pressure from my members and much against my original plan of stocking young growing fish, I found myself having to buy a total of twenty six carp, from a known overstocked water, most of which were old and stunted, at weights between 5 to 8 lbs, the largest being a very old looking common of 11½ lbs. They were introduced solely to give the members some sport, while we waited for better, larger fish to become available. Truthfully, I never expected these carp to do anything, apart from fill out a bit on their stunted lengths. Imagine my surprise and this is where the slice of luck comes in, when the old looking common broke 20 pounds within two years, while other members of his brethren were making weights in the upper doubles. Another specimen from a different source, achieved a seven and a half pound weight gain in its first year, followed by five and a half pounds in its second year. Today that fish is well over thirty pounds, and while the original stunted commons have not done as well, a large number of them are now into twenty pounds, as are some of their first year offspring.

Now waters holding a stock of twenty pound plus commons are far from common in the British Isles, and where such a situation does exist, the reason for it is usually said to be because the carp were of excellent pedigree. This is clearly not the case. Redmire fish one would presume would be good stock, as they can be traced back to the stockings by Mr Leney. However many of these fish have since the early seventies been transferred to other waters, and apart from the rare exception, have shown little or no growth at all in their new homes. The one exception I know of being those purchased by Roy Johnson which were put into a water containing only trout. Some of those fish showed exceptional growth rates, before the population multiplied. Those fish like my own had no competition for food, and this is surely the key to producing big fish in the British Isles. Abundant food and low stock intensity is far more important than pedigree. Get all three right, and perhaps the better temperatures of the south coast, and fifty pound carp should be a real possibility, particularly if no fishing was allowed for the first five years after stocking. Also food must exist for when the fish are large enough to eat big items, ie. such as swan mussels. So if none exist, I would recommend introducing them.

Back in the sixties a great deal of correspondence between the late Dick Walker and myself revolved around Swan and Zebra mussels. Now although we knew carp ate them, it was our conclusion at the time that they were only eaten when dead, when the shell was open and the muscle tissue could be extracted, or that there were times when the shell was extremely soft and the whole mussel could be dissolved. Since that time we have all learnt that this is not the case and that mussels are eaten hard and whole. My personal best fish at the time of writing, a 58 lbs 8 oz carp from Lake Cassein, excreted a very large swan mussel as I weighed it. The shell was still intact, yet somehow the meat had been extracted!

I think without a doubt with the correct policy, carp in England would reach over fifty lbs, whilst in Europe particularly in the southern warmer climate, somewhere carp around the 100 lb mark are swimming around today. Don't ask me where, I don't know, but if you do, give us a buzz.

Safely does it, as I slip the net

Smiling, like you do, with another fabulous forty

Lady luck smiles again, giving me this superb fifty four and a half monster

Hooked for life . . . straight through the hand!

My last fish of the trip, an immaculate 21lb mirror

Chapter 28

Cassien '85

The Pressure Starts

Throughout my carp fishing career I've been very lucky to be at famous waters when they were absolutely at their peaks, and before they became spoilt. There is an awareness at such times, that nothing lasts forever, that this is it and milk it for what it is worth. In years to come, you cannot look back and say "I wish I'd done this, I wish I'd done that", time waits for no man. People change, places change, things can never stay as they were, so if it's there to be done, go for it. Cassien 1985 was such a time, such a place. After just two trips, I had a fantastic confidence in myself. It was as if I only had to turn up at the water and I'd be rewarded with lots of big beautiful carp. It didn't matter how I got there but when the obsession is with you and you are on a roll, you just have to follow it. So come September I was off again.

The holiday could not have got off to a worse start. Driving down the M11 heading for Dover, the roof rack complete with boat and rods decided to leap off the van, tearing off in the process the rim around the doors. Still 900 miles from my destination and two rods had already been crushed to pulp. Not a good start, but that wasn't going to stop me. Cassien here I come. By early morning I was in France and by lunchtime, approaching Paris. Just after joining the frightening Parafrique ring road the motor decided to clap out on me, creating a traffic jam of horrendous proportions. Horns blaring, agitated gendarmes waving their arms around like windmills on acid, it was utter chaos, utter bedlam. With neither party able to speak the other's language, the world hovered on the verge of World War Three.

By the time I arrived two days late at St. Cassien my head was numb. Just to twist the knife in further, the lake itself was wall to wall anglers. Every swim that had ever produced so much as a double, had at least one angler in it. Ones that had produced really big fish, had two or three anglers in them! I felt like turning the motor round and heading home. The crowds and the pressure of English waters that I had run away from, had arrived at Cassien. Things could never be the same again. What was really ironic was that half of the anglers I spoke to had been inspired to head for the place after reading reports of what I had caught on my previous two visits! Talk about not being able to have your cake and eat it too, how true it was.

For three days I did nothing but lie in the sun sulking, hanging around Chez Pierre's and generally eating and drinking, just trying to get my head straight. By the fourth the urge to fish had returned, but where to fish was the problem. The south arm looked as though it had a match in progress on it. One of the other arms had to be explored if I was going to get away from the crowds and find some fish. At that time to my knowledge neither the North or West arms had been carp fished to any degree, and very little was known about them. I spent the morning just lying in the sun at the top of the North arm sunbathing, just watching for signs of fish. One or two fish were seen, but it was hardly inspiring to know that the depths in that area ranged from sixty to ninety feet. Early in the afternoon I moved up into the West arm, pulling the boat in on a small beach. It looked inviting, yet at the same time dead. After downing a couple of lagers, that and the sun combined sent me into the land of dreams. I awoke around three thirty to the sound of leaping fish. It was an unbelievable sight. Everywhere all along the arm, carp were throwing themselves from the water. Within a half hour period well over a hundred fish must have leapt or rolled. It was as if every fish in the lake had moved from the pressure of the south arm into the relative quiet of the West. There was not another single angler on the whole arm, yet I could not take advantage of the fact. I'd left half my tackle back in the van at Pierres. That would be put right the following morning.

Well, it should have been, unfortunately that evening I made my third deliberate mistake. Driving around the track at the top of the South arm on the lookout for fish, I managed to drop the back of the van into a gigantic pot hole. With the engine staring up at the stars there was nothing I could do but wait until the following day to get towed out. That night I slept like a bat, hanging by my feet. By the time I'd been towed out and had breakfast etc., it was nearly midday as I headed the boat towards the West Arm. Turning the corner on the dogleg of the arm, something was wrong. I could see a line of markers out in the mouth of the arm. They had not been there the previous afternoon, my heart sank. On turning the corner my worst fears came true.

The small beach I had been on the previous afternoon was now full of anglers. Indeed every likely looking spot for a hundred yards or so had rods poking out from it. It was nobody's fault of course, only mine for not making sure I was there first, but that knowledge did nothing to take away my disappointment. Making the best of a bad job I set up as best I could on the opposite bank, though my position at best could be described as perilous, so steep was the bank.

Within half an hour of arriving the anglers opposite started catching. Runs came thick and fast to them, while my indicators stayed motionless. Shortly afterwards another boatload of anglers turned the corner into the arm. It turned out to be Ritchie MacDonald, Johnny Allen and Bob a friend of theirs. They had just arrived, as had so it transpired a coachload of anglers from England. Seeing the blokes opposite me catching, Ritchie and the lads elected to set up further down the arm on the Americas rock. Word must have got around very quickly about the amount of fish present, for every few minutes it seemed more anglers arrived. Within a couple of hours, every swim in the arm was occupied. It was time to move, I'd blown it.

It would have been oh so easy to lose myself in a bottle of wine, but something told me to stick at it. I still had that feeling that I only had to find some fish and I'd catch them. Something kept drawing me back to the top end of the South Arm. True it was packed with carp anglers every day and they were not catching, but I was convinced that there just had to be some carp in the area. Compared to the rest of the lake it was relatively shallow and so rich in food.

The following morning I rose at 4.00 a.m. to make sure I'd get the swim I wanted opposite the bridge on the far bank. As I made my way across in the darkness, a fish leapt out just in front of the boat. I hoped it was an omen. I set up in darkness, putting six bait stringers on all rods, as I didn't wish to scare any feeding fish off by baiting up over them. Just as I was about to cast the first rod a fish rolled about 20 yards out to my left. I dropped my bait straight in the vortex left by the fish. As I tightened up, the line was pulled from my hand. I was in, first cast. I'd waited a long time for that run, no way was I going to lose it. Never once letting it get up a steam, I had it in the net within minutes. At 33lb 8oz I was well pleased with my first fish of the trip. I fell asleep, satisfied, with my efforts.

I awoke to the sound of an irate French voice. Even without knowing the language, I knew this guy was swearing and cursing. Looking around the point to my right, I could see this man pulling and tearing at the small electric motor on his boat. The propellor was obviously tangled up in something and he was stuck fast. Then the penny dropped. He was directly above the spot where I'd staked out my carp sack! The sack had been torn to shreds, but that was of little consequence. Unfortunately the carp had not survived the battering from the propellor. I felt like crying, losing such a magnificent fish in such awful circumstances. It felt as if the trip was doomed. Would nothing go right?

As the sun rose, so the fish moved out into the deeper water. Looking around in the boat, I was amazed by the amount of bubbling going on out in the middle of the lake. I was certain they were being made by carp stirring up the bottom and once back at the swim, I set about finding out. Taking the baits out by boat, I searched around until I found a patch of bubbles, then I dropped the bait down amongst them, followed with half a dozen or so handfuls of corn and peanuts. I didn't have long to wait before the rod top hooped over and line poured from the spool. As the bait was in the region of 100 yards from the bank, I jumped straight into the boat, winding down furiously, until the pressure drew the boat directly over the fish. Looking down into the water, I could see it was another very big fish. In many ways it would have been better if I hadn't seen it, for suddenly I was all a-tremble. The fish must have sensed my panic, for suddenly it gained a second wind and started tearing off up the lake, towing me with it. Eventually though the pressure told and I knew as I lifted the net around it, that I'd caught my sixth fish over forty pounds. The scales proved my estimate to be correct, 43lb 12oz to be precise.

That day a pattern emerged that was to stay for the rest of the trip. It appeared that until the sun rose from behind the mountains, fish would feed in the margins. Once the sun was on the water, the fish continued to feed but out in deeper water. For some reason around midday the fish moved off out of the area only to return later in the afternoon between three and four o'clock when once more they would feed out in the deeper water. Two more runs occurred that afternoon, unfortunately one was lost, due to the run coming whilst I was out in the boat playing a fish. The one landed was a plump Italian looking mirror of 28lbs.

I think it is fair to say that I was a much happier man in Pierre's bar that night. After all the disasters of the previous few days, it was great to get a result again. I also knew that I'd have to be up early to get the swim again, as I'd hooked three fish in full view of about twenty carp anglers.

Arriving in the swim, an hour before dawn, I felt uneasy. On the journey across the lake I'd not heard a single fish. The air had a strange chill to it, without the slightest hint of any breeze. Dawn rose but brought with it a thick eerie fog. The rod tips being high in the air, looked as though they were supporting lace curtains. The spiders had been at work weaving an intricate web between the tips. Suddenly the calm was shattered by an almighty eruption directly beneath the rod tops only inches from the bank. As quietly as I could, I quickly wound in one of the baits, dropping it amongst the bubbles left on the surface by the disturbance. For an hour or so nothing happened, then I spotted the rod top knock. Without waiting for further indication, I put my hand over the spool and struck hard. Momentarily I thought that I had hit a snag, then the snag moved! Without ever giving the fish an inch, I played it out on the short line. All it could do under the immense pressure was thrash on the surface. Within a minute, it was in the net. I knew it was another monster. In fact I recognised it from photos I had been looking at, only the previous week. I checked the tail. The frayed edges showed that it had been sacked up in the recent past. Even before weighing I knew that I'd caught my third fifty pounder. The scales confirmed my belief, 54lb 8oz of beautiful leather carp. Was I pleased? Is the Pope a catholic?

Once the fog thinned out, it was back to chasing the bubblers in the boat. Which is when the fun really started. With the rod held in the rest, and the pick up off on the reel, it was simply a case of carrying the baits out one at a time and dropping them into any bubbles I saw. However with two rods already out, and the third bait in my hand, I was searching some eighty yards or so out for more bubbles, when a bird's nest developed at the reel. Suddenly the whole lot jammed solid, jerking the size 2 O'Shaugnessy hook straight into my hand! It felt like I'd been hit by a gigantic electric shock. With the electric motor of the boat turned on full, the boat ploughed on, pulling the hook deeper and deeper into my hand. I managed to turn the boat back towards my swim, gained a bit of slack and bit the line, but not before the hook had been driven in so hard, only a small part of the shank and the eye could be seen. Back on the bank, I was in a mess, I felt sick with the pain, while my body shook uncontrollably from the shock. The logical thing to do was to go to hospital, but I didn't fancy that. I was due to leave the following afternoon and I didn't want to waste a day hanging around hospital, besides which the English were hardly flavour of the month in that neck of the woods and I doubted if my case would be met with much sympathy. Not that it was met with much sympathy by the English anglers opposite me on the other bank. A request for a pair of pliers or tin snips was met with "serves the sod right for catching so many!". So there I was, sitting on this rock, still shaking, staring at my hand in disbelief, when out of the blue this rod butt lifted up off the floor and smacked me in the face. "Have a word, leave it out, stop mucking about, can't you see I'm in pain". I looked around; who the hell I was supposed to be talking to, I didn't know. There was no-one there. Then it dawned on me I had a bloody run. Have you ever tried playing a crazed carp with a hook through your hand at the same time? I assure you it was not easy. The dialogue went something like "Come here baby, aarrhh you bastard, I'll do you for this. That's it, easy does it. We don't want to hurt each other do we? Arrhh, you dirty bastard. Want to fight dirty do you? Well take that, wallop. Don't like it up you do yer. Arrhh."; more blood curdling screams followed. Believe it or not, somehow I landed the fish, and it was the most beautiful thing you could ever set your eyes on. Butter wouldn't melt in its mouth. It was hard to believe that this gorgeous creature only moments before had me stretched out on the torture rack and had shown no mercy.

At 30lb 12oz it represented the fifteenth carp over thirty pounds I had taken from the lake in three visits. Maybe the catch was meant to be etched on my mind, for that day marked the end of an era for me. The following morning I was beaten to the swim. Three anglers were installed by the time I arrived. The pressure was on and nothing was sacred. True the fish were genuinely exceptional but the lake was becoming just another carp water. One where people did what they had to, to catch fish irrespective of whether it upset other anglers or not. Luckily enough by taking the baits out long range in the boat, I was still able to catch a couple of nice twenties, from the position where the anglers who had taken over my swim had previously fished.

However, later that afternoon, when a boat packed with anglers and complete with a Lowrance Fish Finder moved over my baits. I knew the honeymoon was over. Suddenly there was a great excitement in the boat, as a huge fish showed up on the screen. With that a marker was quickly dropped down and a hundredweight of dry peanuts quickly despatched around it. Such behaviour would not be tolerated in England, yet in France some individuals behaved as if they were Lords of the Manor. It was as if there were no rules and it was every man to himself. It was time to go home. I knew I would be back, but things could never be the same again.

Chapter 29

A Short Interview with the Author '80

Question: Rod, is there anything or anybody who has dictated your approach to carp fishing?
Hutchinson: As a youngster I would watch herons in the reeds, moving, but without sign of movement. I have tried to move around lakes in that manner. Yes, I would say herons have dictated my approach. Either that or the booze.
Q: Are you serious?
H: Certainly, I didn't get a nose like this drinking Coca Cola.
Q: You're pulling my leg?
H. Sorry, was I? I didn't realise.
Q: What would you say has been the greatest development you've seen in the years you've been carp fishing?
II: Teabags.
Q: Come on be serious.
H: I am serious. You should have tried buggering about with a billy can in the old days, or drinking 24 hour old tea from a flask. It tasted like the last dregs of a sailor's jock strap.
Q: Who is the angler who has impressed you the most?
H: Chris Yates.
Q: What would you say is the secret to Chris's success?
H: Lovely legs.
Q: Come on now.
H: It's true, Dick Walker was the same in his heyday. All top carp anglers have lovely legs. They have very little else in common, so that has to be the reason.
Q: That's a fact is it? What are your legs like?
H; Keep you hands to yourself sailor. I know you ex-naval types. All rum, bum and bacca.

All top carp anglers have lovely legs . . . I haven't so I hide them with carp

Q: Somehow, you have acquired a reputation for being anti-social. Do you know why this is so?
H: I've no idea.
Q: Surely you must have?
H: I said I hadn't pig face. So shut up before I nut yer.
Q: Sorry Rod. What in this age of tackle development would you like to see all carp anglers having in their kit?
H: Boxing gloves. You should hear the din some nights on crowded waters.
Q: What brought you into carp fishing in the first place, Rod?
H: The same old story, I'm afraid. A broken heart. I was jilted by the first love of my life, Winifred Slack. Slack by name, slack by nature was Winifred. She ran off with a bloke down our street called Johnny Large. I couldn't understand it, I told her I had a small endowment. So it was either the Foreign Legion or carp fishing. Having a bad back stopped me from making the Legion.
Q: Oh, yes, what's up with your back?
H: I've got a big yellow streak down it.
Q: Why do you think you've lasted so long in a branch of sport that sees so many people drop out?
H: Because it's all about dreams. If our dreams come true, what is left? I like living in dreams, it's reality I can't take. After all reality is only an illusion caused by lack of alcohol.
Q: Rod, if you had one wish, what would it be?
H: To bring back the old days. Do you know, we used to enjoy it more when we were catching nothing.
Q: Finally Rod, have you any regrets that so much of your life has been spent in the pursuit of carp?
H: Yes, without doubt. I really wanted to be a ballet dancer, but I could never find a dress to fit me.

Afternoon delight

Chapter 30

Carp Fishing in the Future '80

NO one can forecast the future with any degree of certainty, but as involvement in carp fishing becomes more intense, certain avenues which at the moment are only being glimpsed (by what are believed to be freak captures) will I'm sure be opened up. One of these, I'm sure, will be by taking advantage of a carp's predatory instincts. The majority of a carp's diet is made up from living animal tissue, and whilst in the main part those animals are small beings, at various times larger animals are eaten. Whether those times correspond with a lack of small food items, or it is that larger items are only eaten when they are easy to catch, is open to conjecture. It is rare to see carp actually chase small fish, yet common to see small fish scatter when a carp enters their midst. The small fish are obviously aware of those predatory tendencies, and so should be the angler. Many years ago, I caught a carp on a small lip hooked livebait, while fishing for perch in amongst a shoal of fry. Every close season on one of my local lakes carp can be seen feeding amongst huge black clouds of tadpoles. On a number of lakes, I have observed male carp feeding on spawn, as it was being emitted from the female carp.

All these items offer a higher link in the food chain. Yet they are only eaten when they are still young, weak and easy to catch. Once these items have grown and move faster and further, the energy output is not replenished by the amount of food a carp can catch in this way. If these older, stronger items are able to form a major source of food, it is only for fish like pike, suited for the fast chase. If we accept that small fish, tadpoles, newts, etc, may be eaten when easy to catch, then small deadbaits would seem to provide an answer. I know quite a few carp have been taken on deadbaits, when anglers have been after eels, but as yet the method is not widely used for carp. I believe in future years that it will be, along with small fry livebaits when carp are disturbing fry shoals. As

A beautiful 20-plus common from Belgium

20-plus linear from central France

more and more deadbaits are used, probably in conjunction with prebaiting methods, so the carp will become more accustomed to finding them, and the success of the method will be increased.

I do not believe we will ever see the "ultimate" bait, a food that will catch carp every time it is used. It is just possible we may see the "ultimate" scent, in a given water, something which will always trigger off a feeding instinct in carp. However the carrier of that scent will always need to be changed, or at least all the superficial qualities which a carp can identify. I do not think any scent or attractor will ever work to the same degree in all waters. Most of the attractors are synthetic, unstable chemicals, reacting to the pH value of a given water. Theoretically, it is possible to balance a chemical to a given pH value – but the length of time this would take to apply to all the waters an angler might fish would leave no time for fishing!

There are now known to be many substances which provide stimuli, creating a short attraction period. I can see the time coming when an actual bait (i.e. a particular food) will become obsolete, what is on the hook being only a carrier of an attractor and of no food value whatsoever. This carrier will probably start off in the form of some type of synthetic sponge, which in time will be itself associated with danger. I should think the nearest one could get to the ultimate carrier would be some colourless jelly substance that continually changed shape with water movements, much like an amoeba. Once such a bait is arrived at, I am certain it will be made into a commercial product obtainable by all. Not all anglers will buy it though, because one of the attractions of carp fishing is the challenge. Many will carry on with their own baits, trying to improve them.

The fact that carp do become afraid of something which resembles an item they have previously been caught on will surely see the use of additives which relax the nervous system. A side effect of this relaxation might be hunger symptoms. Although at present most of the substances which perform this function are found naturally in minute quantities in certain plants or foods, and their cost is prohibitive, I am sure greater refinements and synthetic substitutes will one day see their widespread use. One might think that a totally relaxed fish is hardly likely to be afraid of a bait, and so the carrier's productive period would be likely to be prolonged. However, it's not likely to fight much either!

In the normal course of events carp in waters of high food stocks never need to go hungry, and it seems that it is not hunger which decides when a carp should feed, but conditions. On a given day, it is pretty certain that the same amount of food is present at all times, yet the carp will only feed for perhaps a limited time during the hours of darkness. A period of overcast, cloudy weather may also bring on a feeding spell. So it is pretty certain that conditions dictate when a carp feeds. Unfortunately the angler is not always able to fish at those times when feeding conditions prevail, but he still wants to catch fish. With this in mind, I can see the time coming when feeding conditions are artificially created. I don't know the exact formula for those conditions but there are some things which certainly are relevant. Probably the most certain of these is low light intensity. Earlier in the book, I mentioned the feasibility of dragging a swim for carp. This would colour the water and prevent much light from penetrating. On the same lines, I am sure it is possible to make some substance that will artificially cloud the water for a certain period and then disperse. Many years ago I used to fish for roach on a canal at a point where a small culvert entered. Two or three times a day water would be pumped from the culvert into the canal. It was only at those times when the water was coloured, that any bites were forthcoming. One day when fishing with a friend I decided to see if I could create these pumping conditions. I stood astride the walls of the pumping well, and threw buckets of water over into the canal as fast as I possibly could. My friend fished into the area I was disturbing and started getting bites.

In that case the feeding conditions were artificially created, and I am sure they could be with carp. Although not relevant to feeding conditions at all times, in high summer I think additional oxygen may help. I mentioned earlier how high winds battering into banks provide an influx of oxygen and that carp feed regularly in those conditions. I also know of three lakes which have aerators in them for use at times of low oxygen content. Whenever the aerators are switched on, feeding spells start. I have read of things like "Alka Selza" being advocated to provide oxygen. I must admit to not liking the idea. Used on any large scale, the solution of aspirin could be detrimental to a water. I could however see the use of a small battery driven aerator, as used for tropical fish, having a beneficial effect. Even something like a length of hose attached to a foot pump might be helpful in margin swims.

Much as I dislike the idea, I am sure artificially reared large carp will, sometime soon, start re-appearing from the continent. Carp fishing is many things to many people, and just like all other sports there are those happy just to take part for the enjoyment value, whilst there are others who will always want to be top dog. Some will demand the stocking of bigger and bigger fish, irrespective of how those fish were reared, and how hard to catch they may be. Many owners of commercial fisheries will be alive to this demand, and fullfil the need merely for commercial interests. There will be certain anglers who will feel the need to catch such fish regularly, to promote sales of products they are associated with. I can see the time when there will be several forty pound carp waters all plying for trade in competition with each other, in much the way some trout fisheries do at present. Each water will want the biggest fish available. Unfortunately there is only a certain size to which a carp can be grown on food alone, and the demand for replacement fish will mean that size must be achieved in the shortest possible time. In the farming industry, where this situation has gone on for years, there is now widespread use of hormones, to increase bulk quickly. There is no doubt in my mind whatsoever that this will eventually happen to carp fishing. Side effects of sterility and short life span will mean little, once the rat race is underway.

There will however always be the angler who doesn't have to catch the biggest, or the largest number of fish to enjoy himself. The man who can blend with the landscape, and take in all nature has to offer. The man who is content to pit his wits against the master of another environment. It's up to you whether you join the rat race or not.

Footnote 88

Not a lot has changed, because as outlined in the bait chapter, thinking about baits has stagnated in the intervening years. There are still many ideas there to be followed through. The importation of large carp has not happened and I now doubt if it will. If people really want to catch really huge carp, they are now willing to travel to other countries, plus the situation has now arrived where large carp are now as valued in their country of origin, as in England. Carp mania has now spread around Europe. Commercial carp fisheries have now spread everywhere and while they are businesses it would be wrong to criticise them; they give thousands of anglers pleasure and that can't be a bad thing.

Chapter 31

When It All Comes Right and Wrong '88

A friend in Belgium had passed on tales of huge carp in a certain area of Northern France. Unfortunately from my point of view, huge was not specified by weight but by length. It was said that a fish of one metre thirty centimetres existed, set up in a local tackle shop. By my rough calculations this fish was somewhere in the region of forty inches long and there is simply no way of knowing what such a fish might weigh. If it came from St Cassein, in all probability it would weigh over fifty pounds, whilst such a fish from Savay Lake would most likely come in around thirty-five to thirty six pounds. The fact that all the fish were said to be commons threw another spanner into the works; what if they were "wildies"? The largest true wildie I have ever heard reported also came from France, if memory serves me, its weight being twenty eight pounds. For those not sure about the true definition of a wild carp (count me in on that), they are supposed to be descendants of carp introduced in the middle ages by monks, as indeed most European carp were. However it is when the population has been left undisturbed and no additional stockings of other carp have occurred that they are regarded as true wildies. Other stockings would create cross breeding and most likely better growth, but the blood line would be broken. There are those who say if mirror carp are present that fish cannot be regarded as wildies, but this is not strictly correct. While spawning between commons does for the most part produce commons, the occasional mirror and more rarely a leather will be produced. I can think of one water now holding approximately two hundred carp, of which just two are mirrors. These fish are the produce of twenty four common carp originally introduced. Had those fish been wildies, even allowing for the fact that breeding had probably taken place between the couple of mirrors and the commons, I would still regard them as wild carp.

Be that as it may, tales of forty inch long carp had to be investigated. The area we were put onto was alive with beautiful reed fringed lakes. Every one looked inviting, despite the fact we never actually saw any carp. Most simply felt carpy. When faced with choice, I follow my instincts and go for what appears to be the quietest water, which is what I did. However it is lucky that I am not superstitious, because there had to be a reason why a large beautiful lake saw few people, particularly when locals assure you that the lake is full of fish, with very large carp being present amongst them. The old abbey nearby, from where it was said, on a quiet night you could hear the ghosts of monks being tortured and executed during the Inquisition may have put people off, or the rumours of war time traitors' bodies being disposed of in the great depths may also have had some bearing on the matter. Personally with so much water available I was more inclined to believe that most people given a choice of fishing small waters with easy access or a large lake that entailed a long walk through marshes, would go for the smaller ones.

The lake was approximately half a mile long, probably six hundred yards across for the most part. It ran west to east, the west end being a large dam wall while at the eastern end the lake ran off into two arms, a peninsular being present between the two arms. As the prevailing south west wind broke on the peninsular, it seemed as good a place to start as any.

Plumbing around found a most unusual bottom. While the margins averaged between sixteen to twenty feet only a rod's length out, one hundred yards out directly in line with the point of the peninsula was a plateau like area, roughly circular in shape, approximately twenty yards across. This plateau was alive with small zebra and pea mussels, the depth of water above it being no more than six feet.

It seemed logical to me that any carp coming down on the prevailing wind would feed on this plateau before going off into the two arms, which were heavily weeded, to feed again.

With the aid of my inflatable boat, I went out and put polystyrene markers on the extremities of the plateau, before baiting quite heavily with sweetcorn and boilies. Between my fiancee and myself we had six rods, which we intended using with corn and boilie baits alternately. The plateau however was not large enough to efficiently fish that many baits, so we decided to fan two rods either side out into the arms, whilst having one bait apiece on the plateau. Both arms also had markers put into them, around which we again baited with sweetcorn and boilies.

Having first gained permission to fish at night "if you dare, we won't mind," we commenced fishing around four thirty in the afternoon. It was warm and sultry, a light south westerly gently lapping into our bank. Around five thirty we heard a fish crash, but missed seeing it as we were playing chess at the time. However the large flat on the water between our markers on the plateau confirmed it was a fish on our baited area.

Six o'clock was signalled by the sound of my Optonic, and line tearing off through the rings. Pick up in, wallop. The rod bent over to its maximum and I found myself backwinding like fury. Remember this was at a range of at least one hundred yards and the fish was going at such speed, all I could do was hang on and give line. I have done a lot of long range fishing in my life but never before had I encountered anything like this, at one point one hundred and eighty yards of line must have been out from the spool. Even when I'd turned the fish, it was never easy, but a hard bruising fight all the way, my arms aching like crazy. Thirty yards off and the fish turned into the arm to my right. I piled on the pressure but could do nothing to prevent the fish from diving into the weed.

The bottom in the arm shelved very gradually, allowing me to wade out in order to get a better angle on the fish. Maintaining steady pressure throughout, I was about ten yards from the fish when I felt it moving. Suddenly the water erupted and a tremendously long common carp back rolled on the surface. My initial response was "bloody hell, it's fifty." I pushed out the landing net, the fish rolled again and dived once more into the weed. I could feel its head burrowing in deeper and deeper. Applying steady pressure again, I felt the fish move once more when suddenly the lead pinged by my head. The hook had torn free. In time honoured tradition I threw the rod up the bank. To say I was disappointed would be an understatement. I have always denied having ambitions but at that moment I realised I did have one. To catch a fifty pound carp from somewhere other than St Cassein. Now that would be nice.

The evening and night were uneventful apart from a singular carp crashing around midnight and owls periodically trying to scare us off with their haunting cries. The following day turned out to be very hot indeed, without a breath of wind. Out in the centre of the lake several carp could be seen cruising about. The binoculars confirmed that all were commons, but at such distance it was impossible even to guess what size the fish might be. That afternoon we repeated the baiting proceedure, using around five pounds of sweetcorn and two hundred boilies around each marker. The boilies being a very simple preparation of one pound of boilie mix to which was added ten ml. of Shellfish Sense Appeal. The sweetcorn had also been soaked in a dilution of crayfish flavour. The two long range rods out on the plateau were armed with eight pound breaking strain main line, attached to fifteen pound leaders, while the rods fishing closer into the arms were equipped with fifteen pound line throughout. All our baits being fished on a dacron hair tied off the eye of a size four hook of my own design.

Both long range rods also had stringers attached, one with three small boilies, while the other had about twelve grains of sweetcorn threaded on micro thread P.V.A.

The previous day there had been signs of fish by five thirty but that afternoon and evening we saw absolutely nothing, which was probably due to the lack of wind. It seemed that we needed a wind blowing into our faces to bring carp into the vicinity of our baits.

It was well after dark, somewhere around eleven pm when the rustling of reeds, indicated a wind had sprung up, luckily in the direction we wanted, straight into our swim. About thirty minutes later we heard a carp crash over the long range rods. Within minutes a carp crashed on the marker in the arm to our right, quickly followed by another on the baited area to our left! By midnight there was the incredible sound of fish rolling simultaneously on all three baited areas! The water was alive with feeding carp. It was fill your boots time.

I was just starting to get impatient, thinking "why aren't we getting any runs", when the boilie baited rod, fished into the right hand arm, roared off. The speed of the take was incredible. It seemed one second the fish was in front of me, the next second fifty yards to my left. And that was when the trouble started. All of our rods were suddenly flying. Due to our lines being high in the water over the top of weed beds, the fish had picked the lot of them up on its initial run! It was now towing six leads around and umpteen yards of line. Every damn line got pulled into a weed bed, all the rods wrenched off their rests. The night was pitch black and we didn't even have a torch between us to sort out the chaos. I had no idea at all where the fish was! Like Queen Victoria I was not amused. All I could do was wind in until the line from another rod snagged in the rod tip. Then it was a case of biting that line off, winding it around my hand until it was all on the bank, while all the time praying that the fish was still attached to the original rod. Meanwhile, the carp out on the baited area were going bananas. Unfortunately I no longer had baits in their vicinity. What an utter balls up.

For the next hour I went through the bite the lines, wind them in routine, throwing the discarded rods behind me. In the confusion at least one rod got stood on, the sickening crunch really bucking my spirits up. Slowly, almost imperceptibly, the crashing out in the lake subsided. I knew I had to get a bait to the fish before they mopped up all the ground bait and moved on, but I couldn't do a thing about it. I still had a fish on, with every available line attached to it!

God knows what time it was when the net slipped beneath the fish amongst a mountain of weed and line. It was too dark even to weigh it, let alone fix up fresh tackle and start again. The carp was put in the sack for the night, while I jumped straight into the sleeping bag, all thoughts of further fishing that night forgotten.

The next morning the swim looked as if it had been hit by a bomb. Rods and lines everywhere, the bivvy drenched in weed and mud. The previous night whilst playing the fish, my mind had not been tuned in to how big it might be. I was more concerned with getting a bait to other feeding fish. However my eyes lit up on opening the sack. The fish was on its stomach, so I could not see the girth. The length of the back though was incredible. Once out of the sack, its length belied its weight. What could have been a forty pound plus fish weighed in at twenty four pounds and eight ounces. Its scaling, length and general appearance being more like a chub than a carp. It looked like a wildie and had fought like a wildie. As far as I'm concerned, it was a wildie. The following night I caught two more identical in appearance, the largest going just over nineteen. Which makes me wonder about the first fish I had hooked and estimated at fifty pounds. Chances are it was another big wildie, probably half that size. Which all goes to show how many carp you may have caught, we all make mistakes.

Was it wild? It went absolutely crackers

Twenty seven years on — a special moment

Chapter 32

An Occasion of Sorts '88

There are times when I just need to be beside a lake. Times when the rods are out but really are of secondary importance. After a period of being stuck indoors, I simply need to feel the cool night air upon my face, I need to talk to angling friends of good times past and hopes for the future. My mind at such times is not really tuned in to the fishing but all the same I might just as well try to catch one while I'm on the bank.

This was such an occasion, I needed to be out and my friends from Sheffield, Dave and Russ were due to fish the lake on the Saturday night. I arrived around four in the afternoon, finding I had the lake to myself. The cool October wind was blowing moderately into the south west corner of the lake, this also constituted the deepest area and after a week of light frosts looked far and away the most promising area. However as I said earlier sometimes the catching of fish is of secondary importance. Ann my fiancée and the children were due to join me later and although the children could sleep in the camper, Ann and myself were hardly geared up for Autumn nights and the prospect of the chill north east wind in our faces did not appeal to me.

The east bank is protected from the winds by hills and felt ten degrees warmer than the opposite side. Two weeks earlier when walking round I had seen a great many fish half way along the east bank feeding in the last remains of a summer weedbed. Obviously there would still be food there, but considering the weather of the previous week it was doubtful as to whether the carp would still be there, as the water depth was under four feet. The east bank definitely was not the ideal spot but it was warm and comfortable and there was always a chance of a fish early in the evening before the water cooled, then again later the following morning, after the sun had been on the water a couple of hours.

I cast around a few times until I found the remains of the weedbed. Much to my surprise the bottom was relatively clean. I expected to wind back black rotting weed, instead I found short two or three inch stems of fresh green weed impaled upon the hook and around the leger bomb. It looked promising, all I needed was a water temperature high enough to entice carp into the shallow water. It was hardly likely however to rise high enough to bring large numbers of fish into the area, so I catapulted out only twelve free offerings. They were what I call 'samplers'. Not enough for a carp to gorge itself before finding the hookbait, rather just enough for it to be looking for more.

Earlier in the season, I had noticed that the carp were much less tolerant of tight lines than in previous years, their intolerance being more acute in shallow water, so with that in mind, after casting I slackened off, putting a small piece of 'anglers weight', a putty like lead replacement on the line beyond the rod tip, ensuring that the line would lie on the lake bottom. The only problem here is that you have none of the tightness of a tight line set up which ensures pricked fish becoming hooked fish. In this situation you have to make sure that your terminal tackle hooks the fish for you. With this in mind, I set up a fixed 3oz (80grm) lead, with a short 3'' (7½cm) hook length. The boilie was fixed tight to the shank of a size 2 hook.

The theory being that it was virtually impossible for a carp to pick up the boilie without taking the hook in its mouth, while the heavy lead only 3 inches away should provide the jerk necessary to set the hook.

Dave and Russ duly arrived, expressing surprise at my choice of swim. I could only offer the explanation that I had not yet got our cold weather clothes sorted out and it was the warmest spot on the lake. They quickly made off for the deep water area, hardly believing their luck that I was not already entrenched there. It transpired later in the conversation that the deep water swims that they had chosen, had in other seasons been autumn hotspots regardless of conditions. Now although I had suspected that the area would be a likely autumn and winter holding area, I did not actually know for sure, as I had not fished the lake after early summer before. Had I had previous experience I would have taken enough clothes, sleeping bags etc, to ensure I could fish in any conditions. A cold wind certainly would not have put me off.

Ann and the children arrived about half an hour before dark and while the children walked the dog, we sat surveying the swim. It looked as dead as a Dodo. The wind had dropped off, the lake was flat calm and the temperature was dropping rapidly. Many is the time I sit and imagine that I'm a big old carp rooting through the weedstems, searching for food but that evening all I could think of was, my swim would be the last place I would be if I was a carp. I'd chosen a bummer.

However, I was not there just to fish and half an hour or so after dark, Dave came round, silly grin on his face, armed with cans of Foster's lager. We went through our full repertoire of jokes, some dating back to the Christopher Columbus joke book! The kids laughed, the dog went in for every rat and coot which swam the margins and while I had resigned myself to catching nothing, life felt good. It was not long before the kids were asking when we were going to the pub! Now I was not really bothered but you have to keep the children happy don't you, besides which my stomach thought my throat had been cut and the temptation of the local chip shop afterwards was too much to bear. Around 10 p.m, thirst quashed by several pints of Guinness, arms full of parcels of fish, chips, curries and other gastronomic delights, we arrived back to find Russ doing battle with a big one. He had been playing it for fully ten minutes yet had never had it closer than fifty yards from the net. Another ten minutes elapsed, without the fish getting any closer, when suddenly the hook pulled free. During the excitement I had not noticed that a light drizzle was falling, however it soon became apparent that the sky had clouded up and the temperature had risen appreciably.

Back at my swim, Ann laid supper out while I did the necessary with the rods. I think my feelings were best expressed by what I said to Ann (or what I meant to say as my speech was somewhat slurred by this time.) "I can't say I'm confident but I shouldn't be surprised to get one now." Supper was superb, cod, chips, fishcake and curry was washed down with a bottle of chateau plonk. "What more could a man ask for Annie?". Then thinking, "well a nice big carp".

Suddenly one of the Optonics sounded, followed by the smooth clutch of the Baitrunner. In my usual manner, I slid all the way to the rods, across the wet grass on my backside. Picking up the rod, in that nonchalant manner which implied I always do it this way, I slipped on my bum again. Annie started laughing and I got a fit of the giggles. The fish was a long way off and from the vibrations I felt up the line, had obviously made its way through some weedbed I knew nothing about. I tried vainly to get to the top of my sloping swim to get a better vantage point from which to play the fish but in trainers on wet grass it was impossible. Every time it looked as though I might make the top of the bank, the fish would give a sudden tug and I'd go sliding down again.

Several minutes later after removing half a weedbed from my line, I had the fish twenty or so yards out. It was at this point that I realised that I'd have to wade out to land it, as my swim was only inches deep up to ten yards from the bank. At this point the event turned into an utter fiasco. Ann, a little perky from lager and vino, kept tripping me up as she tried to put the Derriboots on my feet. I'm there perched on one leg like Jethro Tull trying to play the fish, while she is trying to force a right boot on my left foot. It seemed an age before I realised that Ann was wearing boots and the obvious thing was for her to net it. "You mean you want me to net it" said Ann, swaying gently in the breeze, for truth told she was now getting a little the worse for wear. "Yes I'd be grateful if you don't mind". "Oh no I don't mind, if you really want me to", "I'd be grateful if you would". "Alright then — pause — how deep is it?". "Three to six inches that's all", "Oh that looks o.k then", said Ann, picking up the net and marching off into the darkness. It was so dark with the heavy drizzle coming down, I could hardly see Annie. It was like watching your telly on the blink, just shadows in a snow storm. "How you doing Annie?", "How deep did you say it was?, the fish is still ten yards away and the waters coming over my boots". At this I played the old trump card trick, "Sorry about that love but do your best please?". The crunch line, "I think it's a bigun". In ploughed Annie further, 'good un' that she is. Either the drizzle had eased or the interference on the telly had cleared, for I began seeing her quite clearly. She'd stopped giggling and I could see from the determined look on her face that she was going for it. I heaved hard and the fish rolled about three feet from Ann. She pushed forwards and the fish just tripped the nylon cable of the net. I heaved hard again and Ann scooped the fish in the huge net.

Almost on the point of netting Russ arrived and in that low undertaker like voice of his asked, "What's thee doing?". Before I could answer Dave appeared letting rip with "Come on you wanker, wind the bugger in". I was not used to this bombardment of high intellect otherwise I'd have had a witty answer of sorts, all I could say was "We've landed her". "It's a big fish Rod", said Annie from the water: "Eh ah lass, give us that", said Dave taking over the net. "You've got a big fish here old lad", said Dave, "It's a beast, get the scales and weigh sling out, get the torch". I was rather embarrassed to inform the lads, I had none of those things. "You pillock", said Dave, "go get the sling and scales Russ".

At this point I still had no idea as to the size of the fish. But when Dave unfolded the net, I could see it was a good one, one I actually recognised, having caught it the previous June. But I distrusted my eyes as this fish appeared far larger than it should have been. Russ arrived back, panting and I sensed that he and Dave were excited: of course this could have meant they were coming into use, but I had the feeling it was the fish that excited them. We discussed what it might weigh, or rather I did; Russ and Dave stayed quiet. I was going on, "Well in good nick it should be in the twenty sevens", when Russ announced "Thirty pounds, two ounces", "Congratulations", said Dave, "me and Russ are very pleased to be present at this historic occasion, your very first Lincolnshire thirty". I'd never thought of it before but after 27 years of fishing all over England and the continent, I had never before caught a truly big fish from my own neck of the woods. ''Ooh, that's nice is that'', said Ann smiling and you know it was. I appreciated that fish and I think so did Dave and Russ. Twenty seven years is a long time: I think I deserved it. The moral is of course, get yourself out there, even the bleakest days can turn into something of an occasion. So if you ever ask yourself ''should I go fishing,'' always remember the man from Delmonte. He says ''Yes''.

Chapter 33

A Never To Be Forgotten Evening '85

Fishing Lake Cassien in 1985 had been the stuff dreams are made of. There were lots of holiday makers admittedly, but very few anglers. The carp behaved as all carp do in a natural unspoilt environment, and catching them for the most part was not difficult. Any difficulties which came were due to the nature of the lake itself, rather than any refusal by the carp to feed on our baits. At times it almost felt like cheating, landing huge carp on extremely crude tackle and using methods which ten years previously would have had the hardened English carp laughing at you. But just catching the big beautiful carp of Cassien was only part of it. Throughout the summer and early autumn the climate had been superb. As my friend Roger Smith had remarked "being the weatherman at Cassien must be the easiest job in the world. All you have to do is to get up each morning and say 'today will be bright and sunny, with light variable winds'. If he ever got it wrong, he would deserve to get the sack." Whilst at home, when I let my mind drift back to Cassien, fish rarely entered the scene, instead I felt the sun on my back, could taste the lobster sauce floating on the soup de poisson, feel the chill of the local Rosé trickling down my throat. I simply loved the place and everything about it. But our late October 1985 trip was a mistake. It was cold and wet, a chill wind blowing down from the Alps. In Chez Pierre's cafe there was no atmosphere, while our favourite restaurant appeared closed most of the time. It simply wasn't Cassien as I knew it. True the fish were still there, but there is more to fishing than the actual fish!

It did not help my mood at all the vast amount of tackle we were losing either. The water level must have dropped twenty feet from my previous visit and some of the new areas we had to fish in, seemingly contained under water forests. Added to this, water was being drawn off at the dam, creating a tremendous flow through the lake. I felt like crying at times when after putting the marker out, and baiting around it, I'd return to the bank only to see my marker heading off in the direction of the dam. Baiting had to be precise, yet on occasions, I had no idea where I'd baited up. By the third morning, I had had enough, and tried vainly to talk Roger into returning home. But my attempts fell on deaf ears. Roger was made of sterner stuff than I, besides which he had already caught fish that trip and he had come equipped for fishing in late autumn. Me, dreamer that I am, had imagined the weather would still be like an English summer, and had only T-shirts, shorts and a track-suit with me, apart from my old parkha.

I was down, things weren't going well back home, I wasn't enjoying the fishing, I simply wanted to be away. Roger eventually agreed to shorten our intended stay, two more nights and that would be it. Great, just two more nights, freezing my cobblers off, catching nothing, and feeling miserable.

Around lunchtime we moved across the lake to a new area, where I'd seen a fish crash early in the morning. We set up on a small beach approximately 20 yards wide, about 200 yards above the first cafe on the southern arm. I took the southerly point of the beach while Roger set up about 12 yards to my right. We plumbed around a bit during the course of which I lost a few more leads, which really bucked me up. Around three in the afternoon, the wind changed in direction, blowing straight into our faces, bringing with it a shower of large hailstones, which you certainly don't appreciate when you've got ears the size of mine! God was I pee'd off, huddled beneath the brolly with nothing to do but stare out at the bleak landscape, listening to Roger snore.

Around 5.45, just as dusk was falling, my left hand rod tip bent over, the line pinged from the clip and my clapped out, rain sodden buzzer emitted weird sounds, something like a flatulent frog. I picked up the rod and jumped straight into the boat, Roger rapidly following me. As I wound down furiously, Roger set the motor running, directing the boat towards the fish. We had not got 20 yards from the bank when all went solid. The bloody thing had snagged me. We tried every trick we knew, all to no avail, eventually having to pull for a break. Just to stick the boot in, the old man upstairs opened up the heavens, completely soaking us before we could make the shelter of the brollies. "Have you got a revolver I could borrow?" I asked Roger.

The next twenty or so hours passed uneventfully, save for the odd earthquake or two, and a succession of chub over five pounds which kept impaling themselves on our hooks. Believe me, when you're really down, cold and fed up and everything seems to be going against you, then the buzzer suddenly goes and you strike into a chub, you are hardly chuffed.

"What you need is a few lagers down your neck" said Roger. "I need more than that Rog. I've had more fun knocking nails in my feet," I replied. "A nice drop of Glenfiddich, that will sort you out. Come on, let's get some stuff down us," tried Roger again. "I would do Rog," I replied, "but it's five o'clock now and I had that run at a quarter to six last night. You know if I went in the boozer now, the mood I'm in, I wouldn't be out till they chucked us out. Besides we're going home in the morning, it's my last chance." "I didn't think I'd ever hear you turn down a drink," replied an amazed Roger, "Shame on you." "I'm not," said I, "jump in the van, whip up to Pierre's and buy a bottle of scotch. You'll be back in five minutes." "Good idea." said Roger.

Half an hour later, I'm thinking, "Where's Roger? He should be back by now. The fish could come on any time." Another half hour passed, it was six o'clock and still no sign of him. The wind was blowing a right hooligan. "Come on Rog, come on." Half an hour later with the brolly being bombarded with hailstones the size of marbles and all chances of a fish now dismissed from my mind, I was pleading, "Please come Roger old chum, I'm dying for a bloody scotch. I don't even mind if I catch nothing and you get a whacking great fifty, just please hurry back with that scotch." Quarter to seven, and still no Roger and I'm starting to be worried about him. "Hope the silly old bugger hasn't driven the van in the lake. Hell, he can't swim!" – pause – "No, the size of him, I'd have heard the splash miles off." During the next five minutes, everything passed through my mind, "He'd had an accident. How? Probably forgot to drive on the right. Had he had a couple of drinks before his accident and been done on the old nose bag? No, he's been fishing Seafoodblend all week. No-one, but no-one would get *that* close. Come on Roger, I'm gasping," I bellowed in a voice meant to break the glass in Pierre's windows, one mile away.

I was awoken from my self pity, by the click of the line clip, followed a full second later by just two croaks from the buzzer, (yes, you've guessed, it was the old frog farter buzzer playing up again.) "What the hell's going on," I said out loud, talking to myself. "Bet it's a bloody chub." I put the pick up in and whacked hard. The rod arched over into something solid. "Oh shit, I've snagged." So there I was, thoroughly dejected, with this rod bent over stuck hard into a snag, when I gradually found myself being pulled into the water. "Christ, there's a fish on." I fumbled at the clutch, unscrewing the tension, and whacked the fighting level right over. The clutch screamed like nothing I've ever heard before. I ran for the boat, screwing back hard again on the clutch as I did so. I literally fell in the boat, hanging on to the rod with one hand, trying to untie the mooring rope with the other.With the line cutting the air like a cheese wire and me hanging for dear life on to the rod, I heard the slow rasping like sound of the rope coiling across the sand, and

Chubby here, took three 1½" boilies, the fish took four!

felt a slow irresistible pull, move the old boat out. I suddenly felt that things were starting to go for me.

"Right sunshine, come to daddy." I slackened the clutch quickly letting it scream, so that I could get my rod upright, then clamped it down tight again the moment it was up. I wound down as hard as I could, bringing the boat directly over the fish. For the first time, I felt in full control. It felt good. It felt slow, it felt big. I felt good, I was having that fish. I knew it was in mid-water. There we were safe, no snags. The tackle was good, it was mine. I just let it tow me, that would tire the fish, before it tired me. The fish slowly moved off southerly, and it says much for the line and the fish, that the boat was crashing through waves any powerful rower would have struggled against. Within minutes my back and knees were killing me, yet the old carp kept ploughing on. She seemed hell bent on going up the river at the start of the south arm, at least that was the impression I had as we turned the corner and I saw the bridge loom up in front of me. Only twenty or so yards from the bridge, I felt the fish bump hard, and its movements stop. We had obviously hit shallow water, the fish just laying on the bottom having a rest. I thrust one hand out over the side of the boat, and using my hand as a paddle, manoeuvred the boat into the side.

Leaping from the boat, rod in hand, I made for the nearest rock. I had to sit down and straighten up because my back was absolutely killing me. I tried to light a cigarette but my fingers were that cold, I could not feel the matches I held, and only succeeded in burning myself. Meanwhile the fish just lay on the bottom, not a care in the world, as though it was getting a tan on the beach at Cannes. After a few minutes, the feeling returned to my hands while my back, though still hurting, would at least move from the bent position I'd been stuck in the previous fifteen minutes or so.

"Right sunshine, let's be having you," I heaved on the rod for all I was worth, but all remained solid. Walking up the bank, I tried pressure from different angles, but still I couldn't budge it. I was beginning to think it had snagged up and there was nothing for it but the old stones trick! I lobbed several fist sized stones in its direction, yet still it didn't move. I yelled for Roger for assistance, but there was no reply. He was still missing, presumed dead. Getting back in the boat, I wound down hard again, pulling the boat towards the fish. When I thought I was directly over it, I dropped another stone down close by the line. I can only presume that I scored a direct hit because all hell let loose. The boat spun round and I was being towed again back in the direction I came from. I yelled Roger again, but in vain, he still wasn't back.

Passing the corner where the river mouth joins the south arm, I heard a buzzer go. Line was being ripped off at a furious pace. The bleeps got faster and faster, until suddenly they stopped, followed by a sound not unlike a rocket taking off, then a distinct splash. It was clear the chance of carp number two had gone. Meanwhile I was still hanging on. My back was so stiff it felt like I was wearing a strait-jacket. My hands didn't exist any more, they were just two numb blobs on the end of my arms. Such was the pain I was in, I had to resort to laying flat on my belly in the boat, (well as flat as you can get with a beer gut like mine.) The bottom of the boat was by now about an inch deep in water from the relentless rain and hailstorms, my tracksuit clinging like frost to my body. I couldn't stay in that position long, and forcing my way back on my knees looked up to see the cafe, 200 yards north of where I had hooked the fish, now disappearing behind me!

The fish just ploughed on slowly, relentlessly, down the lake. I looked at my watch. The fish had been on for forty minutes! Another buzzer burst into life back on the beach! It was obvious a shoal of carp had moved through. Where the hell was Smithy? I tried to ignore the sound, but it just kept on, beep, beep, beep, getting faster and faster, then swoosh. "We have lift off, you're looking fine Spirolite 2, everything is A.O.K." said a voice in my head.

The wind was gaining in force, waves crashing over the bow. Hail had turned to rain, and the night was very dark. I began to fear for my safety. If the boat capsized, I doubted if I'd have the strength to swim to shore. Yet the fish just went on remorselessly. The lights of Pierre's cafe could now just be made out through the rain on my right. It was all so peculiar. The fish felt big, in the slow way it moved, yet other big carp I had hooked in St. Cassien had done nothing. My largest two fish previously have both been on the bank in under five minutes! Whilst some fish had taken ages to land, particularly those in the 25 to 35 pound range, this was definitely not one of them, it simply moved too slowly. I could only hazard a guess that I had foul hooked one of the big ones in the tail, which was why I had so little control over it.

For some misguided reason, I believed or hoped that the fish would ground itself on the shallows in front of Pierre's cafe. No such luck, on reaching the end of the south arm, it promptly turned left and headed up the west arm. By this time, I'm talking to the fish, "Do what you want sunshine. You can't keep this up forever. I'm going to have you, so why don't you give in like a good boy." I think I was trying to convince myself as much as the fish, for truth told, I was in agony with my back and was definitely feeling the effects of exposure. Coming up to the bridge where the North arm enters, the fish stopped for a few moments in midwater, as if confused about which way to head next. This daft thought of the carp tossing a coin up and saying, "What should it be, North arm or West arm?" came in my head. Suddenly the boat spun round and we were heading for the south arm again! "Fooled you there," said the carp. "Too right you did sunshine," said I.

On entering the south arm again, the full force of the wind hit the boat. It was really tossing about, and my bottle was slowly but surely going. Where were my brown corduroy trousers when I needed them? Truth was, I was

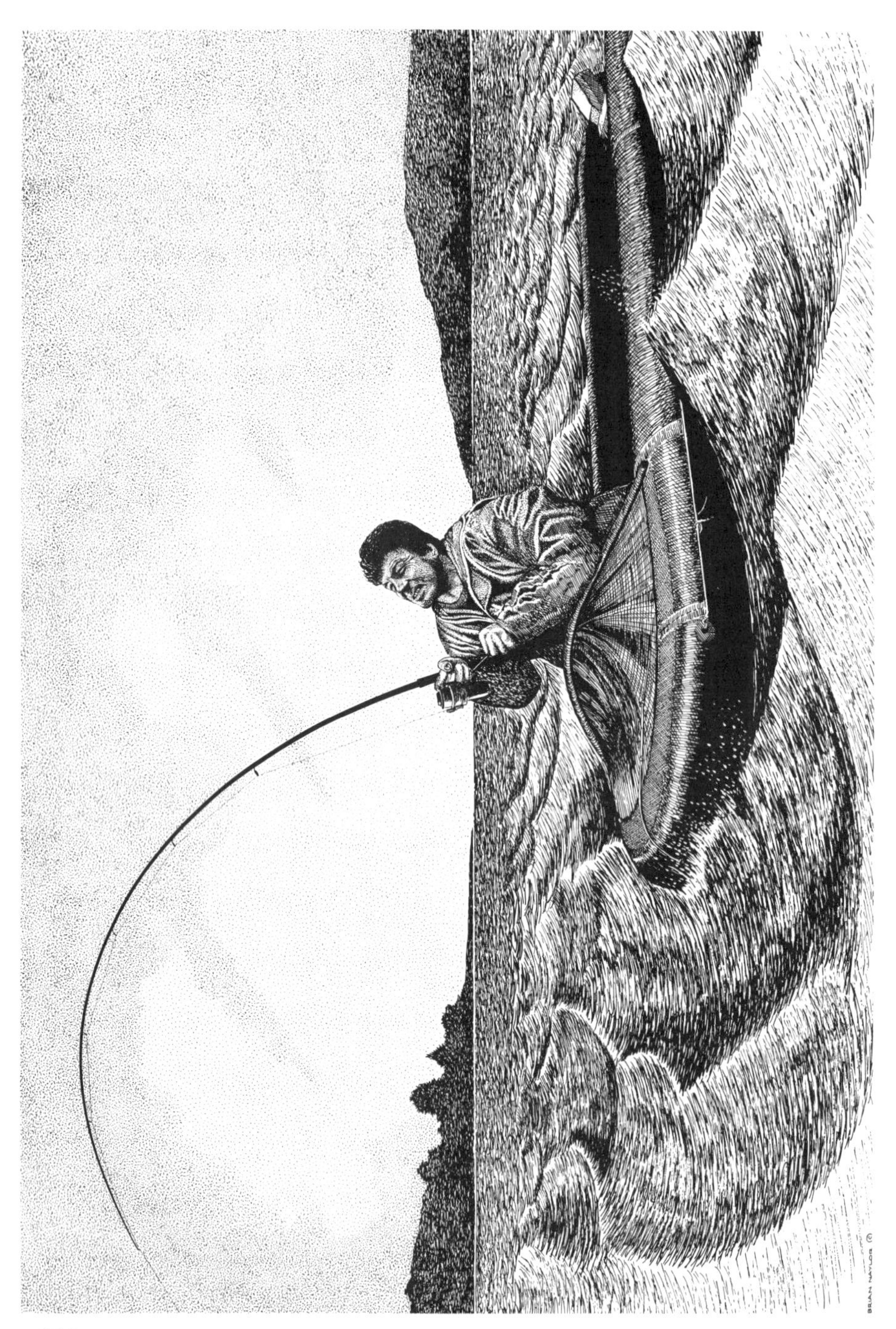
BRIAN NAYLOR ©

getting scared. I knew I couldn't last the night out, I'd have been dead from exposure. Half way up the south arm, I had to go for it, it was shit or bust, I'd had enough. I tried to relax, taking deep breaths to get my strength up. In the distance another buzzer sounded! It was Roger's. It kept on running, Roger was obviously not back yet. Pulling my way up to the front of the boat, I got up on my knees. "Right baby, here we go." I wound down as hard as I possibly could, the old rod, bent double, creaked beneath the corks, I wasn't going to give it an inch. At first nothing seemed to happen, then I realised water was gushing in over the front of the boat, while the stern was literally out of the water! "Christ, I'm sinking!" I threw myself backwards, landing on my bum, righting the boat in the process, thank God! As I did, the fish crashed on the surface in front of the boat! It was a bloody great catfish, that had to be getting on for eight feet long! All manner of things flashed through my mind. "What do you do with a cat that size? What if I landed it, would it take a chunk out of the boat? I was in an inflatable, with forty feet of water beneath me! Worse still would it take a chunk out of me?"

Before I could work out a plan of attack, the fish shot off north. I was getting fed up of this, I'd just been there. The rod was pulled hard over my shoulder and I felt the tight line cut straight into my neck, and blood trickle down my chest. "God, it's decapitating me, beam me up Scotty for Christ sake!" Sheer panic followed as the boat spun uncontrollably around. I could think of nothing but self preservation, as I pulled the pick up off, and let the fish run.

For maybe five minutes I just lay in the bottom of the boat, trying to control the shaking of my body, while the boat just drifted back towards Chez Pierre's. After getting myself together again, I yelled like mad for Roger. If I was going to land that fish, I had to have assistance. But there was still no reply. It was doubtful anyway if he'd have heard me, had be been back, because of the wind, (or was it really Roger with the wind?). By the time my head was together, the reel had been stripped of all 300 yards of line. I was hanging on by the knot! Gradually I wound back, pulling the boat back up the lake as I did so. This was slow and tiring and took fully fifteen minutes before I found myself directly over the fish, which had gone to ground in front of the cafe, just 200 yards from where I had initially hooked it. I yelled again, but Roger was still not back. I'd have to land it myself.

I wound down hard again, nothing happened. At the third attempt I felt the fish come off the bottom, but after gaining maybe six feet of line, the fish surged powerfully for the bottom again, nearly pulling me over in the process. In panic I knocked the anti reverse off, the reel handle spun furiously, rapping across my frosty knuckles. There was blood everywhere. I could feel it trickling down my back and stomach from the cut in my neck, while my left hand looked as if it had been through a food blender. I was starting to lose heart. "Right, this is it," I told myself as I wound down again. "This time you're coming through the rod rings sonny.'' The rod bent and creaked, as did my back, and once more I felt the fish lift up off the bottom. I was determined that nothing it would do would let me give it an inch of line. Slowly but surely the fish came up in the water. The rod and line were making weird unbelievable sounds, a bit like a Yoko Ono record. I guessed its depth at no more than five feet when I felt its tail flap followed by an incredible surge of power. I held on. The rod bent over and over, the tip being pulled into the water, then it shattered, with a loud crack like a pistol going off! I looked down and saw that there was just a cork handle left in my hand. The old ''Big Pit Special'' victor of many battles had finally had its day. Yet the fish was still on, the butt being pulled powerfully from my hand. I knocked the pick up off, giving it line. But, I was done for, I'd had enough, my body could not take any more. Biting the line I said out loud, ''Sod you. If you want to stay in the lake that much, stay there.''

I pulled the boat into the nearest land, knowing I had no chance of rowing against the wind. I can only describe my mood as I made my way back across the rocks as being one of total dejection. As I came up to the beach, I saw the lights of the pickup come down the track. ''Where have you been Rog? You've been gone two and a half hours.'' ''I've just been having a little drink with Pierre,'' he replied. ''You'll be happy, I've got a bottle of scotch, and Pierre has sent you some waterproofs to borrow.'' He looked around a bit, as if confused. ''Hey, where's your rods? Hang on, one of mine's missing as well, and where's the boat?'' ''It's a long story Roger,'' I replied, ''break open the Scotch and I'll tell you about it.''

I slept well that night, due more to the whisky than any feeling of contentment. Just before dawn I got wet again, when getting out to net a fish for Roger. It turned out to be a bloody chub! Just after dawn, his buzzer sounded again, waking me. I ignored it and went back to sleep. I wasn't getting wet again for another bloody chub. Inside a couple of minutes, Roger had landed it anyway. It weighed fifty-five pounds! Good luck to him, he deserved it: however, I don't think I deserved what I got that night.

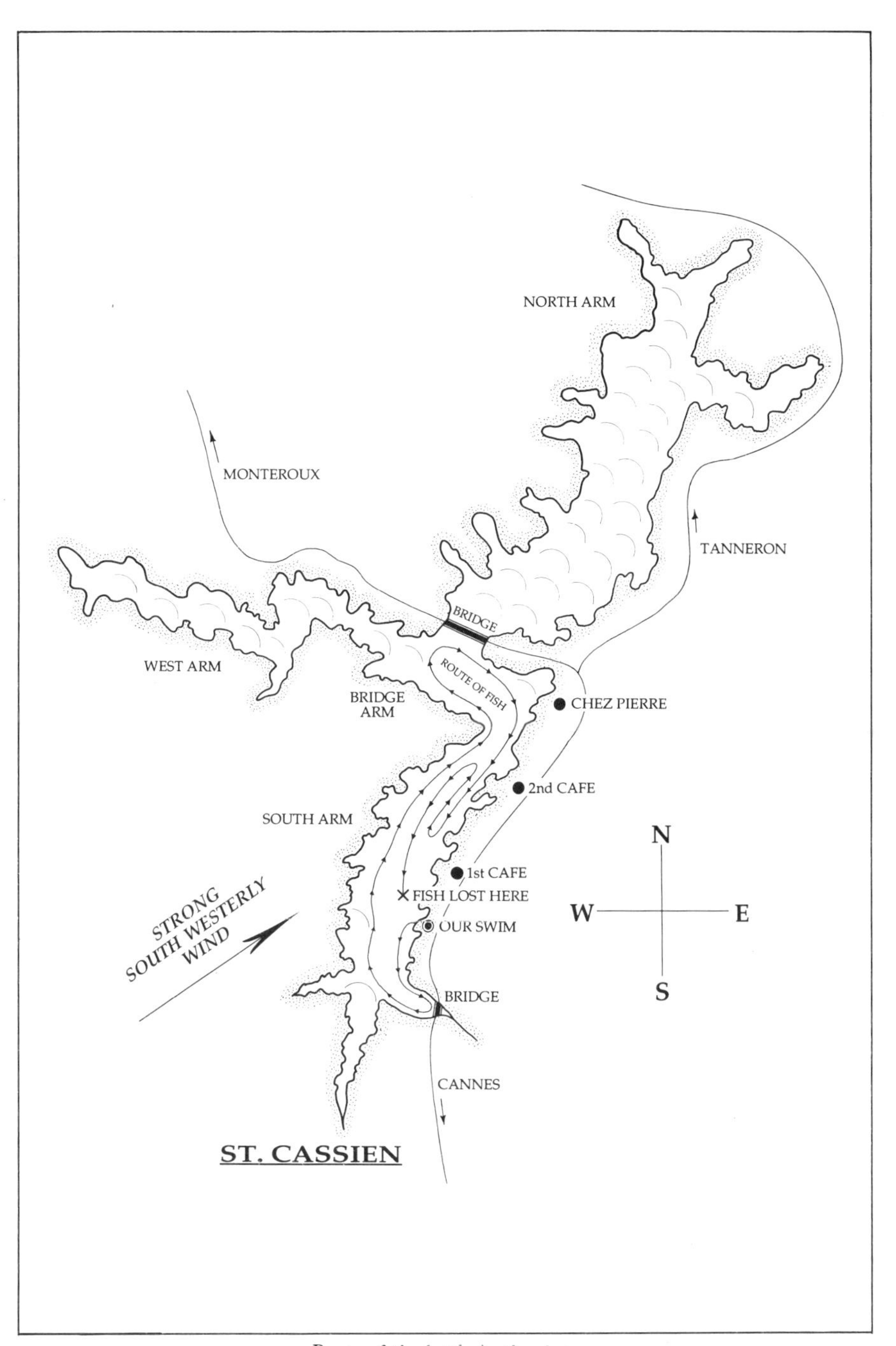

Route of the battle in the sleet

Would you like to share a boat with this? Johnny Allen's huge cat

Another 'Chub' for Roger . . . all fifty five pounds of it!

Chapter 34

Memories From Far and Wide '88

Life felt good laid out on the wooden benches in the rose garden of the Welsh border pub. Chris and I were downing a few, full of ourselves after both catching twenties that day. The local scrumpy had gone to our heads, leaving us giggling like a couple of silly school girls. It was the perfect June evening, the air adrift with the mingled scents of a thousand flowers, alive with the songs and chatterings of countless birds. Amongst the birdsong a strange sound stood apart, leaving us guessing at its origin. ''Squeak, squeak, ooh, squeak, squeak, ooh, squeak, squeak, ooh ooh.'' ''I reckon it's a mouse making love to a pigeon'', said I. ''Give over'', said Chris ''how do you make that out?'' ''Easy, squeak, squeak, the mouse, ooh, ooh, the pigeon''. Old stagers amongst you will realise that I was brought up on the unlikely story of the mouse making love to an elephant. The elephant unfortunately stood on a thorn and let out a loud scream. ''Sorry'' said the mouse ''did I hurt you?''. But I digress, this sound was neither mouse, pigeon or elephant come to that. It was old Ivor, one of the local country folk, walking up the lane to the pub. The squeak, squeak belonged to the new pair of boots he was breaking in, the ooh, oohs reflecting the pain he was in.

Sweat was pouring from his forehead and the twisted look on his face, confirmed his agony. Taking pity I leapt from the bench to greet him. ''Good to see you Ivor, what you having?'', ''I'll have a p,p,p,p,'', ''Pint'', I said, like you do when confronted by someone with a stammer. ''What will it be, cider, bitter, lager?''. ''M,m,m,m,'', ''Mild,'' I said. Ivor raised his thumb and gave me an old fashioned wink. This meant I'd got it and should not be confused with the wink that accompanies the old "you're a fine strapping lad, ever been to sea," routine.

Returning with the drinks, I could see from the tears rolling down Chris's cheeks that Ivor was breaking his heart with tragic tales depicting the sordid history of his troublesome feet. I had been feeling hungry but the thought of Ivor's feet completely threw me. Pushing the menu aside, my appetite had completely disappeared. Scampi in veruka sauce wasn't to my taste. Ivor moved towards one of the benches. Dropping on it with some force, he let out a painful cry. "Cor, me b,b,b,b," "Boots", I said. "No me b, b,b,b,b, bollocks, I've trapped em," stuttered Ivor.

When you visit a lake you know nothing about for the first time, you pull out all the stops. The lake in central France was no exception, I put out three rods for myself, two for Ann and two for young Gary. Gary was quickly into a fish and he was hooked for life. No sooner had he landed it, than one of Annie's rods was off. He was on it like a shot and bent in before Ann or I could move. "Looks like he's taken over your rods as well Annie", I said. "I don't mind, he's enjoying himself" replied Ann. Only minutes later one of my rods was away. Gary was on it like a rat up a drain pipe. "He's after all seven" said Ann. I'd seen nothing like it since the days of Andy Barker on the fens. There he was patrolling up and down checking on all seven rods, pausing only every few minutes to knock a few small ones out on his roach pole! I should have guessed what he was going to say as he made his way towards me, "Could we fix the pole up for carp fishing Rod?". Seven rods out and he wants more!. "There's a future Savay member if ever I saw one", I said to Ann.

Back home another time, I'd been crouched behind a bush for about half an hour, waiting for fish to move in on my particles, laid out in a small gully, tight to the margins. Small bubbles started appearing and I sensed the carp had arrived. I tensed in anticipation, as did Mister Tuesday the dog at my side, as if to say "Come on, we're going to have them". Slowly a tail appeared breaking the surface, immediately another followed. Crash, the dog was in and had one by the tail. He couldn't understand it as I wrung his neck, he was only trying to show me how to do it. One hour later at another part of the lake, I'd got fish going on the particles again, when all hell broke loose behind me. Suddenly a bloody great swan came crashing through the reeds, with the dog well and truly stuck firm on its backside. More screams, more eruptions and the dog's left there with a mouth full of feathers! But he wasn't having that. In he marched and the next thing I knew there he was swimming around the centre of the lake, still chasing the swan. Ann and I were screaming at him but he'd have none of it. You could see from the determined look on his face that he was saying, "I'm going to have you, you hose piped necked bugger". It was fully half an hour before he dragged himself up the bank, completely knackered.

Opportunity taken . . . with just a 5ft telescopic rod

Another time, another place . . . a brace of double-figure wildies

"That's the last time I bring him fishing with me Annie. He's a bloody hooligan", I said fuming because he'd ruined my chances for the second time that day. But you know what, I must be getting old or soft, because I've taken him with me on every trip since that day. Sometimes I catch, sometimes Mister Tuesday ruins it but one thing's for sure, something always happens.

Like it does taking the kids fishing. "Hey look what I've caught Rod. Look Annie, I've caught a lovely little mouse", said Gary, face all lit up, proud of what he'd done. There in the bottom of my best landing net which Gary was wielding was the biggest bloody rat I've ever seen in my life. (On my life for Jewish readers).

That last little quip reminds me of the time my brother Dave and I were scaffolding and doing property repairs in the Finchley, Hampstead, Golders Green areas of north London. One night after a few bevvies, we came up with a simple idea which would double the amount of work we got. On the printed cards we handed out or posted through letter boxes, the wording had been changed slightly. "High Class Property Repairs, at the best prices around. Ring the experts Dave and Hymee Hutchinstein." Which hasn't a lot to do with fishing I admit, apart from the fact we were only working there in the first place so that I could fish Savay and Harefield. Such is life.

Chapter 35

In Conclusion '80

BY the time this book reaches the reader, I will be in my twentieth year of carp fishing. In that time both carp fishing and I have undergone many changes. Yet one thing has not changed since I first cast out a ball of magical honey paste all those years ago – I still enjoy every single minute in the pursuit of my chosen species.

Throughout those years, I've not only enjoyed catching carp, but have gained close friends, fished in beautiful surroundings, and gained a feeling of being close to nature. As I've tried to learn more about my quarry, I've also gained immense satisfaction just by learning and the gaining of knowledge. This pursuit has led me into fields of interest I could never have envisaged at the beginning, and if you find some parts of this book deadly serious and a bit heavy, let me assure you that I still take everything light-heartedly.

Over the years, I've been pretty successful at carp fishing, yet I may have had that success despite what I believe. Success could have been due to entirely different reasons. I don't believe there is such a thing as a carp fishing expert, rather there are successful carp anglers. Until someone devises a way of seeing into the carp's tiny little mind, there will be no experts. I can now see alternatives to beliefs I myself held only a couple of years ago. Little points which once appeared as freak happenings, start appearing too often to be discounted. I'm sure you will recognize these inconsistencies in your own fishing. Carp fishing is to be enjoyed and yet as a thinking man's sport is in a continual process of progression. In two years' time, I will undoubtedly hold different views to some of those I now hold.

If you are to derive the most from your fishing, you should in no way gear your success to that of others. Values held should at all times be your own, regardless of what others may think. Some people want to catch every fish in a lake, while others are happy just to catch one fish. Some of my happiest times have been in the company of good friends, just soaking up the feel of a lake, even though I've failed to catch a single fish. There are far too many variables to take any one angler as a guide to how successful one should be. The waters being fished, the conditions at the time of fishing, the time available, the actual need to catch, are all different things to different anglers. Only the individual can decide just how successful he or she may be, within the confines of the time and waters at their disposal.

As regards the size of the fish one catches, I think it is true to say that everyone hopes to catch large fish. But large carp will always be in a minority and can only provide a small part of a season's total. It is only natural to be disappointed when landing a small fish, when one's stall has been set out after larger specimens, but don't despise the small ones, enjoy them for what they are, and the fight they give, which is often far more spectacular than the big old fellas. There is an old French saying which, although not directed at carp, somehow rings true, "Better the little one that wriggles, than the giant that snoozes". So enjoy all fish, they all have much to offer, in their different ways.

Success in itself does not necessarily mean enjoyment. The constant pursuit of success by perfecting technical items and methods and delving into scientific fields, brings joy to some and despair to others. So if some aspect of the sport doesn't suit you and you don't enjoy it, simply leave it alone and get on with what you're happy about.

For myself, I love the total involvement, the continual thirst for knowledge, the sheer wonder of nature, the good friends I've fished with, being able to observe the changing of the seasons, day by day. All are part of the whole and as long as I can continue not to take myself too seriously, the enjoyment will last.

So if I were to give one piece of advice, it would simply be this. Always keep an open mind and be willing to learn. But above all enjoy yourself, and as the man once said, "Don't forget to smell the flowers along the way".

Footnote 88

Eight years on the obsession is still with me, I guess it is in my blood. Once you've experienced the excitement you want more. Smell the flowers, smell the hops, smell the curry, smell the flavour of frying bacon drifting across the lake on a winter's morning. If you're a carp angler, carp fishing is a vital part of your life. Life is short, so enjoy it all, enjoy every minute. Good luck, good fishing.

Rave on dew dripping from the swaying reeds
Rave on stars that watch but never betray
Rave on bluebacks gliding through the weed
Rave on lilies flapping on a windy day.

Rave on hearts that pound
Rave on lines that sing in tune
Rave on balmy days and frosty nights
Rave on friends that stay, though life has gone.

Rave on wildies full of youth but wise in thought.
Rave on Cassien, Savay and Redmire Pool.
Rave on the farmer's pond.
Rave on, rave on, rave on, rave on.

(Apologies to Van Morrison)